An Architect's Guide to Fame

For Henri and Kate

An Architect's Guide to Fame

Edited by

Paul Davies and
Torsten Schmiedeknecht

Photography by

Julie Cook

ELSEVIER

AMSTERDAM • BOSTON • HEIDELBERG • LONDON • NEW YORK • OXFORD
PARIS • SAN DIEGO • SAN FRANCISCO • SINGAPORE • SYDNEY • TOKYO

Architectural Press is an imprint of Elsevier

Architectural
Press

Architectural Press
An imprint of Elsevier
Linacre House, Jordan Hill, Oxford OX2 8DP
30 Corporate Drive, Burlington, MA 01803

Photography
back cover: Front and back cover photography (c) Julie Cook
inside book: Photographs by Julie Cook

British Library Cataloguing in Publication Data
A catalogue record for this book is available from the British Library

ISBN 0 7506 5967 X

For information on all Elsevier Architectural Press
publications visit our web site at: http://books.elsevier.com

Typeset by Newgen Imaging Systems Pvt Ltd, Chennai, India
Printed and bound in Great Britain

Working together to grow
libraries in developing countries

www.elsevier.com | www.bookaid.org | www.sabre.org

ELSEVIER   BOOK AID
              International   Sabre Foundation

Contents

Contents

Foreword

Stephen Bayley

Vets became professionalised in 1791, architects in 1834. Only dentists are younger. They got their diplomas in 1855. Only surgeons require more training, but their responsibilities are different. Surgeons can bury their mistakes, but we all have to live with architectural errors. Flaubert may have been going too far when he wrote in his quirky *Dictionnaire des Idées Reçues* that architects are 'Tout imbeciles. Oublient toujours l'escalier des maisons', but it does suggest their uneasy status ... something that remains today. So, far from being the oldest profession, architecture is very nearly the youngest. As a defence against unease, successful architects have always developed big egos. Fame is the consequence.

But architects and artists have always flirted with fame. Great buildings and pictures were the first branded products, the author's name adding value to stone or canvas. Driving through Tuscany with Giovannino Agnelli, he said to me 'That's my house'. I said 'Very nice. Who designed it?' The reply? 'Michelangelo'. A point had been emphatically made.

To put down his mercurial and unputdownable colleague, Georges Braque once said 'Picasso used to be a great painter. Now he is just a genius'. Braque meant 'genius' was that ambitious condition obtained by dutiful supplication to the votive gods of celebrity. Fame is to an architect or an artist what brand value is to soap. You can charge more for it. Knowledge is merely power. Fame is money. In 1896 the masterful American architect, Louis Sullivan wrote an article 'The Tall Office Building Artistically Considered'. If Sullivan were writing today, the adverb would have to be changed to *'financially'*.

So the City of London is a good place to look for architectural fame doing what it does best: advertise itself. Norman Foster's ego apart, the greatest monument in the financial district is still St Paul's Cathedral. Inside, Wren so memorably inscribed the legend 'Si monumentum requiris, circumspice'. Foster, one imagines, is working on the translation.

The City that was once John Donne's 'frozen sea of calamity and tribulation' is now a mighty urban engine, pulsing bits and bursts of digitised money to all corners of our globe. What rivals Wren's austere and magnificent St Paul's today? The ludic and odd, even erotic to some, forty-storey headquarters for Swiss Re. It has been criticised as meaningless shape making. Architecturally that may be true, but that misses the point. As a fame-generator it is a work of genius. In any case it is not a meaningless shape. On the contrary, it is often compared to a young green pickling cucumber, or gherkin. The detumescing intromittent organ of a baboon has been suggested as an alternative source of the profile. Exactly what these ludicrous culinary and sexual associations might do for the corporate identity of a proud Zurich insurance company is a matter for specialist debate. What they have done for Norman Foster is make him even more famous.

Never mind the powerful psycho-sexual aspects of imposing enormous erections on the public, the architect's natural tendency towards megalomania has been greatly enhanced by recent advances in technology. While Marinetti, Sant'Elia and Frank Lloyd Wright could only dream, computer-aided design makes anything you can scribble on a napkin functionally possible. But, continuing the psycho-sexual theme, this same empowering technology has emasculated the architect. The bitter truth is that construction companies can build a perfectly acceptable forty storey tower without the intervention of a single member of the RIBA. So, architects in search of fame are driven towards extremes of willful expressionism. They invent startling shapes and finishes. To describe these bravura affects (and none is more bravura than Lord Foster's vitreous pickled cucumber), Tom Wolfe coined the brilliant term 'kerbflash'.

Kerbflash suits business clients in pursuit of visual equity, but may be less well-adapted to the needs of real people. First developers realised that a corporate building must have a recognisable and memorable image as you swept past it on the freeway at 55 mph. Well-considered, even fussy, detail, in this context, was a waste of time and money. It may be that architects wired into the spirit of the age are unwilling to negotiate spatial complexities, or other subtleties, but that's fine because developers don't want them. What's needed is instant iconography. *Kerbflash* is an instantaneous architectural image which excites desire then tickles the itch to consume. Artistically, architects are coruscating on thin ice. For all its superficial excitement, kerbflash disguises a poverty of content. Nearly twenty years ago, Ada Louise Huxtable wrote 'Today architects are looking at some very big buildings in some very small ways. The larger the structure, the less inclination there seems to be to come to grips with the complexities of its condition and the dilemma it creates'.

We live in an age of metaphors, many of them cruelly mixed. Describing a new systems development, Steve Jobs of Apple Computer said 'This architecture has great legs'. And in business this is an age of metaphysics wherein the shifty post-industrial voodoo of branding promises great riches from the insubstantial stuff of image. The most famous architects help their clients with their brands and in so doing, in a masterpiece theatre of synergy, build their own brands the while. You have Foster values, Rogers, Alsop, Calatrava, Koolhaas, Botta, de Portzamparc and Libeskind values too. They all have values. And prices. Go to any sales conference, and papers about *'building brands'* dominate the programme. Everyone wants to do what Coca-Cola has done so brilliantly for one hundred and twenty years: insistent advertising and strong graphics have turned a superfluity into a necessity. Coke is the most famous product there is. And now the talk in the property sector, in a neat inversion, is about branding buildings. Developers need to shift all that square footage. In products and vehicles, the sharp distinction between design and branding got blurred long ago. And now it is happening to the mother of the arts, as architecture rolls up its skirts and wallows in the trough: a credible rival, in terms of morals and deportment, to the very oldest profession.

A structural shift in the relationship between architects and property development has changed the nature of architecture itself. Once architecture was about finding solutions to a client's brief, now it is about speculation and seduction on the developer's account. That's a signal passed at danger to the moral minority. No longer a serious endeavour about problem-solving in building design, nor propaganda for revolutions in taste, the chief end and aim of architecture is to attract tenants.

And famous architects are just as busy turning themselves into brands. So a developer's prospectus announcing a 'Foster building' does not mean that his Lordship has been up all night fretting about circulation or floor loading, it means that years of diligent production by a disciplined team has created a recognisable style which has all the favourable associations and expectations which define great brands. But just as the difference between commissioned solution and speculative seduction has implications for the architect's autonomy, branding buildings has implications for architecture itself.

In *Reality in Advertising* (1961, Knopf), by far the most intelligent book ever written by someone from the fairytale kingdom of adland (although that is not saying a lot) Madison Avenue's Rosser Reeves explained what brands do:

'They establish contact with the subconscious of the consumer below the word level. They do this with visual symbols instead of words . . . They communicate faster. They are more direct. There is no work, no mental effort. Their sole purpose is to create images and moods'.

When you read that, does an image of Swiss Re swim into focus? The catchpenny immediacy suggested here is ruinous for architecture.

There is always corrosive danger in discussing brands before products, whether that product is a frock or a car, but specially so when it is a building. The tenant may be momentarily seduced by 'an exterior envelope consisting of a slab-supported metal spandrel providing continuous vision glass from credenza height to finished ceiling height' (I paraphrase from a real document), but when the shine has worn off his mirror finish credenza how long will it take him to realise he may have bought a very long lease on a very crappy building?

Still, the professional pursuit of fame through sensational shape-making and a winning way with the media may today be the best professional asset an architect can have. It is certainly more exciting than drain schedules. Long-term exposure to celebrity is toxic, but in small doses it can be stimulating. The novelist John Updike warned that 'celebrity is a mask that eats the face'. I suppose he could have used the word 'façade' instead.

Prologue

Charles Rattray and David Vila Domini

I'll tell you the story as briefly as I can. In the square, not far from the temple of Fortune, there stands an ancient and holy chapel, known only to a few, and dedicated to the goddess Fame. Since whoever enters it will live forever, its priests keep close watch so that no one enters it by chance. There are four priests there who continually keep guard, examining the life and character of anyone who approaches. They are Wealth, Power, Action, and Opportunity.

So wrote Leon Battista Alberti in '*Fama*' (Fame), one of a number of satirical fables he gathered as *Dinner Pieces* in the 1430s.[1] In the story, Power and Wealth hold the temple doors open to merchants, but 'foolish literary scholars' are unable to take the chance that Opportunity offers them to live forever. As a literary scholar himself, one might have thought that Alberti was on home ground here, but he wasn't only commenting on celebrity: he was courting it too. His writing – in stylish Classical Latin – was contrived to appeal to the cultural aspirations of fellow Humanists and the wealthy patrons of fifteenth-century Florence.[2]

In the 1440s, Alberti returned to the theme of fame in a hilarious tale about the perverse and bloody-minded god of fault-finding, Momus.[3] Expelled from heaven by Jupiter for insubordination, Momus goes to live on earth where, in a memorable scene, we find him transformed into an ivy vine and creeping through a window to rape Praise, daughter of the goddess Virtue. 'Every time he worked himself up to commit the crime, he couldn't help shaking like a leaf', Alberti tells us, but the ghastly deed is done. Praise has 'barely put her thoughts and hair in order' when she gives birth to 'a horrible and revolting monster'; its name is *Fama*.[4] Jupiter's punishment for Momus is severe. He is to be chained to a rock on the seashore, his body submerged beneath the waves forever. But for Jupiter's wife, Juno, this is not quite enough. In an ascerbic coup de théâtre she gives her husband a kiss and advises that Momus be castrated first.

Even in an allegorical tale one might expect such a judicial gelding to strike a warning note to fame-seekers everywhere: there are consequences to shameless lusting after praise. But the pursuit of personal recognition was part of a new Renaissance mindset which celebrated man's individual talent. As Jacob Burckhardt has it, to the 'inward development of the individual corresponds a new outward distinction – the modern form of glory'.[5] This new individualism would not go away. Because of it, the Medieval guilds would eventually lose their guardianship of professional secret knowledge and the Medieval view of art as a quasi-anonymous expression of divine truth would fade. As if quite suddenly, St Benedict's advice to his monks that 'we descend by self-exaltation and ascend by humility' was old hat.[6]

Initially, what brought Alberti fame in building circles was probably not so much his designs or his built work as his reputed understanding of the principles of Ancient Roman architecture. This he collected in the treatise *De re aedificatoria* (*On the Art of Building*), the first such work to be written since Antiquity. In it, Alberti demonstrates his more formal side. The writing is grand, self-controlled, rhetorical in the style of Cicero. It shows that he is the first to conceive of the idea of the modern architect who is not a master mason,[7] portraying him instead as a talented individual who relies on his own powers of reason, knowledge and ingenuity. He begins with a Prologue in which he writes:

> Before I go any farther, however, I should explain exactly whom I mean by an architect; for it is no carpenter that I would have you compare to the greatest exponents of other disciplines: the carpenter is but an instrument in the hands of the architect. Him I consider the architect, who by sure and wonderful reason and method, knows both how to devise through his own mind and energy, and to realize by construction, whatever can be most beautifully fitted out for the noble needs of man, by the movement of weights and the joining and massing of bodies.[8]

In writing *On the Art of Building*, it is probable that Alberti set out to improve on, as well as emulate, Vitruvius and his *De architectura* (*Ten Books on Architecture*). Alberti is critical of Vitruvius' language (in Book Six he comments that Vitruvius 'might just as well not have written at all, rather than write something that we cannot understand'[9]) but nevertheless chooses to follow his ten-book format and base much of his information on the Ancient work. Both authors address fame but whereas Alberti has mocked it, Vitruvius is more circumspect. He has bullish competitors, after all, whose pursuit of commissions is unscrupulous. There are always some who desert their principles:

> I [...] never devoted my efforts to making money by my art, but rather thought that I should pursue modest means and a good reputation – not wealth and infamy. Thus up to this point little fame has followed upon my work, yet I hope that once these volumes are published I will be known to future generations. Nor is it any wonder that I am unknown to most people. Other architects make the rounds and ask openly to work as architects, but my teachers passed on the tradition that one was asked to take on a responsibility, rather than asking for it oneself. An honest person will blush from the shame of seeking something questionable.[10]

But Vitruvius himself not only wanted recognition; he also courted patronage from the top. Significantly, his *Ten Books of Architecture* may be as much concerned with gaining commissions (or at least recognition) as with the selfless transmission of knowledge. One need read no further than the Preface of Book One to find a direct approach to Caesar Augustus:

> So long as your divinely inspired intelligence and your godly presence, Imperator Caesar, were engaged in taking possession of the world [...] I dared not, in the midst of such concerns, publish my writings on architecture [...] for fear that by intruding at an inappropriate moment I might incur the disdain of your keen spirit. When, however, I perceived that you were solicitous [...]

for the construction of suitable public buildings [...]
then I thought I should not miss the opportunity [...]
given that I was first recognised in this field by your
Father [...][11]

And so on. The context for this effusion is summarised by
Caesar Augustus' boast that 'I found Rome built of bricks; I
leave her clothed in marble'.[12] Augustus, in other words,
was the patron and potential client par excellence;[13] every
ambitious man's career was in his gift.

The machinery of the state aided Augustus' fame. It was
the state that allowed him to patronise so many building
projects and that publicised his deeds in texts such as the
autobiographical testament *Res gestae divi Augusti* (*The
Achievements of the Divine Augustus*).[14] For Augustus, then,
Wealth, Power, Action and Opportunity all played their part.
By contrast, Vitruvius' achievements in his own lifetime were
relatively insignificant. His long-term fame depended on the
fact that his was the only architectural treatise that survived
from Antiquity. Fate or Fortune – or both – leant a hand
when Alberti's officious priests turned their backs on him.

And so the figure of the Renaissance architect might be
seen as restoring a connection not only with the forms of
Antique architecture but also with concerns for personal
reputation which were present in that Pagan world.
Vitruvius provides some indication of the esteem in which
particular architects are held: for example he compliments
Hermogenes for his innovations in Hellenistic temple
design[15] and, as we have seen, also alludes to rivalry and
competition. More evidence of this recognition of individuals comes in the form of names that have come down to us
through history. If some are lost (surprisingly, for example,
the architect of the Pantheon[16]), many survive. At the

Athenian Acropolis we know of Ictinus and Callicrates (the designers of the Parthenon), Pheidias (in charge of the sculptural programme there), and Mnesicles (the architect of the Erectheion and the Propylaea). Even so, such fragmentary historical evidence of authorship in Antiquity is in marked contrast to Giorgio Vasari's systematic recording of the lives and works of Renaissance artists and architects in the sixteenth century. Vasari used a biographical-historical approach similar to that of Suetonius, applied it to art and, in the process, more or less invented art history.

Aside from his considerable achievements as an architect, Vasari's fame rests on his *Lives of the Painters, Sculptors and Architects* of 1550. By his writing, he promoted artists to fame; by his skills as an artist and impressario he promoted the rule of Cosimo I de' Medici through elaborate artistic projects. The only living artist included in the first edition of *The Lives* was Michelangelo, whose reputation as a creative genius was such that he was given the epithet 'divine' (*il divino*). Divinity, in Ancient Rome a status only achievable by an emperor, was now in Renaissance Italy bestowed not on a ruler, but upon an artist.

Vasari praises Filippo Brunelleschi, too. While the youthful Alberti was at work on the *Dinner Pieces* and *Momus*, Brunelleschi was over-seeing the building of the dome for Santa Maria del Fiore. He has 'generosity of spirit [...] sincerity of heart, and [...] nobility of soul',[17] says Vasari, a far cry from Momus' divine – and monstrous – offspring *Fama*. For innocent Praise had spawned a creature 'as thick with eyes and ears and darting tongues as its ivy parent had been with leaves [...] Even more disturbing was the fact that it had been overly endowed with untimely loquacity; indeed, even while it was being born it had tried to speak'. And 'every time Praise slapped or hit it, its voice, body and strength grew'.[18]

This suggestion of the autonomous spread of reputation traces a progression from Virtue (or *virtù*, in the sense of gifted ability and activism[19]) to Praise (deserved) to *Fama* (dubious) and, indeed, within a hundred years, as James Ackerman argues, 'the development of the architect's freedom and social stature' would become 'more important than the establishment of standards of workmanship'.[20]

But that was in the future. At Santa Maria del Fiore, the problem of raising a dome over the crossing of the Gothic cathedral was considerable and Brunelleschi's solution a major feat of engineering. It was built without the use of centring (the span would not allow it) in a series of horizontal courses. A double shell reduced weight. The pointed profile exerted less outward thrust than a semi-circular one. The techniques employed showed that Brunelleschi had studied Roman construction methods and the successful result was the spanning of a width similar to the Pantheon. This proved to Renaissance man that he was capable of comparable achievements to those of Antiquity. It was a significant factor in engendering confidence in man's innate abilities, and debunked the historiographical idea that humanity had peaked with the Classics and that the vigour of the Ancients had subsequently run out. The dome was not Renaissance in terms of its architectural style, but in terms of technological and engineering achievement it proved incontrovertible evidence of a cultural Renaissance and the skill of its designer.

It was also incontrovertible justification for his fame. Brunelleschi had been imprisoned briefly in 1434 for not paying his dues to the the Masons' Guild (a Medieval institution). Now whether his incarceration was the result of a trumped-up charge or of court intrigue,[21] and whether his early release hints at equally distasteful political manoeuvrings, is beside the point. Just as Brunelleschi had been set free from prison and the bonds of the Medieval guild system, the artist was released to pursue an individual career. It was the beginning of fame in architecture as we know it.

Notes and references

1. Alberti, L. B., 'Fame', in *Dinner Pieces* [*Intercenales*], tr. David Marsh (Center for Medieval and Renaissance Studies, State University of New York, Binghampton, 1987), p. 80.
2. Grafton, A., *Leon Battista Alberti* (Allen Lane, The Penguin Press, 2001), p. 45ff.
3. Alberti, L. B., *Momus*, tr. Sarah Knight (The I Tatti Renaissance Library, Harvard University Press, Cambridge, Ma., 2003).
4. Translated in the story's context as 'Rumor'.
5. Burckhardt, J., *The Civilisation of the Renaissance in Italy*, tr. S. G. C. Middlemore (George Allen and Unwin, London, 1890), p. 139. The relevant section is part 2, chapter 3, entitled 'The Modern Idea of Fame'.
6. Benedict, *The Rule of St Benedict*, tr. Justin McCann (Sheed and Ward, London, 1976), p. 17.
7. See, for example, Robert Tavernor's comments on Grafton *op. cit.* in *Architectural Research Quarterly* vol. 5, no. 2, pp. 187–188.
8. Alberti, L. B., *On the Art of Building in Ten Books*, tr. Joseph Rykwert, Neil Leach and Robert Tavernor (the MIT Press, Cambridge, Ma., 1988), p. 3.
9. Ibid., p. 154.
10. Vitruvius, *Ten Books on Architecture*, tr. Ingrid D. Rowland (Cambridge University Press, Cambridge, 2001), p. 75.
11. Ibid., p. 21.
12. Or at least Suetonius' claim to quote him. Suetonius, G., *The Twelve Caesars*, tr. Robert Graves, revd. Michael Grant (Penguin Books, London, 1979), p. 61.
13. And one who, quite apart from his building projects, became very famous indeed. Older readers will recall Luke 2, 1–5: 'And it came to pass in those days, that there went out a decree from Caesar Augustus, that all the world should be taxed [...]. And Joseph [...] went up from Galilee, out of the city of Nazareth [...]

to be taxed with Mary his espoused wife, being great with child'.

14. Augustus (the name itself from the Greek *Sebastos* meaning 'revered') was, in contemporary parlance, a master of spin. See Jones, P., *An Intelligent Person's Guide to Classics* (Duckworth, London, 1999), p. 78.
15. Vitruvius, *op. cit.*, p. 49.
16. For speculation on the designer of the Pantheon, see Wilson Jones, M., *Principles of Roman Architecture* (Yale University Press, London, 2000), p. 212.
17. Hyman, I. (ed), *Brunelleschi in Perspective* (Prentice-Hall, London, 1974), p. 72. The quotation is from Vasari's *Lives of the Painters, Sculptors and Architects,* of 1550.
18. Alberti, *Momus op. cit.*, p. 71.
19. For a definition see Alberti, op. cit., p. 426.
20. Ackerman, J. S., *Distance Points: Essays in Theory and Renaissance Art and Architecture* (The MIT Press, Cambridge, Ma., 1991), p. 378.
21. King, R., *Brunelleschi's Dome* (Pimlico, London, 2001), pp. 131–134.

Acknowledgments

Our grateful thanks go to the students of the London South Bank University whose portraits appear throughout this book. These first-year architectural students were entrants in September 2004, and are discussed in Chapter 15.

Paul and Torsten would like to express their thanks to Jackie Holding at Architectural Press for her guidance, help and patience during the production process.

Torsten Schmiedeknecht's research was supported by the AHRC (Arts and Humanities Research Council).

Arts & Humanities
Research Council

The AHRC funds postgraduate training and research in the arts and humanities, from archaeology and English literature to design and dance. The quality and range of research supported not only provides social and cultural benefits but also contributes to the economic success of the UK. For further information on the AHRC, please see our website www.ahrc.ac.uk

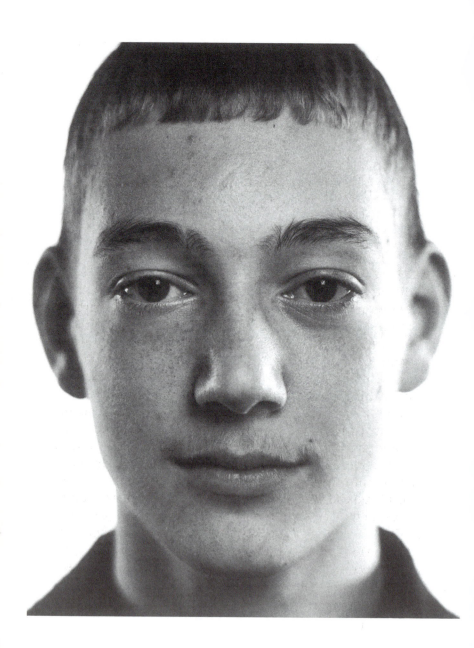

Introduction

Paul Davies and Torsten Schmiedeknecht

As Jon Goodbun and Karin Jaschke say, Architecture is a 'soft' subject, neither a rational science, nor exactly a creative fine art. Deciding what is good in architecture is largely the preserve of those who are already architects. This is a top-down, rather than a bottom-up, process. The jostle for attention at the top, the struggle up the ladder to recognition, has traditionally taken a long time. Architects are famous for reaching their *prime* late in life. Whether it is the shear, unremitting struggle that accounts for their reputation, or some maturity, is a moot point. However, in a culture that we are given to believe thrives on the energies of youth, the struggle for attention is certainly vivid, as is the distance struck from consumers of architecture, the public (if one considered the public passive to the machinations of architectural popularity, which of course they are not, just look at the *success* of the Guggenheim museum in Bilbao). But Architecture can never be the new *rock and roll*. The world of architectural culture as it stands today, could never accept Gene Simmons' maxim of the values of his rock band Kiss; that 'it's not about good taste, it's about what tastes good'.

Not unless, that is, the whole gamut of PR people, educational swengalis, ambitious academics, editors, art directors, curators, directors of foundations and trusts, movers and shakers in political circles, professional bodies and, of course, the *starchitects* themselves, all suddenly shared some kind of *Road to Damascus* moment. And if they did, we posit, *Architecture* would disappear.

Given that, it is the mechanisms of recognition we focus on. We shall not talk about the buildings as if they were the innocent content of architecture, but rather about the media that is the message.

> Above all, it is the reference principle of images which must be doubted, this strategy by means of which they always appear to refer to a real world, to real objects, and to reproduce something which is logically and chronologically anterior to themselves . . . As simulacra, images precede the real to the extent that they invert the causal and logical order of the real and its reproduction.
>
> Baudrillard, J. *The Evil Demon of Images* (Power Institute Publications, Sydney), 1987, p. 13.

This is a book about famous architects, which discusses the means by which they have become famous, and it is also a join-the-dots exercise in understanding the current state of architecture, history and anecdote intended to fill out the space which, in most volumes on the subject, for some reason, there is complete silence.

While most architects actively push for their projects to be acknowledged in some form of media, for obvious commercial reasons, generally they also deny this activity with vigour. Most successful contemporary architects claim that their careers are based solely on their architectural merits rather than on their social skills and networking successes.

Whatever, an army of architectural writers and journalists is out there on the look-out for new material to publish in their magazines, and the editorial offices of all these magazines are similarly swamped every day by material sent in from optimistic architects. Despite its confinement mainly to the realm of the profession and interested bystanders, publicity, in the case of architecture, has more repercussions for the general public than one would at first glance assume, for there is a reciprocal relationship between mainstream architecture and the signature buildings designed by those architects whose projects and ideas are held up for adulation, and whose reputation reaches beyond the boundaries of the profession into the broader realm of contemporary culture.

This is unsurprisingly true in architectural education as well as it is in practice. The majority of architecture students consume (but don't always digest) the stream of images and ideas constantly being disseminated through the various media networks. They go on to process this information and to use those images in their designs. There is nothing especially wrong or surprising about this, except if in the absolute legislation of which images and designs are currently being assessed as acceptable by a group of paranoid maniacs.

A student's adventure into the world of architecture is quickly marked by the experience of *the crit*, a rather curious but absolutely standard mechanism whereby the student submits his or her designs to the vociferous opinion of a gaggle of staff and, occasionally, specially honoured visitors. There is nothing especially wrong or even surprising about this either; except, perhaps, it's speciality to architecture and the eyebrows the crit raises in almost anyone, from any walk of life, when witnessed for the first time, or the significance laid on the event by both the student and staff. Having a *good crit* becomes the currency of student achievement. Yet the crit is overall a poor mechanism of detached evaluation or assessment, it is partial, self-interested and unpredictable, and there lies the rub of architecture as a *soft* subject. So, even at the outset, progress within the world of architecture is social, and the further you go, the more social it gets.

The status of the *profession* of architecture is unstable. It is hardly like that of a doctor (whilst if you were going to be very generous, it could be seen as analogous to it). Legal protection of the title *architect* in the United Kingdom was nearly lost as recently as 1994.

R.W. Brunskill, author of *The Illustrated Handbook of Vernacular Architecture* (1971) proclaimed the death of any truly vernacular architecture at all by the second half of the twentieth century. So by then, presumably, architecture was everywhere in different forms, spelt with a small 'a'. Architects would be busy writing health and safety programmes (or if you were a member of Archigram, staring at the walls and wondering 'What is a Room?'). Every construction in the western world would be constrained by a complex set of permits and protocols, and all these tasks might demand the services of architects. Even computers had architecture. However, few of these were necessarily related to any high-minded appreciation of architecture in built form. The shear ubiquity of the term 'architect' threatened to overthrow its exclusivity.

But out of the mist, like Clint Eastwood, came the *starchitect*.

Against all odds, architecture has, at the very beginning of the twenty-first century, perhaps briefly, but nonetheless certainly, become fashionable.

Suddenly architects are behaving like celebrities, and attain *signatures* in a run-away construction industry. Petty quarrels result in the airbrushing of associates out of team pictures. It is no longer a case of the professional architect doing business over dinner, or at the club. These architects are truly international, flying in to Tokyo for a meeting, then on to Yale for a seminar.

The effects have not been so enthralling at the bottom, at the more prosaic end, of the building industry – once a bastion of a publicly funded architecture, local authority architecture departments simply disappeared. Where once architects were socially important, invisible arms of social policy, they were now privatised, competitive and disposable.

The explosion of opportunity in the media was never lost on a profession of stereotypically gargantuan ego. As early as 1963, Denys Lasdun, on winning the competition for the National Theatre in London, was apparently apoplectic to be knocked off the BBC evening news by the assassination of JFK. Recently, lines snaked around the block when one enterprising television company decided to hold auditions for possible architectural television presenters at the RIBA in Portland Place. Yet few of these potentates were interested in the staple diet of makeover DIY that predominates the schedules. They were interested in what they believed was *real* architecture. They were lining up outside the RIBA not to subscribe to the reserve of a professional class, but because of the glamour of the star.

A few years ago, a colleague teaching first year architecture students at the University of Liverpool made, during a marking session, what seemed to be a passing remark, 'It is not about their individual creativity' he said, shocking all those tutors present who did spend their time – and have since continued to do so – drumming into their students' minds the importance of *original* concepts, creativity, passion and so on in architecture.

In the context of this book our colleague's comment is of some importance since it highlights the dilemma in which architects, architecture and architectural education has now found itself.

The acceptance of celebrity culture at any price, placing individual effort and success above anything else, has led to an atmosphere in some schools of architecture where one might think thousands of years of history of architecture had never happened. Every diploma student now thinks they need to be original.

Until about 200 years ago, architect-designed buildings accounted for very little of the built environment and most of what they designed was on a civic, religious or otherwise monumental scale, hence architects were not or seldom involved in the design of *ordinary* or mundane buildings.

Now we are in a situation where never before has what students want to learn – and a lot of staff want to teach – been so remote from the actual building tasks awaiting the young graduate.

In response to the reciprocal relationship between publicity and everyday architectural practice, *The Architects Guide to Fame* examines the mechanisms by which architects seek publicity and manage to establish themselves. Our intention is not to provide a conclusive history of how which architect employed whatever means to stay ahead of the game, nor do we want to cast any judgement on any architect or patron. There are too many architects these days keen to sue, and careful readers will notice even with our inclusive intent, there are conspicuous omissions from our roster of stars.

However, through careful selection of specialist contributors, we hope that we have enabled the reader to find a way into an understanding of the complex relationship between what they see as the built environment and the unwritten stories behind how it has come about.

There have always been famous architects. Architects have to court and impress clients, and the means by which they do such things (as opposed to the media by which they do it) hasn't changed so much from the days of Pheidias at the Parthenon.

So, for context, we begin with David Vila Domini's and Charles Rattray's Prologue on the fame game in the Renaissance. Following that, the book is structured into segments. First, we look at the curious phenomenon called 'Paper Architecture'. Understanding that architecture might not mean building is a concept hard to grasp amongst those outside the hermetic world of architecture, yet within it, attempts to extend the potentialities of architecture and the role of the architect are explored in essays concentrating on the British scene of the last half century. Charles Rattray focuses on the *extraordinary* career and media manipulations of Alison and Peter Smithson, Paul Davies discusses the group Archigram, while David Dunster ponders Alvin Boyarsky's influence on the Architectural Association in London. The fourth essay in this section by Jon Goodbun and Karen Jaschke looks at the changing role of the drawing and the way that it is being used both in the production of architecture and in its social and political ramifications.

Next, 'Bricks and Mortar' proposes to take a look at various international scenes and their dealings with fame: Rob Wilson traces Mario Botta's path from the vernacular of the Ticino village to global superstar, Andrew Peckham looks at the relationship between the writings, drawings and buildings in Aldo Rossi's work, Hans van der Heijden sheds some light on the *real* Rem Koolhaas, Torsten Schmiedeknecht investigates the role of the German magazine *Wettbwerbe Aktuell* and its impact on the country's competition scene, Javier Sánchez Merina and Halldóra Arnadóttir look at the role of the editors in Spain and theory and practice in Daniel Libeskind's involvement in Ground Zero is scrutinized by Markus Miessen. The essays in this section examine regional particularities and investigate how private and public patronage, and for that matter economical processes and cultural politics, are inextricably linked to the establishing of contemporary architectural figureheads and fashions.

Four essays collected under the heading of 'Conduits' then look at some of the intermediaries involved in the establishment of fame and fortune for individual architects: Matt Witts and Ryan McCrudden trace the history of *Architectural Design's* editors back to the early 1970s, Laura Iloniemi takes a look at the role of the publicists employed by architects and clients. ARB and RIBA are subject to an investigation in two essays by Judith Farren Bradley on why and how architects saw the need to get together to pursue their collective aims in the first place.

Last is a series of portraits which might be understood as more conversational and anecdotal. The Portraits (Paul Davies and Julie Cook), Art, Architecture, Artists, Architects (Edward Winters), A-List Architects (Torsten Schmiedeknecht), The Fall and Rise of Craig Ellwood (Paul Davies), Situating Dalibor Vesely (Richard Patterson), The Psyche of the Unit Master (Carlos Villanueva Brandt), The Psyche of a Depressed and Disappointed Unit Master (Jonathan Harris), Seeking Peter Zumthor (Kit Allsopp) and The Chapter According To St John (James Soane) are each trying to illustrate the human dimension of architecture both in triumph and tragedy, since we believe that there is an increasing interest in the history of architects as vulnerable and fallible human beings, as opposed to the heroic picture painted by most of the twentieth century architectural history.

While we have approached and commissioned all of the authors with a given working title for their essays, it is important to stress that each contributor has used their own initiative to expand the scope of the *brief* and to bring their own views to the subject. Needless to say that hence, while we agree with most of what has been said, we also enjoy disagreeing with some of it. As the essays came in, we were hence thankful to believe that the whole was going to be better than the sum of its parts.

Most of all we hope that the book as a whole will be able to contribute to and to stimulate thought on where we've been rather than joining in the clamour for whatever fresh avant-garde, or emperor's new clothes, the denizens of the latest architectural republic want to foist on the public, and encourage a meditation on just what might (or might not) be going wrong.

Last but not least, Paul and Torsten would like to very much thank all contributors without whom, needless to say, this book would never have happened. May you all become famous.

Part I

PAPER ARCHITECTURE

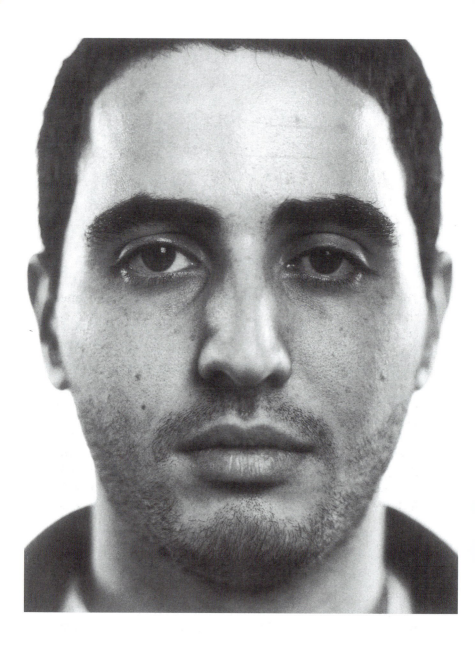

What is it about the Smithsons?

Charles Rattray

The view from the west as you approach is the famous one: the flat landscape held and defined by the blocks, the skeletal steel framework, the generously proportioned upper floor, *that* water-tank tower. All are familiar from the early black and white photographs and the architects' perspective drawing. For this is an icon as well as a building: it is Hunstanton School in Norfolk, the first built work by Alison and Peter Smithson.

The open competition for the school was won in 1949 when Alison was aged 21 and Peter, 26. 'We were just children' he would say later, 'just out of school'.[1] Newly-wed, they worked on the scheme at nights and weekends in their lodgings and made the final drawings with Graphos pens. There would have been much nib-soaking to stop the ink drying, much pen-cleaning. Affectionate gazes and necking, too, one hopes. For, beyond, it was a time of rationbooks and landladies, a time of continuing depression for the UK's post-war economy. Looking back on the period, Evelyn Waugh would describe his literary response to such wartime privation as 'a kind of gluttony [. . .] for rhetorical and ornamental language'.[2] In architecture there was a parallel reaction, seen most clearly in the effete material decoration and picturesque composition of much of the Festival of Britain: a serious departure from the Heroic Modern. The Smithsons were anti all that. And just as the work of 'The Angry Young Men' of 1950s British literature (John Osborne, Alan Sillitoe, John Braine) would displace more declamatory writing by language that was colloquial and down-to-earth, Hunstanton School would stand as an indictment of architectural self-indulgence and as a celebration of something completely different: the ordinary, the everyday. This is the crux.

There are counter-arguments to this interpretation. Reyner Banham cavilled that the literary angries were 'as English and dated as last week's pools coupons' whereas the architectural ideas espoused by the Smithsons were 'live international currency'.[3] But a more important objection is that, however much one admires the creative chutzpah of the young architects, theirs was an intellectual response to a set of social and economic circumstances as much imagined as real. A vision of a new, modern Britain had been an ongoing national preoccupation from the last years of the war, with public housing, new universities and a free health service as national priorities. The characteristic and pervasive optimism of the time was implicitly denied by the Smithsons' fidelity to material circumstances 'as-found'. Perhaps, after all, it was not so much a time to look back in anger (to coin a phrase) as to look forward to a decade in which a UK Prime Minister would boast that 'most of our people have never had it so good'.

Whichever, peers and critics were quick to see that Hunstanton was a landmark in Modernism. It was polemical, too, from its hermetic courts to the makers' trademarks embossed on the steelwork to the exposed piping in the lavatories. The icon-makers were iconoclasts. For Philip Johnson it was 'an extraordinary group of buildings ... the opposite of the prevailing trend'.[4] For Banham – an important early advocate – it carried the qualities of 'brutality, *je-m'en-foutisme*, ... bloody-mindedness'.[5] There were dissenters: for the editors of the *Architects' Journal* it seemed to be a 'blind alley', to 'ignore the children for which it was built' and to be 'a formalist structure which will please only architects, and a small coterie concerned more with satisfying their personal design sense than with achieving a humanist, functional, architecture'.[6] Nowadays, partly because of such implied functional short-comings, suspended ceilings, opaque panels and paint have been added to the fabric. How one wishes a purgatorial suffering on the perpetrators! The changes dilute the school's material directness. A pity because, for the architects, the issue – 'the very heart of present-day architecture', even – was 'the invention of the formal means, whereby, without display or rhetoric, we sense only the essential mechanisms supporting and servicing our buildings [. . .] To make our mechanisms speak with our spaces is our central problem'.[7]

Characteristically (as we shall see) it was the Smithsons themselves who described the results of these concerns as the 'New Brutalism'.[8] They were on the map. They had made a remarkable start to their careers. But it was never quite the same again. After Hunstanton came – well – nothing much. There was, as they put it 'a pause in building' from 1954 to 1962, the first of many.[9] The output of 50 years of practice was to be a dozen buildings, a couple of exhibitions and an annual Christmas card. Plus about a million words. They wrote and wrote and wrote.

Now the reputation of many distinguished architects is based on a combination of their buildings and their writings in different proportions: in the Modern era alone think of lyrical Corb; think of Aalto, Leslie Martin, Raphael Moneo; think, even, of the taciturn Mies. For design ideas, one looks to drawings, models and buildings. But for interpretation, assessment and didactics, the pen – famously mightier than the sword and lighter than the spade – contains a promise that brought out the latent Vitruvius in all of them. In the case of the Smithsons, however, there is an extra ingredient: what they thought about themselves. For theirs was a particularly introspective architectural relationship in which they went far beyond either explaining how their own work came to be the way it was or shedding critical light on the work of others. They meticulously recorded, gathered and archived the meditations and classifications of their own lives, too, and to a surprising degree. Moreover, throughout their working life they were almost continually engaged in disseminating these, presenting themselves to others through articles, books and teaching. Their thoughts – occasionally arresting and incisive, but more often arrogant and naïve – ultimately speak of one thing: the Smithsons were the Smithsons' favourite subject. Unsurprisingly, they thought they were very good indeed.

More puzzling is why so many agree. Why, for instance, Sergison Bates say that 'the debt we owe to Alison and Peter Smithson goes further than these notes allow us to express'[10] or why Peter Cook applauds the quality that 'they have many, many times reminded us of their uniqueness'.[11] The answer is unclear. It is not fully explained by the Smithsons' intellectual level (well above the usual architectural practitioner), or their idiosyncratic contribution to English architectural culture (Cook, again, notes *inter alia* 'the in-fight, the wearing of remarkable clothes, the tea ceremony, the heroic pronounce-ment'). It certainly is not explained by their influence on the wider society of patrons and the public (nil).

No, the Smithsons' reputation is based not only on what we think of their work, the products of that charismatic intelligence, but also on what we think of them – on how seriously we take them in their adopted persona (they pre-ferred to be considered as a single entity) of sequestered English intellectuals generating ideas of profound interest to the world. What surprises is less the idea that this carica-ture of the Smithsons might be accurate (after all, there were never any recreations in Peter's *Who's Who* entry) as that they make it without any hint of irony; in short, what surprises is that the Smithsons actually believed it. And in their public output, as they mix narcissistic photographs of themselves with all their jottings, family events and draw-ings, as they intertwine life and work, the reader is brought into a three-fold relationship – a sort of voyeurism by consent – and invited to believe it too. Examples of this pro-jected persona are common. Take three.

When, in 1960, Rudolph Wittkower apologised for the 'unwieldy character' of his *Architectural Principles in the Age of Humanism* and its 'many footnotes in quotations in languages other than English' he was, to a large extent, echoing remarks of ASG Butler made in his review of the book for the *RIBA Journal* of December 1951. Butler, too, had remarked on 'a ponderous thoroughness' and 'the density of the footnotes on every page'. Although, as David Watkin notes, it had become 'fashionable for smart architects to be seen with copies' of Wittkower,[12] Butler – mischievously, perhaps – ended his review by suggesting that a simpler exposition 'might attract our young architects momentarily from the pursuit of ungoverned experiments in engineering'. Whether the Smithsons were stung by Butler's comment, or genuinely upset that the review did not again draw attention to the move from aesthetic to intellectual art history which Wittkower and his Warburg Institute colleagues represented, is uncertain but their first outing in print was a response.[13] 'One had begun to write' said Peter, portentously, and it was the authors (who else?) who would describe it as 'the famous letter in defence of Wittkower'.[14] But it was a shrill 250-word tirade making a withering attack on Butler as 'a person almost wholly ignorant of the state of the profession' and, as John Brandon-Jones implied subsequently (in the *RIBA Journal* of March 1952), it exactly illustrated the sort of over-reaction and lapse in judgement some might say was typical of youth. The fact that the letter is neither important (Wittkower needed no defence) nor famous (it generated only two further letters) is insignificant, then; the fact that in the cool light of the Smithsons' advanced years they could describe it – or rather mythologise it – as both, is.

That self-delusion characterised their working life. Even as the external critical response to their output waxed and waned, their own self-confidence in praising and explaining it remained undiminished and increasingly concerned with fitting it to a historical continuity. As a second example, try this: 'we deal with insights: the thoughts are there for when the need occurs'. A little pretentious, perhaps, but they follow it with this: 'In the tradition of Vitruvius . . . Alberti, Francesco di Giorgio, Palladio, Serlio . . . Le Corbusier . . . our writings are directed at other building architects and their cast of mind'.[15] Ellipsis-clogged, mistaken and embarrassing, it is the Smithsons' writing in microcosm. Leave aside the startling jump from the heroes of *Architectural Principles* to Corb, forget the distinguished contenders for mention in the gap, such as Viollet-le-Duc or Semper; consider instead the character of a couple who, without a second thought, add themselves to the list.

As a third example, and in that distinguished tradition they identify, consider this extract from an audio-visual package the Smithsons made in 1979.[16] Alison is the speaker:

> The next slide is the WC in Limerston Street, London, 1956. [This was the Smithsons' own house.] This is under the influence of Nigel Henderson. He papered his house in Eastern England – it was an old house – and showed how cutting round things, with a sort of taste-ful margin adjusted to whatever old object you were moving round, could renew the place. The signs of occupancy we are also concerned with is [sic] the renewal of place as well as providing the new place that invites occupancy.

Now imagine a seminar where the tape might be played. It would be a scene deeply familiar to the Smithsons as teachers at several schools. Imagine a tutor pre-emptively explaining that the tone would be dead-pan (dead-pan!); imagine the snorts of laughter from students at the mention of 'occupancy'; imagine the group straining to flush out the reason the architects picked a WC from a three-decade career.

Inevitably, the particular bounty of the Smithsons in re-living their experiences for us makes it easy to see their weaknesses. Without humour (invariably without humour), they give us the ill-judged, the arrogant, the trivial: this may be a cruel analysis, but why *did* the Smithsons insist on putting such things forward along with more worthy offerings? Why did they insist on presenting themselves so excessively and so personally?

Various reasons suggest themselves. The first, and most obvious, is that they had no work. As architects they were usually dramatically under-whelmed and this was a side-effect. Little changed over the years. As teachers with time on their hands, an ongoing introverted re-consideration of their tiny output came naturally, but with this self-fixation came a loss of perspective. It became evident in the way their ideas were presented *ex cathedra*, the delivery pontifical rather than analytical or, even, biographical.

A second reason is more practical. The Smithson's friendship with the artist and photographer Nigel Henderson was an essential influence. Henderson was celebrated for his photographs of life in the East End of London. It was his neighbourhood – he and his wife lived in Bethnal Green from 1945 to 1954 – and he liked to take friends on discovery tours of the area, 'pointing out this shop front, that twisted gutter and so on, until they too had become sensitised to the unexpected and apparently mundane'.[17] Having made an observation, gained an insight, on what Alison later called these 'absolutely incredible' walks, it was worth recording them.

A third reason is indirect: Duchamp's advice to Henderson as they hung an exhibition of Cocteau drawings at the Guggenheim Jeune Gallery in 1938. Duchamp said 'throw nothing away'.[18] This advice was reinforced by Peggy Guggenheim's gift to Henderson of Duchamp's *Boîte Verte* (Green Box) of 1934. This was a box (one edition of several) containing 93 facsimile plans, photographs, notes and sketches related to Duchamp's haunting mechanistic masterpiece, the so-called 'Large Glass' version of *La Mariée mise à nu par ses célibataires, même* (The Bride Stripped Bare by her Bachelors, Even) of 1915–1923. The box was a talismanic object for Henderson and his circle.[19] The Smithsons, entranced, also seemed to throw nothing away and to find a place to keep everything. In March 1989, Alison would write 'I find that in November, 1981, – we keep a 'Magic Box' of insights – I wrote of Edinburgh [. . .]' and later in the same piece, the sub-heading: 'Thoughts from October 2nd, 1981'.[20] The 'Magic Box' (magic suitcase, magic trunk?) was well used: a great deal of the enjoyable *Changing the Art of Inhabitation*, for example, is composed of hitherto unpublished notes, some as short as a single sentence yet still dated to the day they were written.[21]

Henderson's concern to capture the East End – its streets, its long-suffering adults and playing children – with an undistorted vision, what he called the 'innocent eye' of childhood,[22] finds a parallel in the Smithsons' interest in the 'as-found'. But its influence ran deeper. The Smithsons' description of a 'microcosmic world in which the street games change with the seasons and the hours are reflected in the cycle of street activity'[23] is at once an observant description of Henderson's streets and a motivating image for their own critique of post-war urban planning. The way they addressed issues such as mobility and individual identity in the contemporary city were extremely influential, not least in the way they contributed to the winding-up of the Congrès Internationaux d'Architecture Moderne (CIAM) – an overthrow commonly understood to be one of the Smithsons' main achievements. The subject is well summarised by Banham[24] and fully examined (of course) by the architects themselves.[25]

It was a creative critique. The Smithsons' 1952 project for Golden Lane in the City of London owes and acknowledges a debt to Le Corbusier's *Unité* at Marseilles (designed from 1946 and much published before its completion in 1953). But the Golden Lane proposal fully develops the idea of 'streets in the air' to the extent of having yards associated with kitchens on the deck (or 'street') levels and encouraging characterful places by nuanced deck plans. This reflection on Le Corbusier's work was both a re-thinking of a celebrated formal configuration and a revitalising response to it. It also marks one of the few ideas of the older generation (those heroes of the pre-war CIAM conferences) to survive the challenge to orthodoxy effectively mounted by a younger generation including the Smithsons, van Eyck and others at CIAM 9 at Aix in 1954. This group, given the task of organising CIAM 10 in 1956, effectively destroyed the parent organisation and founded Team 10. The emphasis now was on 'human association rather than functional organisation' as Theo Crosby put it.[26]

The Smithsons gave a simple explanation of the radical change in *Architectural Design* in 1955: 'each new generation feels a new dissatisfaction, and conceives of a new idea of order. This is architecture'.[27] In more detail, 'it seemed that through the very success of CIAM's campaigning we were now faced with inhuman conditions of a more subtle order than the slums'.[28] The famous CIAM 4 – the sailing trip of 1933 – had formulated four rigid zoning categories of *housing, work, recreation,* and *traffic,* and had advocated 'high, widely spaced apartment blocks'. For the younger generation, however, 'town building was beyond the scope of purely analytical thinking – the problem of human relations fell through the net of the "four functions" '. The Smithsons proposed less deterministic categories of *house, street, district* and *city.* This concern to go beyond 1930s rational models for housing was already well established.

Aalto, for example, had been questioning narrow rationalism and suggesting its extension to psychology since 1935; by 1951, even Gropius had joined in. The difficulty came with the Smithsons' avowed acceptance of 'the individual urge to identify himself with his surroundings – with familiar objects and familiar symbols' and their simultaneous rejection of 'streets, squares, greens etc., as the social reality they represent no longer exists'.[29]

Their solution was twig-like sprawls of decks which, by their 'unblemishable newness', would 'carry the whole load of responsibility for [urban] renewal in themselves'. Even in the joke decade of the 1960s, this must have sounded far-fetched. By then, there was already considerable sociological and circumstantial evidence that heroic arrangements of prototypes like Golden Lane were problematic. Even on its own terms, Golden Lane seemed conditioned by the model it sought to criticise. As Frampton would comment, an extended version 'appeared to be as much against the continuity of the existing city as were any of the Hausmann-like projections of the Ville Radieuse', its edge conditions 'a series of inevitable collisions between old and new'.[30] Jane Jacobs had documented the true nature of street-life as early as 1961. The Smithsons' assertion that 'with high densities [. . .] we must build high'[31] had been disproved in studies at Cambridge in 1966.[32] Nevertheless, whether through arrogance or ignorance, the Smithsons would not move on. Given a housing brief in the Spring of 1966, they pursued the ideas of Golden Lane as if nothing had happened, only this time in an impoverished form with smaller decks and with yards reserved for only a very few dwellings. Robin Hood Gardens was the result – 'a stark vision of working-class life more in tune with the realities of the early fifties than with the consumerism of later years' as William Curtis put it.[33] The sad reality of its absent street-life is poignantly underscored by the ongoing success of its notional model, the nearby Poplar High Street.

It is for such reasons that some of the key texts by the Smithsons ultimately disappoint. *Ordinariness and Light*, for example (and was ever an architectural title more telling?), is at once a history of good ideas of the 1950s and an apologetic for ideas beyond their time. They say as much in their preface: 'it is a tumultuous rag-bag of a text [. . .] but stuffed with good things' – such as the Golden Lane scheme, whose 'random aesthetic [. . .] has since become part of the vocabulary of "advanced" urban design all over the world, even down to the arrows on the drawings'.[34] Well, perhaps. More likely is the possibility that the authors were too involved with their work to assess it fairly or to generalise about its significance. It is a sort of propaganda that affects readers, too. Would-be critics are disarmed as they find the Smithsons happily, but disconcertingly, referring to their work in critics' language, in terms of periods and shifts in concern – 'the end of our own first period' and so on – and in terms of new theories constructed every few years. Dogmatic and overbearing it might be, but it has produced at least one result: when you mention the Smithsons, people nod sagely.[35]

Of course we can chart the Smithsons' path to fame beyond their own analyses. In the early 1950s their anti-establishment character and creative strength were recognised and encouraged by their peers, including talented contemporaries at the Institute of Contemporary Arts (ICA) like Henderson and Paolozzi. Like the characters in their friend Richard Hamilton's 1956 collage *Just what is it that makes today's homes so different, so appealing?*, the young Smithsons were heroes of a kitchen-sink populism. It was their personality as much as their achievement that mattered

(Hunstanton was not yet finished) and the communal support of the group was protective against the suspicion of outsiders. Later, a crucial shift came with critical support, in particular that of Reyner Banham who became a convenor of the Independent Group at the ICA in the autumn of 1952. Here was an influential staff-member at the *Architectural Review*, and a charismatic writer whose studies – and popularisation – of the New Brutalism stimulated debate on the Smithsons' most important built work and championed their cause.

The path becomes less clear then. In his study of the way in which artists rise to fame Alan Bowness notes the importance of such peer support and critical recognition and suggests that patronage usually follows.[36] But for the Smithsons, patronage proved more difficult. In retrospect it seems as inevitable as it is sad that their own sense of being an avant-garde, of avoiding what Cook[37] calls the 'British trap' of reasonableness, would militate against them. It was a brave client who, from rows of pin-striped professionals, would commission two who proclaimed 'Demand a solution! Demand a vacuum cleaner for your "experts"! The failure of nerve is everywhere'.[38] A career in practice was unsustainable because they were too uncomfortable to be generally accepted.

What is it about the Smithsons? They are a talent hard to classify. When they were good, they were very, very good. One only has to think of the space-making of Hunstanton (1949), the subtle critique of the spec-builder at the Sugden House (1955), the 'charged void' of the Economist Building (1959), the spatial layering of Upper Lawn (1959). But when they were bad, they were horrid. Consider *inter alia* the jumbled and unresolved Amenity Building at Bath (from 1978), the restless triviality of the Porch to University Hall at

Bath (1983), the frankly peculiar Waterlily/Fish Desk (1986). In fact, what the Smithsons intuitively demonstrated was well expressed by Philip Larkin:

> The Golden rule in any art is: keep in there punching. For the public is not so much endlessly gullible as endlessly hopeful: after twenty years, after forty years even, it still half expects your next book or film or play to reproduce that first fine careless rapture, however clearly you have demonstrated that whatever talent you once possessed has long since degenerated into repetition, platitude or frivolity.[39]

An elaborate etiquette accompanies this. It was described in a classic study by Erving Goffman:

> When performers make a slip of some kind, clearly exhibiting a discrepancy between the fostered impression and a disclosed reality, the audience may tactfully "not see" the slip or readily accept the excuse that is offered for it. And at moments of crisis for the performers, the whole audience may come into tacit collusion with them in order to help them out.[40]

How very true of the Smithsons, whose inconsistent achievements and consistent celebrity simply do not match up. Theirs was a youthful promise that was rarely fulfilled. The Smithsons did not see it. They believed in their importance all the time and that belief helped others to accept it and, even, to protect it. If this sounds like the story of the Emperor's New Clothes, then it shouldn't. Here, the emperor is not naked. But neither is he as lavishly dressed as the crowd makes out.

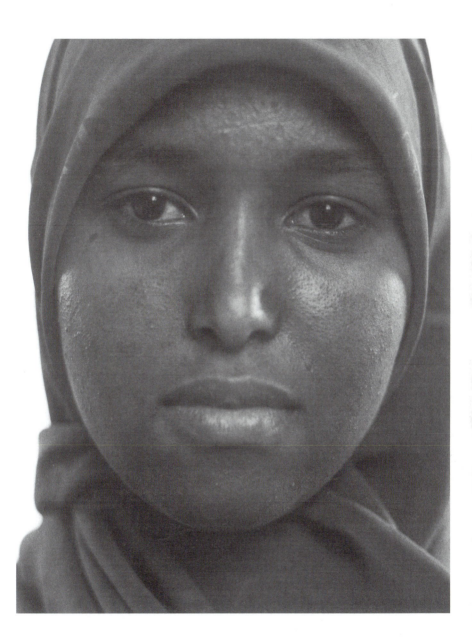

The Archigram Group

Paul Davies

2

Archigram were a group. Previous generations of English architects may have hung out together in the French House or shared tea in the afternoon, but they were not a group. A group like a band, in the 1960s, where the collective effort was more than the sum of the individual parts (of course this brings immediate focus on those individual parts). They were collectively awarded the RIBA Gold Medal in 2003, yet since their inception in 1961, they had effectively built nothing but a small adventure playground in Milton Keynes, now demolished, an irony not lost on anybody at the celebration. Even David Greene, the so-called *poet* of the group, confessed from the platform: 'I'm not sure the RIBA know what they've done'.

This extraordinary feat tops almost everything we find in this book with regard to promotion, publication and power. Most conspicuously, founder member. Peter Cook has become the most important figure in architecture in Britain today, even nominated by a serious broadsheet news-paper as one of the 100 *most intelligent* people in Britain today. Of the others, by 2003, Warren Chalk and Ron Herron were dead, one had just lost his long serving job at the Architectural Association and was virtually working full time on the Archigram Archive (Dennis Crompton). One had just been retired from his professorial post at the University of Westminster (David Greene) and, if you believe the 20-year-old mythology, one was still sleeping on other people's floors in New York (Mike Webb).

We were the ones who loudly heckled that Gold Medal ceremony for Archigram, ex students, shouting David's name, rather than Mr Cook's, Mr Chalk's, Mr Webb's, Mr Heron's or Mr Crompton's. It was a highly unusual occasion. Ours was not exactly edifying behaviour, but the event was sponsored by Hennessey cognac and it had flowed well, and we were, well, fans. We got lines in the press.

As Ronnie Wood and Ian (Mac) McLagan recently remarked, 'the singers usually handle the business side of things pretty well, the musicians, well, we were just out for a laugh'. Now I don't want to overburden this piece with musical metaphors, but I can't resist.

By 2003, Peter Cook was head of the most influential school of Architecture in the United Kingdom, and, as a recognised leader, everybody should have been cheering him. Mr Chalk's nieces and nephews were there for the reception; glum, angelic in a row, while Warren himself had died drunk and anonymous in the gutter years before. Mr Heron has also died, leaving his son, also an architect, somewhat heir apparent, not unlike Jason to John Bonham of Led Zeppelin. Mr Crompton was still the quiet man at the back, Mr Webb the lanky eccentric and Mr Greene the foil for the front man. It did, and does, come down to personalities.

Not withstanding any internal bitterness (for which Archigram were themselves famous), we have to look deeper to find a huge paradox within the mighty successful edifice of Archigram, that, in Cook at least, ringmaster of a group propounding a essentially populist critique of architecture, we find, 40 years on, a swengali figure nurturing the most exclusive of architectural clubs, and furthermore (as Neil Jackson put it, reviewing a recent Peter Cook publication) producing material where 'real people do not exist . . . only architects'. This, from the band of jesters who were authors of, as American critic Mark Wigley put it, 'the most devastating critique of Architecture in the C20th, so devastating it made you want to give up'.

The enduring power of Archigram contrasts starkly with the reputations of other peddlers of 1960s values that have withered on the vine of architectural culture over the same time period. Brian Anson, firebrand of Covent Garden, is now to be found pottering around a cottage in France. Who now cares for the work of Lucien Kroll? It is somewhat spooky to realise that Cook has always, like Phillip Johnson, understood this game way too well.

As far as the work goes, whatever its weaknesses, not least its Arcadian naivety (Paul Shepheard wryly commenting 'the failing gaskets of the walking city are clogged with the dismembered limbs of dead babies'), the Archigram group have become monumentally significant as the benchmark in the consideration of architecture in the technology driven consumer society. The fundamental agenda for Archigram, if it could be said to have one, was the dissolution of the false distinction between buildings and consumer products. Under that umbrella, all Archigram work remains consistent. The *sound* of Archigram is remarkably consistent. However, in its 30 year wake, the lesson, as the scope of the 1960s endeavour was systematically dismantled, is that the institution of Architecture did not, and is unlikely to, change.

Cooks success, a man who appears to professionally espouse no ideology, and certainly no politics, has been largely to maintain his progress within the small and essentially avant-garde community called Architecture. He also appears, via a mixture of anecdotal style, gossip and general geniality, to be a free thinking, jolly, liberal minded, typically self-deprecating ('Well, Mike (Webb) is just a genius') architect wearing funny glasses. What happened is a lesson to us all.

It starts with two meetings of this group around 1961, the elder, Warren Chalk, Ron Herron and Dennis Crompton working for the LCC, the latter, pretty much straight out of college, Peter Cook, Mike Webb and David Greene. The latter already had an Archigram pamphlet, and clearly wanted to make a group. In this endeavour, they were supported, naturally enough given the way the architectural world works, by mutual contacts such as Theo Crosby and Cedric Price. Indeed, it is astonishing, and telling, how often the names of other architects crop up in the Archigram history. Contacts were made, some money was raised (from the Gulbenkian) and an exhibition secured at the Institute of Contemporary Arts to be called *Living City*. The affiliations grew to include almost anybody who was cool in the visual arts at this time (Peter Taylor, Ben Fether, Edouardo Paolozzi, The Smithsons, Frank Newby, Joe Tilson). Peter Cook admits his tendency was to 'bustle about', while David Greene 'was reading the beat poets'. *Living City* was a jumble of tat as far as I can work out, borrowing heavily from 'This is Tomorrow' of the Independent Group, but flashier. But that is not the point, as anybody who is busy struggling around trying to get an exhibition in today's art culture establishment will understand. In the days when working in the cultural industries feels as hard as working down a pit, Cook makes taking on that fledgling art establishment look easy.

The groundswell effort embracing movement, change, exchange, response and metamorphosis amidst a society in tumult would be disseminated in a magazine on which a newly enfranchised, empowered and decidedly agitated student body would feast, and by a whole jamboree of events that went with it. The Archigram magazine *was* Archigram. Direct action, doing your own thing, and doing it right now, was often the key. The proposition, at least my reading of it, was the abolition of architecture in favour of everything, and everything, now. To this end Archigram made amazing drawings, like the posters on your wall, the cartoons in your comic book. Indeed they re-constituted the idea of drawing. How could you make drawings that echoed the relentless turmoil of construction/destruction, consumption/obsolescence? Were they history before they were even finished?

In the beginning, it was a recourse to a starry eyed technological utopia that got the band out of the garage. The image was science fiction, the idea, a new functionalism, and the inspiration, perhaps, a boyhood fascinations with the machinery of war, certainly, the potentials of 'space capsules, computers and throw away packages of an atomic/electronic age'.[1] The kernel question for me has always been, are these real proposals for buildings or not? Somewhat contrarily I insist they are not, typically, and without fancy ideas, Archigram appeared to say they were.

Criticising the *meat* of these proposals from a conventional perspective was easy. There were many who scorned houses as *pads* that became *capsules* and a social agenda that reached no further than an appreciation of a *nomadic* contemporary life (Denise Scott Browne famously declaring, 'all these pods and capsules are fine, but what do you do when mother comes to stay?'[2]).

But drawing was no longer a prescription, as McLuhan called it; propping up the 'Greco-Roman Encapsulation of Space' (pretty much everything architecture had been up to now) but an image, a moment, an event, alongside all others, and whether you believed these drawings as concrete (sic) proposals or not, it would not be until the demise of Archigram and that ruckus of a night at the RIBA, that it became the kind of problematic question that seemed terribly important to answer. For if they were not proposals, then surely Archigram was simply commentary, and, to put it bluntly, Archigram were essentially getting the RIBA medal for being lovable guys, making some pictures, doing a little schmoozing and teaching for a living.

Once started Archigram had soon become the vehicle for each member's virtuoso performances. Even by 1964, Greene had felt 'a bit pissed off', sold his Mini Cooper and sailed on the Queen Mary for America. Greene's drawings for Living Pod (1966), completed in Virginia Polytechnic, USA and sent to London for Archigram's Folkestone bash, show something part potato, part space capsule, part Yellow Submarine, but they do show a definite thing. Later *the thing* problem would disappear for Greene, his architecture, at it's purest, became pure commentary.

Chalk and Herron also went to the USA for a few years, and Webb never returned to the UK. Previously I have wondered at just how the group could still exist under these circumstances, when there were not even fax machines, certainly no e-mail and transatlantic telephone calls were a rarity. But with Cook and Crompton essentially at the helm, this physical dispersal, an inadvertent prophesy, worked in

Archigram's favour. For the young English, America and American things were the touchstone of the age. How could you be interested in consumer products without going to America? Greene proudly displayed Disneyland tickets in his University of Westminster office, and recounted tales of himself, Webb and Chalk, high on something or other, on a guided tour of Cape Canaveral. Even 20 years on, this remained cool, at least to this student.

Beyond the tyranny of *the thing*, the Archigram team would seize on new generations of reproductive technologies, this would include film, sound, collage, Roneo and tape recordings in a (somewhat unconscious but definitely happening) quest to bring the contemporary world in to the production of architecture. In this they crucially extended the remit of *technology* in architecture from the bits and pieces of construction to the means of reproduction, echoing McLuhans clarion call, the media is the message (or massage – take it as you will). A piece such as Herron's *Walking City*, one of the canonical Archigram images, is easily interpreted as a proposal, a doodle, a poster, a collage or a joke. We should also note that *Walking City* is walking on water (the Atlantic?).

The overall trajectory of ephemeralisation and obfuscation of the architectural subject is the surest ground to appreciate Archigram. The most complete representation of this became *The Archigram Opera*, a multi media festival of slide, sound and televisual presentation that remains the benchmark in a period of *happenings*.

Behind the scenes as far as this argument goes, but front of house in terms of presentation, I am not sure either Cook's industrious bustle could be called cool in anything like the same way. Indeed, when Cook eventually went to Los Angeles, it seemed it was to meet more architects.

And here lies a further paradox, and much has been made of the sheer quantity, the work ethic, that produced a vast array of images. It is as if Cook and Herron, in particular, were almost drawing machines, with Crompton grafting away in the repro studio. This ethic predominated in an era where it might appear generally unfashionable. It's not exactly, 'tune in, turn on, and drop out'. Archigram's industry remained solid and positive in an era where comparative London Art scene happenings (for instance, the work of DIAS under the umbrella of the INDICA gallery) focused on destruction and the absurd. By comparison, an Archigram project such as (Cook's) *Instant City*, if it's taken as an actual proposal to strap balloons and airships all over the place, looks just lame.

But within architecture, within a culture that still fostered the *all nighter* as a scrupulous index of commitment (and machismo) and where bow ties were still the norm for such a conventional profession, Ron Herron and Warren Chalk did buy 'Ivy League suits from Austins in Shaftsbury Avenue and looked, for a while, like Steve McQueen and George Raft'[3] and Cook did get photographed with Tom Courtney, Joe Orton and Twiggy for *Queen Magazine*. That, you might think, says it all for the relation of architecture culture to politicised art practice.

By the end of Archigram (Cook, by continuing to draw, hints that Archigram did not end for those who continued to do so) it was possible to imagine, with projects such as Webb's *Dreams Come True Inc* and Greene's *Invisible University*, that at least half of the Archigram team had made the conceptual leap in to comparative inactivity, that of a conceptual approach to architecture closer to the work of sculptor Robert Smithson and away from comic book sci-fi functionalism and all those well is it or isn't it (a building) arguments.

Indeed, Greene's mantra of the later years, borrowed from Cedric Price, was 'the answer to an architectural problem is not necessarily a building', a retreat, perhaps, from the conceptualism of *The Invisible University* (its just a line drawn across a canyon) but a still daring call for a wider consideration of what architecture might be. Now this was much closer to radical art practice. By the very end, which for most of us is marked by the Monte Carlo competition win, Greene was thoroughly off beat, even ready to lampoon drawing entirely with excursions into a further taboo of architectural production, the aesthetics of the shoddy, with a hastily scribbled cartoon for a moveable bikini making machine as an advertisement for Archigram 9 in *Architectural Design* (May 1970).

So there was a lot going on. Separated, it is clear that middle period Archigram became an umbrella term. Cook focused on events and connections with other architects, events like the Folkestone (1966) *Rally* make it clear that Cook, in particular, was very pleased at the actually appearance of a whole host of European and British architects and thinkers, all introduced under the Archigram umbrella (even if he didn't agree with what they said) Hans Hollien, Cedric Price, Reyner Banham and Paul Verillo turned up, Cook making fun of the French intellectual's *Rolls Royce radicalism*. Further on, organisations like Art Net and Addhox would become almost international alternative schools of architecture, generating their own publicity in architectural journals such as the hip *Architectural Design*, all parented by Cook, who even distributed rally veteran badges to regular attendees.

Archigram eventually set up an office, and with the office, came a gallery and lots of friends who wanted to show in it and lots of others who'd turn up on the night. Who was in the office seems still a matter for debate, for an extended

'Archigram family' was now available through contacts at The Architectural Association which had previously been Archigram headquarters. Archigram took on 53 Endall Street in Covent Garden. Out of that *chrysalis* if you like, sprang exhibitions by Wolf Prix, SuperStudio, Bernard Hafner and Co-Op Himmelbleau. The brand identity of Archigram was building (sic).

However, for Archigram, the energy of the masses, so beloved of Chalk, had polarised into the energy of avant-garde architectural practice, meanwhile the actual energy of the masses was clearly demonstrable on the streets and definitively (and inconveniently for Archigram) technophobic. The Vietnam War had made Buckminster Fuller's balding crown in to an American helmet. The ironies were not lost on rock stars. Penning *Street Fighting Man*, when asked of his favourite place for *Architectural Design*'s 'Treasure Island' special (June 1969) Mick Jagger chose, appropriately as it turns out, the stately home of Stourhead, while Chalk chose a trussed and chained Houdini escapologist/artist near the Tower of London. His caption read:

> People tired of being excluded are looking for an evolutionary breakthrough. The involvement of magic might be the key. To seek magic it is necessary to get in on the act, and put some noise in the system.

Greene chose Piccadilly underground with a bunch of daffodils.

Given the well-documented dance with the devil the Stones went through at this time, Chalk's reference to 'noise' in whatever metaphorical capacity, and the chained man, and bearing in mind the fortunes of both Jagger and Chalk, Chalk's lines are prophetically tragic, yet illustrative perhaps of exactly what architecture can't and music can, do. On the tide of mass rebellion, Jagger could get out of jail. However, in the soft room(s) of the Architectural Association, what Cook understood, and Chalk did not, was that architecture was irredeemably trapped, and destined, as it feels today, to eat itself in perpetuity.

Even while separated, a great deal of material was produced and rigorously catalogued by Crompton. The original Studio Vista monograph appeared by 1971. Without Crompton the whole thing wouldn't exist. Forty years of hoarding secured the Archigram Archive to eventually stage the first major retrospective in London at the Design Museum in 2004, and re-publication of the original Studio Vista book, 23 years after the event. The Archigram legacy had been a slow burn, much being made of the absurdity that London had not yet hosted the show that had already toured Vienna, the Pompidou Centre in France, Manchester, NY, Chicago and Santa Monica.

The show included work beyond the lifespan of the *Archigram* magazine from individual members, notably Cook, Herron and Greene, whose naked *shroud* piece was telling.

It was puzzling, with my groovy 1960s style invitation in my hand, to check I'd got the right date for this opening, because instead of the hoy paloy of the usual architectural suspects, I was sharing the room with what looked like a couple of bankers and a Clapham housewife. I had found myself at the *members* opening and the yawning chasm between architecture culture and popular culture. Poetic indeed, Archigram's imaginings o the integration of popular consumer culture with architecture in this vast catalogue, witnessed in relative peace. You see, I had missed the night when all the architects where there, when the exhibition was heaving.

I left rather melancholic, a colleague's daughter, a student of architecture at Cambridge, clutching one of the re-issued monographs. 'It'll be good for you' we said. But for me, there was that thumping bass drum, that Jagger Richards riff in my head; a slight dropping of shoulder, a slight swagger of step. . . .

'Everywhere I hear the sound of marching charging
people,
For summer's here and the time is right for fighting in
the streets boy,
But what can a poor boy do?
except sing for a rock and roll band,
. . . in this sleepy London Town there just no place
for . . . street fighting man . . .'
No![4]

Boyarsky and the Architectural Association

3

David Dunster

Alvin Boyarsky became Chairman of the Architectural Association in late 1971 and died in that post in 1990. Boyarsky was the first *Chairman*, his predecessor John Lloyd having been *Principal*. The change of title signalled a new epoch in the history of the Architectural Association (AA), now virtually unsupported by the state, a condition that would be frozen when Margaret Thatcher was Education Minister in the Heath Government. Boyarsky was on a 5-year contract to be re-elected by a 'forum comprising staff, students and with the consent of the AA governing Council'. In addition, negotiations to take the AA into the Imperial college of Science and Technology in Kensington had finally broken down. Prior to this Boyarsky had taught at the AA while William Allen had been principal, and had left after a severe disagreement. Then in 1970 and 1971 Boyarsky had run the first of many International Summer Schools at which the emerging talents of more extreme design lectured, debated and ran studios with paying students. When he therefore applied for the post, opposed only by Kenneth Frampton, he was not an unknown quantity. During his first 10 years he ran the school surfing a series of financial crises and graduated a suite of architects who have subsequently become architects of note. Rem Koolhaas and his student Zaha Hadid, Peter Wilson and many others came through a system of education which Alvin instituted and which carried his unique stamp.[1] Far from explaining his extraordinary achievement, I want to discuss two major influences upon his approach to architectural education. Neither of these influences should be seen as explaining much less justifying Alvin's approach. Instead they might raise questions for the here and now, like why is architectural education so dull now? Can education be anything other than led by exceptional and therefore dangerous personalities? The blunt end of the armoury Boyarsky deployed to reform the AA into a new operation was his dislike of the English architectural establishment, his distrust of the growth of Universities as sumps of incompetent management and lazy academics, and third, a virulent antipathy to the notion of a curriculum. He enjoyed disputation; arguments based upon perception rather than morals or ethics, and liked to play people off against each other. He also possessed a withering tongue. When Peter Cook was appointed to the chair of Architecture at the Bartlett his comment to me was why appoint AA leftovers? At the same time he was generous especially to those he disagreed with. Sadly this mercurial genius has become buried under a welter of no doubt deserved personal adulation, whereas his position seems to me more subtle, more intelligent even intellectual, and more the product of the two sets of circumstances that I wish to address. These are the context of British Architectural Education during the 1960s and the undoubted influence on Boyarsky of his mentor, Colin Rowe.[2]

To address the first of these circumstances, the post-war construction boom meant big workloads for architects serving in either the private sector, or working for town, city or county councils who, when they had too much on their plate, passed jobs to architects in private practice. At the same time because of the repetition in schools, hospitals and housing combined with politicians demand for speed, industrialising the construction process had been top of the agenda, and implicit in that was a need for architectural research. Some, who had participated in such albeit technical research, were behind an invitation only meeting in Oxford, known as the Oxford Conference.[3] The changes to be wrought were substantially those which would establish architecture as a proper professional discipline within universities, simultaneously requiring that entrants possessed pre-undergraduate qualifications equivalent to their peers in other disciplines. Architectural knowledge thus became a term waiting definition. To Richard Llewellyn Davies, brought to University College London in 1960 by his wartime research unit boss, William, later Lord, Holford, knowledge was precisely what could and should be taught. The emerging science of architectural physics, as Ralph Hopkinson named it, later to become heat, light, and sound, the technology of construction and industrialisation, the psychology of seeing and an understanding of society all formed a backbone for his new course at the Bartlett. There was little place for architectural history and none for theory. The mysteries of design, and the design process, would be elucidated as the Space Programme developed the strange but binary logical device – the computer. Gropius, in his brief tenure at the Bauhaus was Llewellyn Davies' model. Within 3 years Llewellyn Davies had been made a life peer, and this author had signed up to his programme.

In 1963, the Fabian Society financed and published a pamphlet whose title defined the anxiety of post-war

British Architecture. Written by Paul Barker and posing the question: 'Architecture: Art or Social Service'[4] the pamphlet opposed the logic of functionalism against the presumed ethereality of all the Fine Arts (Music, Painting and Sculpture, Poetry) and their self-absorption, the phrase 'art for arts sake'. This polarisation of the purpose of architecture must be read within the context of a large public building programme eclipsing privately financed construction. Architecture, an arm of the political and ideological apparatuses of both left and right, signified the reconstruction of Britain after the war. Only one European country treated architecture in such an explicitly subservient way and for those now travelling to America this illustrated how much closer to the Soviet ideas of socialist realism Britain had steered. The Fabian pamphlet illustrated just how representational architecture was now seen to be, and if this effect was concealed behind a cloak of fashionable sociology it marked a renaissance of the simplistic functionalism of the 1920s, but now with no modernist banner to unite it with the formalists. As the neo-classicism of Lutyens and others was gradually replaced by the obviousness of modernism, and Llewellyn Davies had been brought into the Bartlett precisely to sweep away the Beaux Arts teaching methods of Richardson and Corfiato. A confidence in the obviousness of architecture, indeed its transparency to political and functional purposes, made any concentration upon formal questions appear a heresy.

Following the provocative success of Barker's first pamphlet he, together with the architect Cedric Price and Reyner Banham concocted a further diatribe, this time against planning as it was practiced according to the 1947 Town and Country Planning Act. *Non-Plan*, published in the *New Statesman*, then edited by Barker provoked discussion but few letters. One in support came from Alfred Shearman, then leading an embryonic think-tank. Shearman was later knighted by Margaret Thatcher, as Prime Minister for his services to her in writing many of her speeches. The simple strategy of calling for less governmental control, non-planning rather than state-led planning, from a small group of left leaning people could thus appear to appeal more to the right than to the left. Any provocative statement on architecture or planning therefore had clear political overtones within the British political scene. Architecture and planning were thus not activities whose importance was confined to the internal discourses of the professions involved. They were intertwined in delivering the Welfare State. Both design disciplines could not, therefore, avoid aligning themselves with one side or other of the political divide. Nor could they practice confident in the knowledge that whatever they produced would be accepted simply by virtue of their professionalism. Architecture and planning were not to be trusted, and practitioners began as a direct result to doubt themselves.

It might be thought that the Fabian Society would reach such conclusions about architecture. Since its foundation by the Webbs and George Bernard Shaw in 1884, closely tied to the founding of the London School of Economics and through Sidney Webb of Imperial College of Science and Technology, the Fabian Society provided the framework within which aspiring left-wing politicians and academics could confer. Through its weekly magazine *New Statesman* it provided news comment and coverage promoting Fabian values. Concerned with improving the social, political and economic conditions of the whole nation, Fabians were against the radical and potentially violent politics of Marxist, socialist or communist, preferring to bide their time and strike only when the opportunities were absolutely right. As such the Fabians provided the intellectual backbone to Labour Party governments after 1945. *Architecture Art or Social Science* was but one of a few Fabian tracts published on issues to do with the arts. In Tract number 453 Richard Wollheim, then Grote Professor of Philosophy at University College London discussed Socialism and Culture in the series *Socialism in the Sixties*. He had some pungent things to say about the working class and high culture and socialism's relationship to both. Six conditions are isolated that gave the debate its context. These were that UK 'culture is predominantly literary based as it is upon classical learning', that 'English middle class culture is strongly anti-theoretical' unlike its European counterparts and that it also practices 'intense resistance to any new cultural movement' English middle class culture 'has always contained a very high level of criticism . . . is hostile to professionalism in any form . . . (and) has a strong class character so that the line between education and manners, between culture and convention would be frightfully hard to draw'. I am quoting this description at length precisely because Wollheim addresses problems which have not, 40 years on, evaporated. Towards the end of his tract, while quoting T.S. Eliot with approval and after having given short shrift to Orwell and even shorter shrift to Raymond Williams (his definition of culture as a system of communication was far too vague to mean anything) Wollheim writes:

> The doctrine of Art as Expression gives way in the theory of mass culture to a doctrine of Art as Catering; in the theory of working-class Culture it gives way to a doctrine that may be more attractive but is ultimately no less trivial, that of Art as Hobby.

This is clearly a disaster for the most cosmopolitan philosophers in the United Kingdom, and the only one who dared to admit to undertaking psychoanalysis.

Whatever his conclusion, Wollheim's analysis of the situation gives some clarity to the problems which Boyarsky was to face at the level of Culture when he took on the role of Chairman of the AA. Further up Gower Street, the Bartlett School of Architecture was in the hands of Lord Llewellyn Davies, friend of Ministers, and often mentioned in Richard Crossman's Diaries,[5] senior partner in the architect and planning firm of Llewellyn Davies Weeks. Responsible not only for the new Times Building, his office also took on the Stock Exchange, numerous hospitals in the United Kingdom and abroad, and the planning of first Washington New Town and then the new city of Milton Keynes. Boyarsky had been briefly employed there in the early 1960s but his face clearly did not fit. In 1966 his mentor, Colin Rowe was touted as a future Chairman of the AA. According to Rowe's editor, Caragonne,[6] Banham made very clear his opposition to Rowe in a review of Douglas Stephen's book *British Building 1960–64*. Accusing the authors of constructing an in-group, Banham wrote:

> If the in-group have their way: and Rowe is seriously put forward as the next principal of the Architectural Association School, he will find an underground opposition movement waiting for him.[7]

Rowe did not get the job, and coincidentally when Boyarsky won the Chairmanship in 1971, it was in opposition to one of the co-authors of that very book, Kenneth Frampton.

As recalled by another failed entrant for this post in 1991, Leon von Schaik:

> Alvin Boyarsky came to the AA [Architectural Association] and there was actually a very interesting contest which perhaps explains much of my fascination for the two [education and architecture]. Kenneth Frampton, the critic and theorist, and Alvin Boyarsky were the two contenders for the Chair. Kenneth Frampton's position was everything that can be known about architecture is already known. All we have to do is devise the proper curriculum and teach it rigorously. Alvin Boyarsky's was that the world is a place to be experienced and we certainly cannot deal with that through a curriculum system. When he died, his last words were reputed to have been, 'There will be no curriculum system!'[8]

Is it so hard to avoid the interpretation that Boyarsky was in some sense the agent of a certain revenge?

In fact Boyarsky had taught at the AA in the 1960s before the introduction of the unit system by the academic who was selected as Principal in 1966 – John Lloyd. He had already arranged a return to direct the 1971 International Institute of Design when he was selected as Chairman.[9] Introducing the report of this summer school in Architectural Design, Boyarsky wrote:

> It set out to provide an alternative ambience to the boredom, frustration, futility and waste of precious time experienced by those associated with the universally isolated, statically based, often intellectually under-nourished seats of learning whose institutional hang-ups, narrow professionalism and provincial lore

engenders a lack of urgency and contact with prevailing problems and ideas.

He collected together over a period of 6 weeks 65 participants from 20 countries and orchestrated the banquet with strongly contrasting courses. Peter Cook described Boyarsky's skills:

> Good teachers are too honest to be effective as entrepreneurs. Alvin Boyarsky was one who could do both. Not that he couldn't pedal his own North American formalist canoe among the European rapids that he obviously relished. Wrily pitching a Colin Rowe-ish flag into the scene and gathering together the best juries in years he would deliberately juxtapose (say) a picturesque merchant with a leader of the English Cool with someone from Archigram. He would dig them all in the ribs and get them back again for more. His network was the complete London–Atlantic geography (the only invitation brush-off coming from the Smithsons.) A wit. And a professional academic at work.[10]

In a previously unpublished eulogy Rowe has written:

> Alvin's English career, which was not easy to begin with – a period with Richard Llewellyn-Davies, some teaching at the Bartlett and, later, moving on to the AA, (from which he was fired in 1967).

Rowe adds further to the idea that Boyarsky, after a brief and unsatisfactory interlude at the Chicago Circle Campus, emerged after winning the competition against Frampton as 'an impresario of architectural knowledge'.

Boyarksy established himself with this great and noisy overture as the Bedford Square Maestro, and thus international students were attracted there. He regularly toured America to drum up business and in the 1980s Japan. And he attracted staff – Elia Zenghelis, Dalibor Vesely and Bernard Tschumi along with Robin Middleton as cultural commissar. Lists of the units for the decade of the 1970s shows how he was like a novice bar-tender, mixing and sometimes matching, sometimes messing up and changing mixtures of staff until thematic groups began to emerge who would use the studio as a form of design research organism. Because everyone was on part-time contracts and those contracts only lasted one year Boyarsky had much greater freedom than any other school in the United Kingdom and, apart from his own 5-year contract, managed to skirt the stranglehold of tenure, about which there was much discussion in the 1970s in educational circles.

The content of the work produced by students became increasingly challenging, especially to the Visiting Board of the RIBA in their quinquennial reviews of the course for the purposes of validating it. Successive RIBA validating boards, composed of the great and the good in those days, found the work so challenging that the AA appeared to be continually on the brink of running non-validated courses. Somehow, Boyarsky's mesmerising combination of school bully and snake charmer pulled it off. Other schools either went their own way, which is to say, towards exactly that provincial pseudo professionalism that so upset Boyarsky's mentor Rowe, or there was an effect particularly on the penumbra of schools in and around London of the experimental character of Bedford Square. More important perhaps than Boyarsky's graduate successes was the way in which the AA began to be the school which taught people how to teach. By the 1990s and to the present, graduates of the AA outnumber any other school in the ranks of the teaching profession.

It was precisely Boyarsky's ability to rub up against the tired Establishment attitudes that proved so successful. By rejecting the Establishment in Architecture and in English, particularly London, Culture Boyarksy found that he had a perfect stimulus, the continuous presence of a threatening neighbour just up Gower Street, the Bartlett. During the first decade of his authority at the AA, Boyarsky also developed a marked antipathy to the AA Council, and particularly to the Journal that came out as if from Boyarsky's AA. Finally this was closed down, with much protestation from the editor, Dennis Sharp. Having already established the AA as one of three major exhibitions and lecture programmes in London (the other two being the Alastair MacAlpine financed Art Net supervised by Peter Cook and the emerging programme at the RIBA), Boyarsky set about publishing.

In many ways the Art Net competed with the AA (Cook was perhaps constructing an exit strategy that he would complete when he became Architecture Professor at the Staedel in Frankfurt). From 1972, Cook took a backward step from the AA as Dalibor Veseley, Elia Zenghelis and Bernard Tschumi, more theorists then than architects, began to dominate the teaching programme. Both techno-philia, the idea that technological change equalled the progress that would transform society, and the sociological imperative to ask more questions of those who *use* buildings particularly if they came from that class pronounced with a wide 'a' now fell to the more global concerns of those who had experienced first or second hand the events of 1968. These were, the Invasion of Czechoslovakia by Soviet troops, the anti-war demonstrations in the States and the Democratic Convention in Chicago, the assassinations of Martin Luther King and Robert Kennedy, and the Paris led Student

Revolution. As Boyarksy took over the reins the direction of the AA turned from technological fantasising to theoretical work. This would lead away from the idea that the purpose was to build and towards the direction of paper architecture, or diagrammatic theory. Art Net foundered between these two stools and Cook then took over the Institute of Contemporary Arts where his reign proved once more awkward, pleasing neither the architectural in-group nor the increasingly politicised artists and hangers on of the avant-garde.

It may also be useful to point out that this decade saw an explosion of Architectural publishing. In the United Kingdom, Andreas Papadakis turned a small Kensington Bookshop into a major publishing empire, Academy. In New York, Rizzoli under the leadership of Gianfranco Monacelli, began to threaten the dominance of major publishers there, and in Milan, Electa Edizione directed by Massimo Zellman published a series of major monographs, magazines and the new writing and theory coming from the Venice Institute led by Manfredo Tafuri. But to return to magazines, this was the period of the launch of *Building Design*, of *Blueprint*, the re-vamp of *Architectural Design* chez Papadakis, and most importantly the launch of *International Architect*. Boyarsky was therefore part of a tidal wave. For whatever reasons, the ease and availability of high quality black and white printing and improving standards of colour printing plus the thirst amongst students across the world for pictures and drawings of new work in Italy and America, set up a demanding situation which publishers rushed to fill. By comparison with the present time when the Internet has yet to fulfil any serious demands that architecture students and architects might make on it, the 1970s and 1980s were in retrospect a time of extraordinary increase in the power of publishing. Boyarsky rode this wave, but lacked the ability of more professional publishers to distribute the productions, this despite his often repeated claim that he was the major architectural publisher in the world.[11] With the launch of *AA Files* Boyarksy began his programme of advertising the activities of the AA which he describes as if he were a newly arrived Margaret Mead who chances upon this curiously tribal yet intellectual Feydeau farce:

> For many the AA remains a volatile centre for the invention of radical architectural propositions. The press, the international lecture circuits, the recent popularity of drawing exhibitions, and the AA's own publications provide ample evidence in support of the myth.

> Nevertheless, even the most casual visitor to the AA's traditional club-like premises at Bedford Square where the School, the London and International networks make contact, cannot but be caught up in the momentum of the daily events which have made the AA a centre for the public discussion and display of architecture on a unique and unprecedented scale.[12]

Clearly this is a picture of the AA from the salesman's pitch. But note some key words: propositions, for example, and myth. Architecture, as the Texas Rangers[13] had understood it and promulgated it, needed the *architectural idea*. What this term meant was an idea which could only and uniquely be expressed in the media that architects employ, at best as a building, at worst merely a set of drawings. An architectural idea could only be inadequately hinted at in words, grasped with all the frustration of outsiders perhaps only fitfully but somehow known and understood by those inside the architectural game, a game often of nods and grunts. Boyarksy, fully aware of the power of this thinking for his mentor Rowe, extends this term or perhaps even appropriates it from a neighbouring school, the then Polytechnic of Central London, an equally vital powerhouse of the networks but lacking the *club* that Boyarsky both hated and used. *Proposition* suggests the painterly digression as argument as well as the scientific theories of Karl Popper and Michael Polanyi. No theory without propositions, and no practice without theory, these are the two essential connectives without which the elastic stretch Boyarsky gave to intellectuals and intuitive designers could not have occurred.

And then to distance himself from this show, which clearly he regarded as entertainment of the highest order, Boyarsky refers to the institution which he runs as not only volatile but mythic. The layers implied by this term can only be guessed at. Certainly there must be one meaning implied here which is that all that is mythic is false against the claims of knowledge. But the irony of that meaning may be caught considering that this is also the period during which structural anthropology, in the writings of Claude Levi-Strauss particularly, taught that the production by tribes of myth was an essential characteristic, one which when analysed could offer a complex but nonetheless revealing picture of the human mind. Myth, in this sense is further elaborated by Louis Althusser in his theoretical works. Myth, therefore becomes both a construction of the AA, something that could well be false, and essential to the education of young architects who will benefit from exposure to this complex but international conversation. His description elides his own involvement, yet he had by this time made it past his first re-election and already personified the AA as the Queen personifies the Monarchy. What he enjoyed, by repute, was contestation and confrontation. Stories are legion of his employing people with whom he profoundly disagreed but who he in another and possibly paradoxical way, respected. Passionate debate, rather than simple and calm discussion, was exactly the objective of Boyarsky's clever and irritating microtactics. Only in his office, protected by the redoubtable Micki Hawkes, was there ever a table for reconciliation.

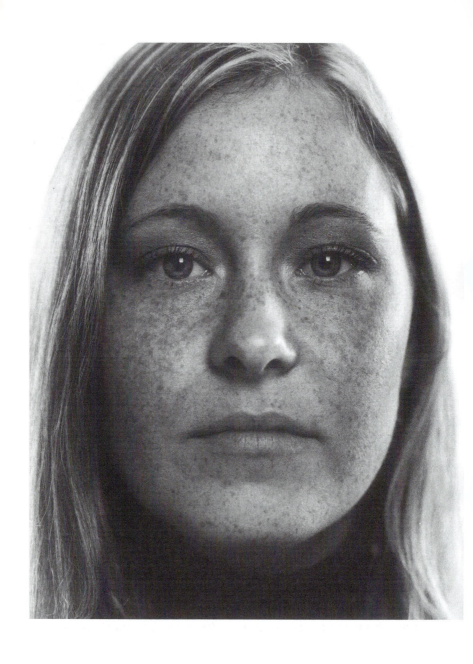

Fame and the Changing Role of Drawing

4

Jon Goodbun and Karin Jaschke

Drawing and the Profession of Architecture

Architecture is a weak discipline. It has no natural or normal condition. It does not have a clearly defined and stable object of knowledge. Not at least, in the way that organic chemistry is certainly defined by various combinations of carbon and hydrogen atoms.[1] Architecture as a discipline is rather defined 'on the wing' through its various historical objects (buildings, spaces, activities, drawings, images, texts) and their specific social modes of production and consumption. This process has involved at certain times in the history of building a particular brand of specialists who did not immediately participate in the actual construction process of the buildings and who are now commonly referred to as architects. In their modern embodiment, what these specialists are defined by most directly and what they tend to produce most directly are drawings. This, once more, is not a natural condition for architecture. It is important to note that although there is evidence that some drawing-like practices have been used at most times and places in building production,[2] it is clear that it has been and is possible to build, and to build large complex structures (such as the medieval cathedrals, or more recently perhaps Antonio Gaudi's Sagrada Familia Temple), without the use of drawings.[3] This does not mean that such objects are not planned or preconceived in any way. It just means that the act of imagining is located in processes and practices other than drawing (such as production technique, model-making or perhaps entirely different procedures such as storytelling). It also means that in the latter situation the social task of imagining can be organised in such a way that there is no necessity for the labour of a professional architect (but rather it can be found in the builder, or elsewhere in society).

The particular role of the professional architect as it emerged in modernity is closely related to developments in architectural drawing techniques since the Renaissance,[4] and the ability of forms of architectural drawing to meet the complex and shifting social and cultural demands placed upon them. In turn, the centrality that drawing has acquired within contemporary architectural practice and discourse affects the production of architecture – most evidently in the works of Star Architects, but with repercussions in all areas of production. Crucially, the development of drawing technologies allowed architectural knowledge to become separated from its primary object, the building or structure, allowing thinking about architecture to be separated from the process of making buildings to an unprecedented degree. Developed at times out of, or with, adjacent disciplines and practices – whether based in the arts (drawing, painting and perspective), sciences (mathematics, optics and geometry), or military-industrial practices (surveying, map-making, engineering and mechanisation) – by the nineteenth century there was a clearly defined set of conventional architectural drawing types in common use by the profession, through which it could imagine, communicate and produce – both itself and architectural objects. These drawing types would include projective conventions that maintained metric relations such as the orthographic family (plans, sections, elevations) and axonometrics, other projective conventions that are based upon metric relations although they do not themselves maintain them, such as the various systems of perspective, and entirely non-metric drawing forms such as the sketch and collage. In recent years developments in digital media have encouraged the widespread use of other forms of image production closely related to drawing and its projections. Following amongst others the work of communications theorist Marshall McLuhan, we are familiar with the notion that all media and technology, including drawing, affect the way we think and communicate; that *the medium is the massage/message*. Drawing does not provide a neutral medium with which to represent and produce reality. It is, rather, a particular historical prosthesis. Whilst it is not possible or desirable for architecture to simply abandon drawing (not least because, as E.L. Eisenstein has noted, that, 'when ideas are detached from the media used to transmit them, they are cut off from the historical forces that shape them'[5]), we should nonetheless be attentive to the particular social, cultural and political effects and histories accompanying them.

Drawing, Space and Ideology

In his book *Why Architects Draw*, the anthropologist Edward Robbins explores the historical conditions of the role that drawing has taken on in contemporary architectural practice. He argues that,

> In privileging and essentialising particular aspects of design and in emphasising the cultural over the social reality of a design, architects may be limiting their capacity to join in the broader discussion of just how buildings should be produced by society. Drawing cannot address issues of cost, of social power, and of the uses social power is put to in the development of the built environment. Rather, by essentialising drawing, architects have shifted the discourse about the built environment to issues that drawing can and does address best; i.e. formal, aesthetic and cultural issues.[6]

The dominance of drawing and image making within architectural discourse has specific effects upon the types of architectural knowledge and objects produced. However, we should obviously not imagine that drawing is in some simple way 'responsible' for this, perhaps limited, condition. Rather, this condition is itself determined by the broad historical demands placed upon architectural knowledge by capitalist spatial production. The philosopher and theorist of space, Henri Lefebvre, has explained that the architect is confronted not with an 'innocent space' which he can develop freely according to his ideas but with 'the space of the dominant mode of production', i.e. a space of competing capitalist interests. And, as Lefebvre noted, 'as for the eye of the architect, it is no more innocent than the lot he is given to build on or the blank sheet of paper on which he makes his first sketch . . . architectural discourse too often imitates or caricatures the discourse of power, and . . . suffers from the delusion that "objective" knowledge of "reality" can be attained by means of graphic representations'.[7] For Lefebvre, contemporary architectural practice is determined by and operates within a small sector of what he calls 'abstract space'. This expression denotes the conceptual form through which capital exercises control over real lived space in all its manifestations (geographic, social, mental) and over the ways in which we currently think about, experience and produce our spatial environments. 'Abstract space' is the commodification and rationalisation of real lived space.[8] The particular properties and effects of architectural drawing media must therefore according to Lefebvre be understood historically in relation to the development of this 'abstract space'. This leads us to ask, 'what are the roles that architectural drawings play in supporting the dominance and control of real lived space by capital through the production and maintenance of abstract space?'

Drawing, Architectural Discourse and Production

At various points in the design process, and depending upon the kind of project being developed, different combinations of drawing types play at least four primary, distinct and almost 'common sense' roles within conventional contemporary architectural practice. These include an imaginative, a social, a technological, and a persuasive role, all of which may be said to have some ideological effects.

First, drawing is an imaginative tool. It is often the primary medium through which architects imagine spatial and formal relationships, often in complex relationships with other modes of thought and practice. Robbins argues that, 'using drawing, the possibilities for innovative design increase. Freed from the time-consuming and costly realities of design while building, architects have greater room for experiment'.[9] However, as with any medium, drawing is always in some way active and present, over-determining the objects it describes. In Robbins' words, 'drawing limits as much as it opens up possibilities. It precludes things that are not amenable to its instrumentality'.[10] This is the case whether we consider the simple sketch as an extension of the hand and mind, or the complex effects of drawing techniques upon architectural thought, as considered in architectural historian Robin Evan's extensive studies of the difficult relations between the development of projection, geometry, and architectural and spatial imagination. In relation to the work of the sixteenth century French architect and stonemason Philibert de l'Orme, Evans states,

> It would be as crude to insist upon the architect's unfettered imagination as the true source of forms, as it would be to portray the drawing technique alone as the fount of formal invention. The point is that the imagination and the technique worked well together, the one enlarging the other, and that the forms in question . . . could not have arisen other than through projection. A study of de l'Orme's use of parallel projection shows drawing expanding beyond the reach of the unaided imagination.[11]

The role that drawing plays in the social production of architecture is equally ambiguous. Drawing not only extends the formal imagination, it also expands the social imagination. It does this through a number of mechanisms. Primarily, as Robbins observes,

> The role of drawing as a form of rhetoric has provided a whole new set of possible social roles for architects as

critics, as visionaries, and as artistic fantasists . . . the new uses of architectural drawing make it possible for the architect to become a major social critic and commentator without a client, without significant social resources, and without, in some instances, ever having realised a building.[12]

In this context it is interesting to note that for Henri Lefebvre architects and artists involved in spatial imagining and production are as much the (perhaps unwitting) agents of a broader, legitimating capitalist myth-construction, even while their media act as the primary site for any utopian resistance and imagined alternative to that same capitalist development. In a similar vein, Manfredo Tafuri examined in *Architecture and Utopia* how two modes of drawing, the plan and the collage-assemblage, were developed by the avant-garde as paradoxically, or dialectically, both the leading edge of concrete capitalist development and as the avant-garde's utopian affirmation of an alternative to that same dominant mode of production.[13] That the actual route taken by historical development is not determined simply from within architectural discourse, but is the result of much broader political and social struggle over space at any given time, is self-understood.

Extending the first imaginative role, drawing also operates as a technological tool in architecture, developing new information about objects and spaces through geometry and recording information from other sources, in contemporary practice almost always in the form of suitably annotated and coded orthogonal, metric drawings. As well as generating, recording and processing information, drawings are the primary communications tools used in architectural practice – that is to say that to the extent to which drawings are based upon agreed conventions of representation they are language-like, and able to communicate, within offices, between building professionals and trades, clients and society at large. Robbins notes that,

> All forms of communication define their own forms of fluency, and their own choices about what is important to communicate. The use of any form of communication is a claim about who is the master of that communication, what it is that needs to be communicated, and how this is best accomplished.[14]

Indeed, this last role expands into the fourth major task of drawing in architecture, namely that of producing the drawing as a persuasive object. Robbins is particularly attentive to this aspect in the context of the social practice and production of architecture. He argues that because of the complex roles that drawing plays in architectural production and communication, it is engaged in the production of what he defines as both conceptual and social realities. That is to say, it has both cultural and social properties and effects, whereby culture is understood as subjective, conceptual aesthetic practices, and society as the network of concrete institutions and relationships through which people live.[15] Importantly for Robbins, architectural discourse is now primarily engaged in the production of cultural rather than social reality. For Robbins the development of drawing played a particularly important role in the shifts that occurred in the social division of labour within building production. It is necessary to understand this in order to comprehend the possibilities opened up by the changes that new digital media are having upon the roles and production of 'drawings' in architecture.

In addition to the four primary roles that drawing fulfils in architectural production, there have been other, somewhat more ideological roles and effects of drawing, normally hidden by the normative mythologies of architectural production (i.e. the first four roles). We might begin by noting how drawing technologies helped to remove the practice of architecture away from the building site. This effected a split between mental and physical labour in the building industry and allowed architects to define their trade as a clean, gentlemanly profession with a particular social and cultural status and simultaneously to expand their business, working with more than one building at a time. Robbins notes that drawing, 'weights the social division of labour in a way that places communicative and social boundaries between those actors whose experience with the making of buildings is primarily phenomenal (hands-on) and those whose experience is primarily noumenal'.[16] And although architects found themselves acting ultimately under instructions from clients and excluded from many of the fundamental decision making processes (dominated by financiers, developers and politicians), drawing 'did, however, provide the opportunities for architects to reappropriate cultural control over how architecture should be conceived and, once conceived, who should control the social process of its design and realisation'.[17]

Drawing and Value

Because of the capability of architects to produce drawings without significant capital outlay, the drawing is in no small way responsible for the tendency of architects to engage in large amounts of unpaid or low paid speculative work. This has direct effects upon the market value and social importance of architectural work because the value or *cultural* capital that drawing and image production generates within architectural discourse does not come primarily from the sectors of society engaged in the production of the built environment. It comes rather from the cultural sector (this would include academia, the professional media, certain commissioning clients within the public sector, especially galleries, museums, etc.). For the necessarily small number of architects and architectural practices that are able to situate their practice within the cultural sector, it is possible to make an at times lucrative living. However, the vast majority of architects and architectural practices attempt rather to position themselves in relation to the broad sectors of general building production. For this group, a paradoxical situation arises. The primary means of their communication with their social sector is itself responsible for economically devaluing their work. This is because the cultural value that architects add to their work (primarily in the form of new drawings and additional designs or extra detailing, etc.) is not culturally valued in this social sector, i.e. the majority of individuals and organisations involved in the production of the built environment. If architectural practitioners as a whole are to increase the economic value of their work, it would seem that there are two possible responses to the above condition. First, architects might attempt to reposition their practice in relation to currently underexploited (by architects) sectors engaged in the production of the spatial and communications environment, where their work might already have cultural capital, such as advertising, branding, and digital and media environments. Second, architects might look for ways to increase architectural cultural capital in the sectors within which they currently operate. This might be by revaluing its current productions, including drawings and images. Equally, it might be by developing new forms of discourse and types of knowledge that are beyond the cultural and social logics of drawing that operate within and contribute to the social and cultural realities of the broad sectors of general building production. Such forms of knowledge and practice might emerge through an entrepreneurial and political expansion of architectural practice 'up the food chain'[18] into planning and property development. Equally, it might be based in the changes in architectural and building production brought about by recent developments in computer aided design and manufacture – changes which architects could exploit to reposition and revalue themselves to some extent in relation to building production.

Contemporary Architectural Drawing Practices

Arguably, traditional architectural drawing no longer offers architects technical superiority in building production. Engineers, surveyors, project managers and contractors are quite capable of meeting most if not all the technical tasks once provided by architects.

Furthermore, the exclusivity that drawing wins for architects is no more than the spoils of a phyric victory: formal autonomy won at the expense of social power. Star Architects, then, continue to lead the profession in the formations described by Tafuri: 'brandishing as banners the fragments of a utopia that they themselves cannot confront head on'.[19]

However, new kinds of architectural drawing have emerged in recent years, often as a result of cross-disciplinary practice.

Lars Spuybroek of NOX, Nic Clear of GLP, John Bell of FXV.org, Robert Venturi, Denise Scott Brown and architects FAT are all in various different ways examples of architectural producers who have developed innovative new hybrids of drawings and other modern visual communications media, producing graphic and video tools that allow architectural discourse and practice to take on new tasks, such as the development of built environments as modern communicative surfaces, incorporating new media and iconography into space. In a related but dialectically opposite manner, Archigram member David Greene has spent much of the last 30 years exploring non-drawing based ideas about a non-material architecture of immersive and ecologically integrated communicative networks. In a different but related way again Will Alsop is a characteristic if bravura example of many contemporary architects for whom video is the medium of choice for their Point of Sale mass visual communications and persuasions. UN Studio, MUF, Space Syntax, Jason Bruges, Cedric Price and MVRDV exemplify in very different ways many practices that have developed new kinds of drawing, often in the form of diagrams and animated 'digital landscapes' that allow them to visualise and design with information previously excluded from architectural drawings, such as programme, demographics and movement.

In addition to the broader possibilities of new multidisciplinary graphic media, new digital tools within architecture and related disciplines have transformed the technological and manufacturing potential of drawing based practices.

Mark Burry has primarily used a mixture of physical models and digital animated geometry as the media best able to understand, communicate and produce Gaudi's design work, in relation to the continuing construction of the Sagrada Familia Temple in Barcelona. Greg Lynn/FORM and WaG Architecture are among many small practices researching the possibilities that are opened by computer aided manufacturing processes. In this area, developments are characterised by significant shifts in division of labour between design and manufacturing – a condition perhaps best described as a digital Arts and Crafts. At a much larger commercial scale, the practices of Sir Norman Foster and Frank Gehry are examples that have both seen computer aided manufacturing and information management transform the role of the drawing in building production. Fully digital environments offer perhaps another location for rethinking architectural drawing, whether in real-time modelling environments such as those of 'Cadai',[20] or in the data based environments pioneered by the likes of Asymptote. Some of these new developments in drawing will no doubt lead to fertile territories for the next generation of aspiring starchitects. Others, however, might suggest the abolition of this class of practitioners, and even whilst the utopian hope of a full politicisation and socialisation of 'drawing' remains elusive, they might promote very different and perhaps more progressive figurations of architectural knowledge within the social production of space.

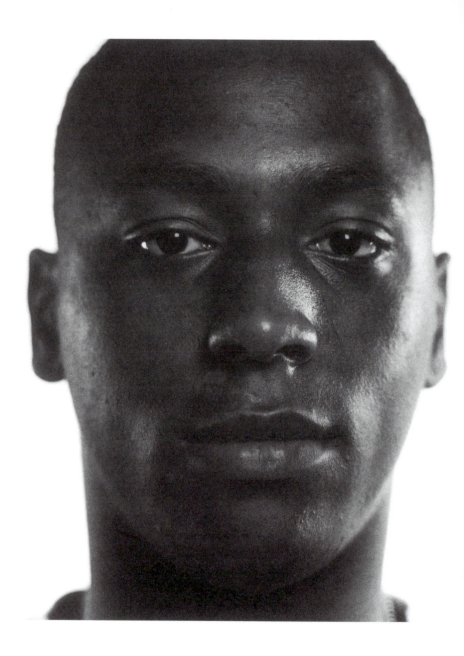

Part II

BRICKS AND MORTAR

Switzerland – Botta: Fame and Scale

5

Rob Wilson

Botta? One of the Great.

With these words Benedict Loderer concluded his introduction to the third volume of *The Complete Works of Mario Botta*, published by Birkhäuser in 1998.[1]

This is a resounding affirmation. But one you'd think unnecessary even as a rhetorical device in such a tome. After two previous volumes you might assume that this could perhaps be taken as read.

It came at the end of a barnstorming 1000 words, in which Loderer presents Botta as some sort of unassailable force of nature, cueing off paragraphs with a series of statements such as: 'Botta builds . . . Botta shines . . . Botta moves' and (less happily) succinct 'Botta is symmetrical' . . . 'Botta remains an artist as did the Italian masters for centuries before him . . .'[2]

The cumulative effect was not perhaps as he intended. In the context of the time, it has a slight sense of 'methinks he dost protest too much' – reading like a robust but rather overblown and desperate defence in the face of a tacit perception by the late 1990s of the relative waning of the star of this once fêted architect.

It was in a very different critical climate, that the first volume had been commissioned back in the late 1980s. Only the third architect's *oeuvre completes* in the series up to then, it shared shelf space with those of Le Corbusier and Alvar Aalto alone.[3] At the time Botta was still only in his early 40s.

But by 1998 Birkhäuser were already firing off a fourth volume in their Norman Foster cycle,[4] which had all been published in rapid succession. Whilst any shifting priorities in their publishing schedule or fast tracking of Foster, does not automatically betray active doubts as to the continued justification for a further instalment of their Botta magnum opus, it is at the very least a significant pointer to the higher volume of projects completed by this architectural peer in comparison with Botta himself.

Foster is perhaps an extreme case, and number of projects is not everything. Yet the 1990s, despite being the decade in which Botta completed his most significant projects to date, such as the Cathedral at Évry and the San Francisco Museum of Modern Art,[5] saw a myriad of other names eclipse his in the perceived firmament of great contemporary architects. Apart from the *wider-still-and-wider* growth of the global church of Our Lord Norman, the last few years have witnessed such phenomena as the ecstasy of Santa Zaha, and the apotheosis of the Blessed Rem, amongst numerous others.

Yet Botta is undoubtedly a highly talented and important architect with huge facility, who certainly justified his early acclaim.

His series of early villas, such as those at Cadenazzo (1971), Riva San Vitale (1973) and Ligornetto (1976) in the Ticino

Region of Switzerland near the Italian border, were brilliant essays in what had become known as *critical regionalism*, working within the language of high modernism but combining this with local vernacular *peasant* building traditions and forms.

In this, he is the most celebrated of a group of architects practicing in the Ticino, who were heavily influenced by the Italian Neo-Rationalist movement – the Tendenza – which had originated in the adjacent Lugano region of Italy.[6]

This movement looked to reinstate the relative autonomy of the language of architecture and its use as the embodiment of social and cultural structures. It underlined the importance of the resource of historical form in architecture, particularly its continued relevance and use in the present.

Botta was in the second generation of this movement, working in the office of one of its founders, Tita Carloni. Significantly though, where Carloni and others exhibited 'a predilection for the masters of the modern movement'[7] in their work (in Carloni's case, Frank Lloyd Wright), Botta actively sought actual contact with them. As a result his curriculum vitae during his tutelage reads like a roll call of twentieth century architectural greats. On making the move to Venice, to continue his studies, he not only gained Carlo Scarpa as a tutor, but through a 'combination of single-minded determination and youthful enthusiasm',[8] got to work on Le Corbusier's project for the Venice Hospital in 1965 and Louis Kahn's proposed Congress Centre there in 1969.

It was Kahn in particular and the ideas of structural rationalism that underlined his work, that would influence Botta. His belief in the validity of logic of traditional forms of building, especially masonry construction, and the referencing of the Romanesque and even the Roman in his late work, resonated closely with Botta's own ideas and practice.

Kahn's influence is clear in the villa projects of the 1970s, with their often stark and graphic forms, and sense of the monumental even on a domestic scale. Simultaneously they are interpretations of the forms, materialities and locations of the local vernacular building traditions of the Ticino, that Botta had grown up with, in particular the barns and bird-hunting towers. The forms of these structures built for 'protection not enclosure' are a fundamental to those of the houses, whose massive outer brick or concrete skins contrast with the suppressed glazed elements and roofs. Their physical locations, often on the edge of a settlement, acting as a marker between urban and rural, also exemplify Botta's notions of 'building the site' – of his projects growing out of, and further reinforcing, existing geographies and patterns of settlement.

It was not long before the strength and significance of this work was picked up on by the critics. Most significantly perhaps it was elucidated in an article by Kenneth Frampton 'Mario Botta and the School of the Ticino'[9] which appeared in *Oppositions* magazine in 1978. In the article Frampton also highlighted two unbuilt urban projects designed with Luigi Snozzi, that indicated for him the wider significance of Botta's work: the 1971 proposal for a new community centre in Perugia and the 1978 project for the expansion of Zurich Railway Station. Both these take the form of the megastructure, but tame this trope of 1960s architectural avant-gardism, with their logical use and application both fulfilling the briefs set whilst solving the particular problems thrown up by their inner city sites. Frampton described these public projects approvingly as 'critical strategies for urban intervention' differing from some of their utopian forebears by being 'specific, limited and realizable'.[10]

In retrospect this article can be seen as forming the bedrock of the international acclaim that Botta's work attracted over the next 10 years.[11]

Frampton condensed the essence of this article over a page of 'Critical Regionalism: modern architecture and cultural identity', as the then concluding chapter of a revised edition of his book '*Modern Architecture: A Critical History*'.[12] It was to be in this context, as part of a worldwide manifestation of 'critical regionalism', alongside other practitioners such as Alvaro Siza, that Botta's work was held up as indicative of the next chapter in the Canon of Modernism, adapting and domesticating it to local conditions.

Not that any great schema hung off *critical regionalism*. Indeed that was its point. It was in its very diverse localness and in the variety of practice that the term covered that it seemed to provide a way forward – a next possible step for the modernist project, saving it from itself. For by the late 1970s with high profile failures such as Pruitt Igoe, Modernism was in danger of becoming stereotyped as a crude indulgent universalist even utopianist experiment on the part of designers and planners, playing fast and loose with ordinary people's lives, anti-humanist and alienating in its effect.

Whatever the subtext, Botta became one of the great white hopes of Modernism and the decade that followed saw him accumulate an amazing number of teaching posts, awards and accolades which culminated in the exhibition *Mario Botta* at the Museum of Modern Art in New York in 1988, its catalogue essay entitled 'Mario Botta and the Modernist Tradition' (note the title inflation),[13] the rejoinder to one showcasing post-modernism and the work of architects

Ricardo Bofill and Leon Krier. He was then just 42. Such an exhibition would appear to be the final acclamation – the tipping point of true fame. Yet his career seemingly set to go stratospheric over the following few years, did not. So what happened?

For one, it was a bit of an overbilling anyway. As the contents of the exhibition demonstrated at the time, he had hardly completed any really substantial projects. Beyond the body of domestic work on which his reputation had been made a decade earlier, these amounted to a handful of significant but still relatively modest office and educational projects and buildings for the Church. Indeed it was still with a project dating from 1972 to 1977 for a school at Morbio Inferiore that he had come closest to realising a public building on a scale that approached that of his unbuilt urban schemes.

In many ways this slow growth of his practice might be seen to be expected. As a *critical regionalist* it would by its nature be more problematic or at least take longer than for another practitioner, with the concomitant need for time to digest and reutilise wider influences, to develop and adapt an architecture to conditions outside a given region. The textbook example of this is the career of Alvaro Siza.

But the character of Botta comes into play here. Whilst it is tempting to stereotype the formation of this in his childhood as the adored boy-child growing up in a father-less Italo-Swiss household – the centre of attention for both mother and grandmother – detectable perhaps in the slightly petulant set of his lips – for whatever reason, he was not prepared to wait for fame. An accomplished and talented architect, he was hungry to assume the mantle of greatness before fame herself sought him out – grabbing her trumpet to blow it himself.

Of course ambition is natural and indeed essential for success in anything. But with Botta there seems to have been a sheer self-belief in his own myth that meant when his possible place in the history of Modernism was tentatively sketched out by the critics, rather than a signifier of present worth and future promise, it seems to have appeared as an affirmation, a chance to set in stone the myth for which he had set out the ground-work. This was the Authorised Version in which he is passed the torch of genius from the Masters of the Modern Movement, their anointed successor, conveniently eliding over the facts that he had only worked in Kahn's office for a few weeks and in Le Corbusier's office only after that architect's death, never actually having met him.

Accordingly throughout the 1980s Botta proceeded to consciously assume the trappings of the Master architect. He took all his cues from Corbu – the classic model of old-style architectural fame, carefully conceived, constructed and presented, with its own very particular tropes, rules and internal logic – and perfectly complementing his neo-rationalist ideas about the *autonomy* of architecture itself.

Thus hagiographies of his work, still composed mainly of unbuilt projects and competition schemes, were bulked out with pages variously devoted to the Master's sketches and the Master's signature and indeed photograph upon photograph of him and his signature look – distinctive round glasses, mop of unruly hair – an architectural Einstein. Thus we find him here photographed with Gabriel Garcia Márquez, there with Philip Johnson, with Arata Isozaki, with Claus Oldenburg, with Tadao Ando, Jean Nouvel, Meret Oppenheim, Mitterand[14] . . . and for dessert: it was inevitable that the afore-mentioned *Oeuvres Completes* followed.

As a result by the late 1980s there was this odd disjuncture between his projected profile – a, perhaps too perfect, simulacrum of the accoutrements of a famous architect – and the actual achievements of his practice to date – crucially the definitive built-Masterworks of Architecture were still missing.

Indeed through the early 1980s, Botta's practice seemed to be effectively just treading water. Not in itself an unusual occurrence in any architect's career, often resulting from the economic climate or other factors beyond their control, yet for Botta this temporary statis would prove particularly corrosive to his career, given his prodigious energy and talent. Up to this point the rapid development of his early work, had reflected this energy, showing a thirst, an impatience even, to learn, digest and master influences – almost as if to tick them off and move on – perhaps too rapidly at times. In some early designs for instance influences seem rather ill-digested, such as at the Stabio Villa, a competent but not overly inspired – indeed rather literal – essay on a Le Corbusier Villa.

Somehow in retrospect, for Botta, the beginning of the 1980s needed to have been his 'tipping' point. The time when without pause, he should have had the chance to make a dramatic professional leap forward and get his teeth into much larger projects which would have cemented and enshrined the sharp upward trajectory of his career. He should have his 'Pompidou moment'[15] – but it wasn't to be – by then it was 10 years too late. Given the time delay between competition win or commission, and finished building, it had actually been in the 1970s that he had missed his chance – in particular to realise one of his great urban schemes such as for Perugia or Zurich highlighted by Frampton. For by the 1980s, the appetite for such modernist megastructural urban solutions had passed.

As it was, his practice – whilst successful – suffered without the fresh impetus of any larger scale projects that would have stretched him. One can almost sense his frustrated talent churning over with few fresh challenges offered by the endless essays on the villa that he was commissioned to design by the wealthy Ticenese. These designs suffer from this lack of creative spark and their higher budgets, meaning the use of more refined, less raw, materials, further removed some of the poetics of his architecture. They appear as bloated versions of his earlier villas – less rooted in an understood landscape – having lost any recognisable grounding in their increasingly plush and anonymous suburban sites.

When larger public projects did come on stream for Botta's practice in the late 1980s, they were of a very different kind to those he had proposed in the 1970s, reflecting a changed climate. Big stand-alone and iconic, institutional buildings like the San Francisco Museum of Modern Art and the Cathedral at Évry reference rather his domestic projects, looking like vastly inflated versions of his villas, as though his practice, invention and repertoire had somehow ossified. These huge striated brick symmetrical monoliths, now 'built their sites' not through subtle moves in response to local geography and tradition but by their sheer bulk: becoming landscape themselves – literally in the case of Évry, with its sloping crown of trees on its roof.

These can be seen as more the precursors of the rash of post-Guggenheim Bilbao icon buildings which glutted the Millennium – models for urban regeneration through statement architecture and 'culture' instead of large scale urban interventions designed specifically to act as a social generator and model. These two projects seem in fact resolutely detached from the cities around them.

Inevitably by this point, Frampton had jumped ship. With the potential of Botta's early urban schemes which he had identified as significant pointers to the future, both aesthetically and socially, not realised, he had transferred his affections to others – such as the tasteful organic progression of Alvaro Siza's career and his beautifully considered, and unquestionably High-Modernist, architecture.

But by the end of the 1980s, the stately progression of the Modernist Canon's caravan had in any case been irreparably disturbed. Whereas it had been exposed in any case as a rather artificial construct by the general climate of comparative cultural studies that mitigated against such old narratives, the picture had been further fractured by Post-Modernism, in all its forms and scions, breaking down the old certainties.

To add insult to injury, despite the undoubted poetics of many of Botta's buildings in the flesh, their primary shapes and unsatisfyingly over-symmetrical forms – arising from his ideas on architectural autonomy of form and of function following form – do not photograph well, appearing exaggerated, crude and overdrawn. As a consequence it is not difficult to see how the Moma exhibition encouraged a case of false memory syndrome, bracketing Botta more in sympathy with Bofill and Krier, rather than in contrast to them, vaguely confirming him in the popular imagination as one of the apostates of Post-Modernism. In the event, his two big public works, Évry and the San Francisco Moma, came to look more like out-of-date codas, two large bookends to a body of work, not springboards to global acclaim.

Indeed what at the beginning of the decade seemed like fortunate timing, with Botta poised to inherit the earth or at least to be in possession of a possible roadmap to the Modernist project, in the event it could hardly have proved worse.

For ironically global critical acclaim remained fixed on Switzerland, but shifted north of the Alps. The observation that Botta's erstwhile supporter Frampton made in the 1970s, favourably comparing the 'quality of recent architecture built in the Ticino – with its population of 200,000 – to the relatively banal, if technically competent work achieved in the rest of Switzerland',[16] had been reversed. A new vanguard of Swiss architects led by Herzog and de Meuron and the Basel boys were producing architecture celebrating, and celebrated for, these very qualities that Frampton dismissed.

Botta, whilst still only in his mid-40s, suddenly found himself caste in the mould of belonging to a previous, and now outdated, generation, perversely caught between the Scylla and the Charybdis of banality and Post-Modernism.

Whilst he took architecture as his autonomous god, practitioners such as Herzog and de Meuron looked to the theories of minimal art. Taking their cue from Judd not Jeanneret, their architecture exhibited a strong phenomenological aspect with its emphasis on material and physical presence through its form, surface and detailing.

This shift also heralded the age of architect as global celebrity – and brand – subsuming the idea of the merely 'famous' architect. This new breed took their inspiration not from past models but from an expanded field of contemporary culture – neither *high* nor *low* – utilising all the new platforms of the media – in particular visual media which has come to so excessively predominate due to the advances in digital technology.

In this new order, Jacques Herzog became one of the key players. His skull-like visage symbolised the new ascetic ideal for the decade of minimalism after the supposed excess of the 1980s. Fittingly, in appearance Herzog is the grim reaper – or perhaps more pertinently a puritanical Luther – to Botta's fleshy, worldly priest.

Stereotypically there almost feels to be an element of old European divisions and prejudices about the contrast – a Mittel-Europa of a whispering concrete immanent order in architecture set against that of the border-country, loudly and rather gauchely hinting at a transcendent one – one building art galleries, the other churches. More pertinently in this new globalised environment, there was not so much a division between Italian and German-speaking Canton-based architects, but perhaps more significantly that between the non-English speaking and their English-speaking colleagues.

Where once he rode the system of architectural fame, Botta became a victim of new rules that he didn't understand. No more a universal reference point and in danger of becoming just a footnote, he suffered a wholesale critical withdrawal – with Frampton playing Saatchi to Botta's Paladino. In this new role he could be cast as a glam-rock dinosaur in the Neue Sachlichkeit of Punk: a doomed antidiluvian species of architect, ultimately just to be studied, classified, and to move on from in the new *her-stories* and (no longer Grand) narratives of architecture.

This proved of course to be as dated and hasty a conclusion on Botta's career as any of the previously over-hyped and laudatory ones. Inevitably with so much architectural practice bedded down in the maelstrom of mass contemporary culture, it has inevitably allied itself to the vagaries of fashion, and the tide has turned again. Much architecture that appeared to define and be identified with a now-dated minimalist lifestyle choice – is last season's style in our über-consumer society. This has inevitably provided a fresh perspective on those tendencies in architecture that celebrate it not as a commodity but for its own formal logic.

In any case, it has become easier to see Botta's work afresh, away from the clamour and at a critical distance and he commands an interesting position. Today leaner and wiser – still just 60 despite the critical roller-coaster he has ridden and still widely known – he now seems liberated from and have passed beyond reach of whatever structures or strictures that the critics can cast over him.

It is tempting to be overly revisionist, but at a basic level the fact that his buildings are not made for magazines, but demand to be visited and experienced in the flesh, seems a highly admirable thing, in an age when buildings disappointingly do not live up to their computer-rendered image – or indeed for that matter do: exhibiting that same generic dead gloss of their computer-generated image.

His own personal image now seems rather refreshingly unmediated. The straightforwardness and unapologetic lack of guile in his pursuit of architectural fame seems like natural, healthy human ambition, and almost modest in comparison with the hubris of the new global brand of architects playing at being scientists, sociologists and world doctors. With every competition shortlist littered with the same names – with corporate buildings as critiques of globalisation – it is not clear whether projects are meant to be read post-ironically hypocritically, and one longs for a simpler world of the common-or-garden famous architect.

Freed of having to build some unwieldy practice as a global brand, Botta has put his money where his mouth is in his own bit of the 'local'. He was instrumental in founding a school of architecture in the Ticino.[17]

And his own practice has moved on and evolved. He uses an increasingly wide palette of materials in projects, regularly ditching the brick that had so often the effect of unnecessarily over-monumentalising projects however small – witness his bus station in Lugano built from 2001 to 2002.[18] This is a structure large in scale yet modest in manner, an elegant steel and polycarbonate sheet canopy that is basically a simple, symmetrical shed. But it fulfils its functional role whilst maintaining an appropriate civic gravitas, as a key arrival and departure point and indeed public space, in the city.

Botta still builds and Botta is still symmetrical, but with the hyperbole now long departed, he seems able now to just get on with the job of being just a good, well-known and well-regarded architect.

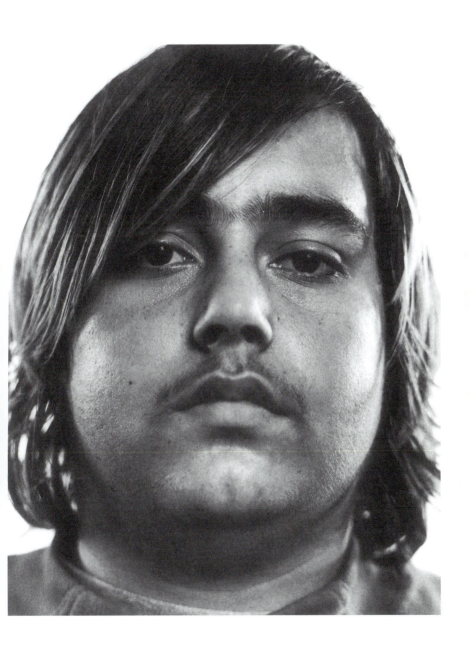

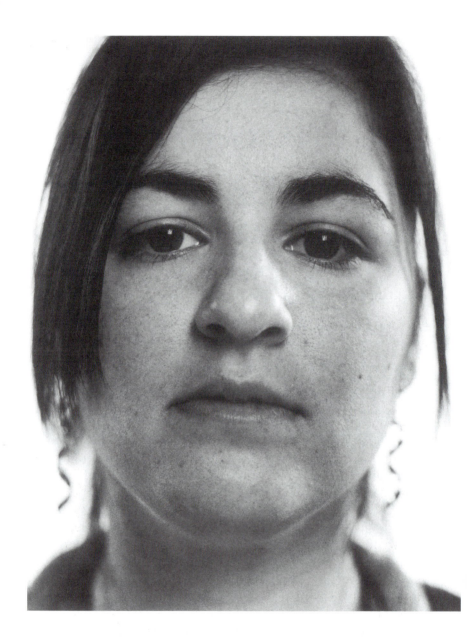

Italy – Rossi: Fame and Familiarity

6

Andrew Peckham

There is a double-edged relationship between fame and familiarity. The better known the architect, the more familiar his (or her) reputation; the more predictable the buildings (and their image) the more identifiable they are, but conversely the less noticeable they become, as all too familiar. In this sense consistency becomes a virtue, but also a limitation, and too familiar a repetition breeds contempt in a culture where the notion of the avant-garde has become an acceptable commodity.

Aldo Rossi's *oeuvre* is inextricably bound up in this double bind, given its formal consistency, and for Rossi (and his critics) the significance attached to the concept of repetition in his work. In spite of the general assumption that this formal consistency is intrinsic to the relationship between his writing, drawing and building, this can, as Carlo Olmo has pointed out, in no way be taken for granted.[1] If the buildings are consistent and the thinking ambivalent; or his ideas develop in phases, associated with stages in the development of his career[2]; might the inherent contradictions and instability of his reflections on architecture not provide a necessary vicariousness as its counterpoint? The drawings; whether seen as an alternative production of 'architecture'; a representation or reflection on it, or more conventionally simply part of the operative process of design, clearly mediate between the two.[3]

Bearing this in mind, the intention is to examine the manner in which translations of Rossi's two main texts, *A Scientific Autobiography* and *The Architecture of the City*, were published in 1981 and 1982 respectively, following an exhibition of his drawings in New York. An associated catalogue *Aldo Rossi in America: 1976 to 1979* effectively acted as an 'introduction' to these books.[4] Peter Eisenman was the principal protagonist in 'framing' these texts and drawings, while the Institute for Architecture and Urban Studies (IAUS) journal *Oppositions*[5] had already influenced the wider reception of Rossi's work in America. By 1980 Rossi's earlier identification as a leading figure of the Italian *Tendenza* had been marginalised, and his teaching in America prompted access to a wider international audience.

If the American publications are an indication of, and stimulus to, Rossi's international reputation as an intellectual, his tea service for Alessi (1980) of the same period, attests to a rather different marketability. How pivotal was this moment for his subsequent development?[6] Subsequently (post 1982) his theoretical work is put on hold, or rather what he does write is modest compared to his previous output. There is a certain inevitability about this, as the balance between writing and building changes. The assumption, often voiced by Rossi and his critics, is that once the theory, or the formal vocabulary, had been established, there is little more to be said than its repetition. This depends on maintaining the conviction that the two are essentially similar in kind, and mutually dependent. Both assertions are open to question.

Similarly, the view that in some way the drawings are themselves architecture, depends on a lack of buildings (or it helps); just as more buildings might condition a more instrumental view Rossi's drawings, no longer 'designs' in a world of their own. Or their predictability might allow more licence for a divergent practice of drawing. Unless, that is, one remains convinced that Rossi's buildings and drawings remain 'tokens' of a fictive architecture (or 'architectural imaginary').

Obituaries September 1997

The obituaries written on Rossi's death (4 September 1997) provide an insight into his reputation at the end of his career. Representative texts published in Italy, Britain and the United States, serve to outline the brief facts of his life, and the key works and characteristics of his architecture. They also address the relationship between his experiences and personality, and the nature of his varied 'architectural' work.[7]

While no reliable guide to its development or its likely future, they do present an indication of received opinion about his work, an 'appreciation' of the depth, or otherwise, of his thinking, and a view of the legacy it represents. The obituary has the virtue of avoiding theoretical jargon, in concentrating on the immediate and accessible. Copy from newspapers and professional journals reveals the summary nature and psychological conventions of the architect's obituary.[8] Inevitably it is fixed in time 'for the record', and conditioned by a degree of emotion and sentiment. These aspects conspire to create a symptomatic, rather than objective, view of the deceased and their reputation.

The question of Rossi's reputation raises several key issues about the extent (in later years) of his architectural production, its identity and relationship with his teaching and writing. There was agreement about the scale, international range and importance of his *oeuvre*.[9] Rossi, viewed as an architect of 'world renown', was seen to have acquired an 'international acclaim' lacked by his Italian contemporaries. But while an aspiration to 'universality' was claimed for his work, there was a degree of ambivalence, and confusion, as to its identity.

National perspectives varied. Italian journals focussed on 'local' difficulties, commenting on 'tendentious' critiques of Rossi's abstraction, while recognising his ability to work both 'within and beyond architecture', at the 'frontier' between architecture and the other 'arts'.[10] In contrast *Casabella* simply presented a single page photograph of Rossi in reflective mood. The only words are in the title: his name and dates of birth and death.[11] This eloquence may mirror the qualities of Rossi's architecture, but is also uncannily reminiscent of the presentation of his drawings in the final issue of the journal *Oppositions*.[12] British critics, meanwhile, claimed his support for their conservative notions of 'modern buildings sensitive to old cities', and the 'creative' use of old buildings;[13] collectively admiring his 'powerful intellect'. The American obituaries tended to identify with the recent award of the Pritzker Prize, and also recognise the influence of the media on aspects of his work. Its 'poetic' character was emphasised, and a cultural interaction between America and Italy identified in his range of interests. While his professorial role was recognised, complementing the influence of his ideas, the formal qualities of his buildings generally took precedence.

A fault-line was apparent in the significance given to Rossi's forays into the fashionable territory of product design. While it was asserted that 'these are better known than the buildings', or they pre-empt discussion of his ideas, others noted that Rossi 'eschewed the fashionable' for a singularity of his own.[14]

A consistent international recognition was given to Rossi as architect *and* theoretician. The buildings (we are told) are epitomised by a monumental simplicity, a 'haunting' silence and beauty, and a sublime character, qualified by a degree of austerity. It is striking how aphoristic dualities informed perceptions of his work, typically seen as intimately monumental, primitive and sophisticated, universal yet intensely personal, warm and dangerous, or simply bold and ordinary. Significantly Italian perception of his work often appeared to disregard these ambiguities. Given such ambivalence, the individual anecdote might reveal deeper insight into Rossi's reputation and personality, and the work that lies behind them.

Visiting the Gallaratese housing in 1982 Jonathan Glancey talked of being 'shocked by what he saw' in the 'almost impenetrable freezing fog' of the Po valley in winter.[15] He was unequivocal about the banal reality of the individual building. Yet Rossi's explanation of the project is equally unequivocal about an autobiographical dimension which emerges from his petit-bourgeois childhood.[16] Alan Powers inverted this perception in proposing the *ready-made* scaffolding erected around the Albert Memorial, as 'the closest thing to a Rossi building in London'.

Describing arrival at Rossi's extension to Milan's Linate Airport (as an *entré* to Milan and the broader Italian context), Thomas Muirhead subsequently extended Powers' notion of a 'found' Rossi project: 'Rossi's masterpiece would be an invisible building that belonged nowhere and did not exist'.[17] The concept of an invisible architecture, at odds with physical 'building', is reminiscent of Rafael Moneo's contention that 'Rossi ... defends architecture as an expression of thought'.[18]

Criticism is voiced in many of the obituaries, often taking issue with the formal abstraction of an architecture characterised as 'anti-human'.[19] There remains a stable consensus, however, about Rossi's debt to the eighteenth century architecture of the Enlightenment, and to the collective research underpinning the *Tendenza* during the 1960s. Manfredo Tafuri, the critic and historian, is regarded in several obituaries as Rossi's theoretical mentor (though he is not a complicit or an uncritical one).[20]

What remains unquestioned in the obituaries, though not elsewhere, is the distance, and process of translation, between the ideas and the architecture.

Publication in America 1979–82

The catalogue *Aldo Rossi in America: 1976 to 1979*[21] (the second in a consistently formatted series) is related to two IAUS exhibitions of Rossi's work: the first in 1976, and the later, in 1979. It collects a set of representative drawings from the second exhibition, dating back to 1974, preceded by Peter Eisenman's preface, and his essay *The House of the Dead as the City of Survival*. Inserted between the two is a short introduction by the architect. Beside Rossi's text, a quietly composed *Urban composition with monument* (1973) contrasts sharply with the fragmented imagery of his watercolour *Architecture Assassinated* (1975), which accompanies the following essay by Eisenman. Dedicated by Rossi to the Manfredo Tafuri, this painting adorned the cover of the American edition of Tafuri's polemical *Architecture and Utopia*.[22] Here, it complements Eisenman's outline of Tafuri's thinking, which might have placed Rossi in its Italian context; instead Eisenman extends Tafuri's conception of ideological rupture to a further level of philosophical 'post-humanist' abstraction.

It is instructive to compare their different attitudes to the drawings. Eisenman claims that, while Rossi's writing, drawings and buildings are seen in Europe as an integral oeuvre, in the United States, students remained fascinated by the drawings in default of reading the texts or experiencing the buildings. This sets out the context for the exhibition of drawings; for Eisenman they provide the opportunity to explore the foundations of Rossi's imagery.[23]

The published drawings are all what Rossi calls *designs*, presumably in distinction to 'sketches' for ongoing projects. These typically incorporate designs of realised buildings, or completed projects, superimposed onto earlier drawings as a composite record.[24]

Eisenman argues that the content of the drawings is primarily about 'emptiness, in-completion and abandonment'; their selection predicated on the *Città Analoga*. There is a prevalent sense of uncertainty in many drawings, induced by foreshortening and transpositions in scale, which suggests an unstable ground condition, or a 'frozen' state of collapse induced by different projections. If many of Rossi's drawings (and buildings) seem redolent of the 'still-life',[25] here they become agitated.[26] A valedictory hand gestures in front of an urban landscape on the cover, and in paired versions of his view from a 'poet's window'.

The second section of Eisenman's essay, reiterates Rossi's paradigm of 'analogy'.[27] He claims:

> Just as it is necessary to read Rossi's book to understand Rossi's drawings, it is also necessary to read his drawings to understand the ideas first formulated in his book.[28]

89

This tautological assumption which asserts a transparent relationship between drawing and writing, becomes, in the final section of the essay, a plea for the drawings themselves as 'architecture'. 'They do not demand to be built' since they are seen to incorporate all the constituents of Rossi's *theory* of architecture. Certainly the drawings obsessively revisit Rossi's preferred catalogue of forms, though it would require a very narrow definition of his conception of *primary elements, monuments* and *locus*, to suggest these are in any way definitively present in the drawings.

Rossi himself sees designing and writing as different 'techniques', describing his drawings (*designs*) as 'a kind of writing'. He discusses the manuscripts of 'the great writers', written out in longhand, and comparable to frescoes; design and writing meet, he argues, in ancient, and modern forms, of hieroglyph.[29] This prompts a view of the logic of his drawings as if 'pages out of a story'.

While Rossi takes a direct 'literary' view of his drawings, endowing them with a narrative status, Eisenman backing away from their iconography prefers to see them as architecture *and* theory.[30] His preceding, elaborate discussion of 'three symbolic "houses"', which he finds repeated in the drawings,[31] argues for their philosophical association with aspects of the 'post-humanist condition'.

Their two different perspectives are intriguing. Rossi finds narrative and material reassurance in the drawings (as if to compensate the absence of building in America). Eisenman reassures himself in his writing that both his professional interests, as architect and theorist, are there to be 'seen' in the drawings. The drawings console the one, and project the thinking of the other. In this respect, Rossi's comments on his 'analagous city' corroborate Eisenman's view. He talks of a 'consistency which almost liberates me from any representational technique'. The drawings seem to be conceptualised as a form of automatic writing, reproducing objects of his affection.[32] But they are not writing; nor are the ideas drawings.

Rossi's *A Scientific Autobiography* was the first of his books to be published in English. The ochre cover and black and white illustrations conform to the model established by *Oppositions Books*.[33] However the title remains misleading. In spite of the reference to Max Planck's own '*Scientific Autobiography*', it is clearly not 'scientific' in character, nor a conventional autobiography, however ironic the scientific label may be. Rossi conceives the book as an 'autobiography of my projects', suggesting they have a life of their own, or that they have a privileged relation to events in his own life.

Displacing an explanatory introduction at the start, a quotation[34] from the main text directly precedes the opening pages. The writing, faithful to its origins in 'notes' written over 10 years, is typically structured into paragraphs of uneven length. Broken into notional, and untitled, sections, the text is followed by a reworked set of twelve drawings, which read as anodyne versions of their originals. Vincent Scully, contributes a substantial postscript commenting on the surreal 'circling' of Rossi's thinking (in contrast to the 'reasoned argument' of the earlier *The Architecture of the City*), and placing it as a reaction to the 'ferociously ideological ambience' of 'North Italian Criticism'. Critics have noted the idiosyncratic character of *A Scientific Autobiography*; its consistently uneven and discursive text overlaid with declamatory emphases, epitomised by the choice of the initial quotation.

A framed image (reduced in scale on a black ground) of a ruined bridge on the Mincio River, is illustrated where the initial quotation resurfaces in the main text. The amalgam of different forms conveys both the passage of time, and its suspension in the agency of the supporting steelwork; an 'illumination', for Rossi, of an 'analogous architecture brought back to nature'. Later he speculates on how to constitute a project out of 'bewilderment' (intangible as that may seem). A house is visualised as if present in a film or a novel, where an indifference to its form (presumably its familiar ordinariness) is 'identified with a kind of malaise', providing the pretext for Rossi to ruminate on 'the order of things', resigned to a loss of idealism.

The passage reveals his highly subjective use of the concept of analogy; a preoccupation with disorder, irrationality, or the circumstantial, as an antidote to a rational order, and a philosophical disposition.

In what way does Scully's postscript respond to this thinking? His presumptions concerning Rossi's 'innocent' poetics emerge from his own conception of how 'Rossi has been able to divest himself of ideology. A tendency towards hagiography becomes increasingly evident. Rossi's painted forms in *Architecture Assassinated*, are said to be exhibited 'in a state of massacre',[35] yet he became increasingly sanguine about the status of the provisional and circumstantial (qualities notoriously elusive in built-form).

Scully elaborates Rossi's conception of an 'analogical architecture' as the embodiment of a classical conception of memory. In a rhetorical figure of speech, an 'ocean of remembered shapes' (or 'the world of forms') is seen, curiously, arranged in Rossi's imagination as if in a catalogue, available for composition.

What specific relationship does Scully propose between Rossi in Italy and America? Early on, he notes that the typological elements of Rossi's formal vocabulary are 'never abstract always Italian'. Later he retracts this claim suggest-ing that Rossi's iconic four-square window represents a 'distilled' affective form, representative of the two respective national vernacular traditions.[36]

Scully discovers similar qualities in Rossi's floating theatre: '. . . a creature, with square cross-mullioned eyes'. The anthropomorphic assertion sits uneasily with a long list of antecedents, which accumulate associative value; the theatre being presented as a strangely familiar presence.

Conceiving a phenomenological archetype beyond the concept of style (or the aspirations of the International Style), Scully notes how 'Fascism haunts' Rossi's rhetorical 'classical' collonade at Gallaratese. He suggests that 'An American cannot fail to guess that Louis Kahn is . . . present';[37] the mute qualities of Rossi's forms parallel the American's call for 'silence'. Concluding his postscript in poetic vein, he dramatises Rossi's projects: 'Speechless, we open our hearts to them, and they guard our dreams'.[38]

Earlier on, Scully compares the planar piers beneath Rossi's Gallaratese housing with Kahn's rendering of the hypostyle hall at Karnak. Displaced from the tactile expres-sion of compressive force, Rossi's piers are seen to constitute the ultimate dream space (as purely 'visual beings'). Scully is, nonetheless, momentarily dispassionate enough to mention the conventional critique of Rossi's buildings as 'over-scaled and gratuitous'.[39] Deferring such a prosaic view, in the light of Rossi's conception of 'unforeseeable functions', he proposes a Freudian reading of the composition at Gallaratese.[40]

In similar vein, he addresses Rossi's 'rite of passage' at Modena Cemetery.[41] The phrase suggests the psychology behind a subsequently consistent series of projects; designs from which he infers significant parallels to American architecture. The drawings, for Sully, evidence 'Rossi's insistence' on 'architecture as a stage set for human action'. Noting an 'expectant tone', he foregoes the contingencies expressed in recurring episodes of the text: the fracture in the housing grid; fog entering the basilica; a still-life animated by domesticity; the granite table to which people come and go in the villa by the lake; a corridor awaiting the 'occasion', and the suggestiveness of the empty theatre or the potentiality of the unoccupied ETH *lichthof*. All represent circumstances with an ambivalent relation to the design of Rossi's buildings.

The Architecture of the City is Rossi's most celebrated text, first published as a book in 1966.[42] Several editions and translations followed; the American translation into English, under the auspices of the New York IAUS journal *Oppositions*, finally appeared only in 1982. The original publication reinforced Rossi's reputation as the leading figure of the Italian *Tendenza*, but by the late 1970s its wider influence had diffused under the international auspices of *Neorationalism*, and Rossi's own influence had became increasingly a singular one.

This emphasises a distinction between what the book 'represented' on its initial publication; and its status in the form of the American edition sixteen years later. No longer directly keyed in with the subsequent drift of Rossi's polemic, it had been displaced by the earlier publication of *A Scientific Autobiography*, and an ambivalence about its content was inevitable. Peter Eisenman's editorial role aligned the publication to the trajectory of Rossi's growing reputation.[43]

Eisenman notes in his preface that the translation was 'not so much a literal transcription' of the text, 'as a carefully revised edition' providing 'the style and flavour of the original' while editing out 'some of the rhetorical and repetitive passages'.[44] The clarity and simplicity sought by Eisenman is contrary to the nature of Rossi's writing, but also to his own theoretical digressions as editor.

Eisenman makes a series of claims in his short, but dense, preface (which precedes his own subsequent 'introduction'). First he asserts the character of Rossi's text as a systematic 'treatise'. This he associates with the practice of marshalling 'ancient' precedent together with built and unrealised designs. Given the lack of any reference to Rossi's own designs or drawings in the text, he is quick to also note Rossi's significant departure from this model. He argues that while purporting to be systematically 'scientific' in his analysis, Rossi also provides 'a unique anticipation of . . . (his) . . . subsequent architecture'.[45]

This claim might be thought entirely uncontentious (in that one thing leads to another). But it is asserted by Eisenman as if it were retrospectively self-evident: he views the book itself as 'an analogous artefact', concretely epitomising the theme which conditioned Rossi's work during the intervening 15 years. Given only marginal reference to analogy in the text, and the poetic licence Eisenman indulges in concluding his preface,[46] there is a certain inevitability to his argument.[47] Eisenman reiterates Rossi's nomenclature in eliding collective 'unconscious' and 'memory' to assert the social value of Rossi's expanding, but increasingly personal, *oeuvre*. What he seeks is a consistency which provides reassurance that Rossi's thinking is at one with what the buildings look like, even if this is contrary to the textual evidence.

Eisenman's 'Editor's Introduction', *The Houses of Memory: Texts of Analogue*,[48] briefly positions Rossi in relation to the

Modern Movement, before launching into the main body of his text titled 'The Texts of Analogue', concluded with a final section 'The Houses of Memory'.

Eisenman's ambition to 'contextualise' Rossi's thinking to date, beyond the limits of the original text, conditions his emphases. The opening sections of his text are headed with carefully chosen and evocative quotations from Derrida and Freud. These directly correlate with Rossi's ideas, and lend a certain *gravitas* to the proceedings. While at the outset, and in conclusion, the text takes a philosophical drift, it otherwise presents an informative *résumé* of the content of Rossi's book. This outline, however, incorporates an obsessive preoccupation with the metaphor of the 'skeleton', and the concept of 'analogical thinking', which overlay the text with themes from *A Scientific Autobiography*.

Eisenman's introduction is marked at the outset by a degree of 'over-interpretation'. He reads a spiral motif in a pictogram of a horizontal section through Hadrian's mausoleum illustrated on the cover of the fourth edition of Rossi's book. But any spiral seems absent in the circular and radial configuration. The association of the labyrinth created by Daedalus with a humanist condition of architecture, seems questionable, as does his conflated connotation of 'unfolding path' and mausoleum. Eisenman's logic spirals in on itself to a hermetic degree. There follows a claim that Rossi is situated at a 'rupture in history'. This dystopian view is aligned with Manfredo Tafuri's ideological critique.[49]

While Eisenman is working within a wider frame of reference than the book itself, he does direct aspects of Rossi's thinking towards his own formalistic conception of a American avant-garde.[50] At the end of his introduction he argues that the 'analogical drawing' embodies 'a changed condition of representation; it exists as a record of its own history', something he sees to have 'evolved directly from the writing of *The Architecture of the City*. In a characteristic displacement, the localised practice of drawing is generalised to become at one with the city.[51] Eisenman the 'editor' returns, in his conclusion, to the figure of the 'autonomous researcher' (with the humanist poet at his shoulder). These generalised persona inhabit a paragraph at once figurative yet philosophically obscure.[52]

But what of the text of *The Architecture of the City* itself? Carlo Olmo comments warily that it can, 'by virtue of its conceptual nature, be used as a theoretical text', while constituting a 'text of architectural poetics'. Remaining sceptical of its methodology, he suggests the text offers no more than 'the rhetoric of a real book of theory', noting a degree of theoretical opacity at the points where Rossi resorts to 'his architectural imaginary'.[53] If it constitutes 'a text of poetics', where does this poetic aspect reside? Claudio D'Amato suggests this is characterised by an expressive or 'literary' mode, which he contrasts with consequentially structured argument. Nonetheless particular 'episodes' stand out: a composite image of the European city devastated after the war[54] constitutes the first concrete description in the main text. Changes imprinted in 'the layers of the city that archaeologists show us' provide signs of everyday inhabitation:

> Anyone who remembers European cities after the bombings of the last war retains an image of disembowelled houses where, amid the rubble, fragments of familiar places remained standing, with their colors of faded wallpaper, laundry hanging suspended in the air, barking dogs – the untidy intimacy of places. And always we could see the house of our childhood, strangely aged, present in the flux of the city.[55]

This image is revealing for its psychological implications; the familiar 'untidy intimacy of places', starkly revealed, are associated childhood memories, no longer immediate but 'strangely aged' as the faded wallpaper.[56] But here the flux of the city is actually its devastation, associated with collective amnesia as much as active memory. In Rossi's mind, it seems, the image projects a concretely experienced suspension of past and present.

A more specific, personal memory emerges later in Rossi's discussion of the Roman Forum: 'I remember in the post-war years the sight of Cologne Cathedral in that destroyed city; nothing can conjure up the power that this work, standing intact among the ruins, had on the imagination.' Rather than an expression of trauma, for Rossi this memory serves as a prompt to castigate the subsequent 'pallid reconstruction' of the city centre around the cathedral.

The recollection of Cologne Cathedral, an icon of national identity, in the banal context of post-war reconstruction, as if in a 'modern' museum display of traditional objects, parallels how an 'architecture for museums' redeems the historical object as an aspect of the 'imagination'.[57] This is a key point in the book, since it is here that Rossi first deploys the concept of analogy, fundamental to his view of his later work and *A Scientific Autobiography*.[58] Eisenman in his haste to extend Rossi's interpretation of the concept as intrinsic to his own thinking, forgoes the problematic origins of this argument.

Lost in Translation

The first significant monograph published after *The Architecture of the City, Aldo Rossi: Buildings and Projects*[59] catalogues Rossi's projects from 1959 to 1983. Preceding Rafael Moneo's concluding 'Postscript', the covers of selected publications are illustrated in a grid format. On the first page the two *Oppositions* books are illustrated in their yellow ochre dust-jackets, to the left and right. They frame the mainly Italian publications above, and emphasise a symmetrical axis.

This aptly summarises their role in defining Rossi's status as architect and intellectual to an international audience. Taken with the IAUS catalogue they plausibly constitute the 'treatise' sought by both Eisenman and Rossi, but one that refers to realised buildings primarily through emblematic drawings and literary description.[60] The three publications strive to present a consistent *oeuvre* of texts, drawings and buildings, through their rhetorical 'framing' of Rossi's drawings and translated texts (whose content is often significantly inconsistent). Ironically the less than immediately explicable *A Scientific Autobiography* is left in principle to stand for itself (if only in the context of Scully's following postscript).

Rossi's final contribution to the *Oppositions* series of publications is his introduction to the translation of Adolf Loos' 'collected essays'. Rossi views Loos as his mentor, and not only for his precursor's visit to America:

Adolf Loos' writings are an integral part of his life's work; together with his designs, his constructions, and his biography, they display a coherence rarely found in an artist of the modern era. The totality of his writings, which arise from a great variety of circumstances and are often fragmentary, nevertheless present this almost systematic coherence, as though it were really a treatise on architecture he was writing.[61]

Eisenman, in the American publications, provides for Rossi (or rather his American audience) what Rossi himself wishes to infer from Loos' varied *oeuvre*.

Rossi introspectively projects his own ambitions, yet Moneo relates how in an earlier text:

> In describing Boullée's attitudes, he discretely conceals any revelation of his own thought through the interpretation of Boullée's work.[62]

This psychology of concealment, or projection, is not unrelated to Rossi coming to terms with aspects of his own personality and experience, in his practice of architectural design. In a parallel conception, he conceives the history of the individual city as affective biography. The unstable relation between introspection and rhetorical ambition in Rossi's thinking, conditions Eisenman's philosophical 'overwriting', so evident in these American publications.

What ultimately informs Rossi' relationship with America? His interest in the mythic America sought by Italian anti-fascist writers, and the association in Visconti's films between the wide spaces of the Po Valley ('lost within national equilibrium') and the 'great open spaces' of America, provide a model for the transposition of Italian experience into the American realm. In taking issue with Joseph Rykwert's reluctance to speculate about Loos' experience in America, he describes how for Loos:

> Resolutely exploring the streets of downtown New York the beauty of this nucleus of American business struck him in much the same way that the beauty of aristocratic and capitalist London had once struck Engels.

If Loos' experience of America, was to be turned to critical advantage on his return to the 'hypocrisies' of Austro-Hungary, the context in which Rossi's work was published in America set out a rhetorical framework for the international 'fame' associated with his later buildings. A retrospective tendency, exemplified in the post-dated drawings in the IAUS catalogue, and the reverse chronology of the translated texts, also surfaces in *A Scientific Autobiography* where a discursive quality animates the text whenever it refers back to the, apparently objective, analytical concepts of The Architecture of the City.

These passages contrast with the otherwise episodic character of the 'notes' that characterise the main body of the text. The previously 'ideological' becomes mediated by a personal vicariousness, while recurrent anecdotes concerning Rossi's own experience, become absorbed into the text's consistently disjunctive surface. Unless read episodically, it remains frustratingly divergent (and less than immediately accessible).

Lobsinger revealingly identifies the trope of repetition in Rossi's work as a form of consolation or compensation for loss. Rossi's retrospective views of childhood experience, cultural authenticity, architectural tradition or critical objectivity, may all be understood in these terms. Eisenman's commentary provides a different kind of reassurance. Placing Rossi's narratives in relation to his own conception of an avant-garde, he conceptualises in philosophical terms, ambivalent aspects of Rossi's architecture – the repetition of form and aspects of contingency. In Eisenman's hands these come to inform procedures for the production of a contemporary formal repertoire far removed from Rossi's.

Rossi's 'influence' may be seen epitomised in the extent of his later international practice. Alternatively it might be found in the work of architects, at one remove from the formal qualities of his architecture, yet engaged with his idiosyncratic ideas. The first depends, to a degree, on the conviction with which the drawings effect a material translation of Rossi's ideas. In spite of the attempt to characterise the American publications as a consistent treatise, this remains an open question.

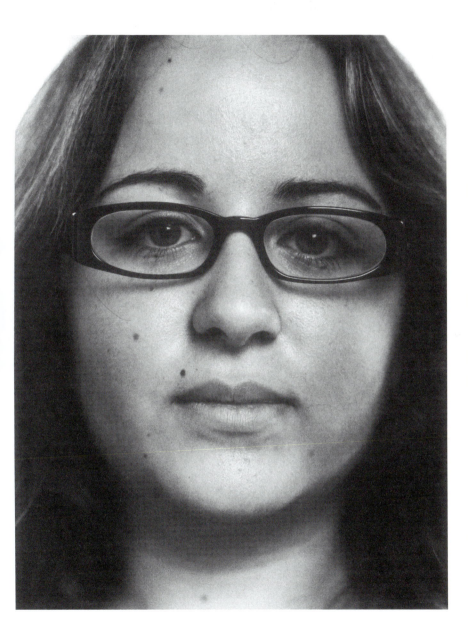

The Netherlands – Koolhaas and the Profession at Play   7

Hans van der Heijden

> When you are young and want to become a film star, you go to Hollywood. When you want to be an architect, you go to the Netherlands. The Netherlands are the Hollywood of architecture.[1]

Is this ironic? Is this a publicity slogan of one of the many institutes promoting Dutch architecture abroad? A mantra? Or is it a fantasy of an eager architecture student? No, this is the serious credo of Canadian/English/New Zealand architects S333, offering their explanation for setting up practice in the Netherlands. S333's case confirms the myth of the Netherlands as a tolerant society, open to foreign contributions to a modern and ever lively architectural debate.[2]

Inevitably, the Netherland's liberal image is tied in with the reputation of Rem Koolhaas and his OMA practice. In S333's terms, Koolhaas is the megastar of an architectural Hollywood. Respected opinion leaders including *NRC Handelsblad*[3] leave little details unmentioned about his personal life, sexual habits and business scandals.

Koolhaas is an adored public figure with mythical properties.[4] Archis' editor in chief Ole Bouman is reported to have said that 'Rem Koolhaas flies to and fro for acquisitions, there are little really interesting jobs in the world'. His words suggest a problematic high level of identification with Koolhaas' boredom, real or pretended, towards the bread and butter work of architectural practice. Nevertheless, viewed from abroad, Koolhaas' case is quite easily regarded as a *pars pro toto*[5] for the sort Dutch architecture so much admired.

Without pretending that Koolhaas is the caricature of the common Dutch architect, Koolhaas' XL status magnifies various local circumstances that have contributed to the rise and fame of Dutch design practice as a whole. This cult of the person obscures the origins of the man's myth. It is therefore necessary to look at the start of Koolhaas' Dutch career, the way various undercurrents in Dutch architecture merged after his appearance on the scene, how the perception of his first built works was manipulated in publications and finally how the Dutch construction practice has informed Koolhaas' work.

Landing

In the 1970s and 1980s, Dutch modernism found itself in a crisis. As opposed to the situation in America and other European countries, the postmodernism a la Venturi, Moore and Graves did not have much impact on the debate, which in the Netherlands took place not so much on an architectural but an ideological level. The debate was coloured, if not dominated, by a paralysing controversy in the setting of the technical university in Delft (the largest of the two architecture schools in the country). The players were divided into two distinct camps, one formed by architects such as Aldo van Eyck and Herman Hertzberger and the other led by Carel Weeber.[6]

As former Team-X rebels, Van Eyck and Hertzberger claimed the humanist morals of the early modernist heroes Rietveld, Duiker, Van de Vlugt and Bakema. Their design attitude, very much reflected in their teaching, was premised on individual artistic skills resulting in singular, unrepeatable 'original' edifices and the promotion of the architect as a classic building master. The magazine *Forum* was their publication platform. Weeber, by contrast, fitted into the rationalist line of architects like Berlage, Oud and Van den Broek, who had a much more institutional perception of the profession. Weeber stressed the new production circumstances of building and was engaged with a modernised assignment of the architect within the construction industry and his camp had a certain affinity with the Italian Tendenza. Weeber combined his intellectual stature with a bulky, but moderately received body of work. Weeber was controversial and, despite not being trendy, firmly on the map of the intellectual elite of the Dutch polder.

The way Koolhaas, being a Londoner at the time, landed between these father figures is a fine example of how a radical can profit from deliberately selecting and cherishing his enemies. Koolhaas was introduced to the Dutch architectural world in a special issue of the magazine Wonen TABK (now Archis) in 1978. In a now famous conversation with Hans van Dijk, Koolhaas violently took position against Forum, especially targeting Herman Herzberger as a moralist whom Koolhaas accused of *Montessori terror*. 'Does Herzberger ever talk about other things than that you should have a special brick to put the milk bottle on? Even the first porn film has more nuanced ideas on the interaction between housewife and milkman', Koolhaas remarked. The inward looking attitudes and self-promotion of Hertzberger and Aldo van Eyck were ridiculed: 'Ignorance is imagined to be a virtue here. Deliberately not knowing things, as a sort of ideology. (. . .) Do you know the phenomenon of polder blindness? Because of the absence of scale reference a hare sometimes seems to be as big as a cow in the polder-land'.[7] Some years later, it proved much more effective to mock Rietveld's Schroeder House than to frantically fight the monopolisation of the Dutch modernist canon by Forum: 'You can see the Schroeder House as sublime, but you can also read it as an overfull seventeenth century genre piece. For the Schroeder House is full. Full of discoveries, full of intentions big and small, full of wishes, full of things, full of colour or at least paint'.[8] In those years Koolhaas' eloquent criticism was very much directed at the roots of Forum's belief system.

As a new kid on the block, Koolhaas reacted strongly against the Dutch father figures and yet he did so differently for each of the two camps. If Van Eyck and Hertzberger were ridiculed without mercy, Weeber was simply neglected and consequently out-smarted. Koolhaas' critique of Forum niche-marketed his intellectual position at the cost of Weeber's. When Koolhaas landed in the Netherlands he immediately claimed a position between the local masters of the time, but he carefully located his actual place of landing in the rationalists' niche.

Part of the attraction attributed to Koolhaas in the 1980s was that he was a much sexier alternative to the moralists of Forum than the ones that had been available prior to his appearance on the scene. Unsurprisingly, Koolhaas' father killing was appealing to younger architects and students. His work was instantly imitated. Koolhaas' black and white plans and perspectives were as precise as computer drawings. His schemes were explained through diagrams, easily legible especially for those familiar with Weeber's Delft rationalism. In the 1985 special issue of *The Architectural Review* 'The Netherlands', he was bluntly categorised as a 'Rotterdam Rationalist'.[9] Although we now suspect Koolhaas is an inherent-by-proxy of Forum's moralism and we now know that his buildings show an equal bias to invention, fullness and paint as Rietveld's, at the time the categorisation of *AR* was regarded as being plausible.

An analogue interpretation was outlined by the historians Michelle Provoost and Wouter Vanstiphout stressing with polemical bias, the importance of the urban studies by Delft academics that were in vogue in the 1980s. Based on the reading of the French *sciences humaines* of Foucault and others, 'their outrageous paranoia seemed to cut right through all strata of conceptions of what the city and history is. The result of the aggressive archive research (. . .) was that the beginning of the nineteen eighties, all at once, could be understood as a whirling mass of ideas, rudimentary apparatuses of knowledge, trances of regulation, lies and mystifications, black holes of ambitions. Historic research had never been this exciting, but what on earth was left to the individual urbanist or architect?'[10] The claim of Provoost and Vanstiphout is that this 'paranoia that always hits the nail on the head no matter where the blow falls'[11] was diverted by Koolhaas. Where he shared a critical paranoia with the Delft rationalists, in the analysis of the chaos of the modern city, he differed in his attitude to the conspiracies that were found. Much rather than to reveal the conspiracies in the western city, his agenda was to set up one of his own, generating the space in which he could design.[12]

Role Model

A 'sublime start of a generation of architects' was documented in the exhibition catalogue *'Referentie OMA'* by Bernard Colenbrander.[13] In 1995, the exhibition and book were, without doubt, premature. Their main merit is the vast collection of anecdotes told by early students in Delft and the employees of Koolhaas. It gives an insight of the poor soil on which Koolhaas' seed fell: 'Design education in Delft was suffering, genuine suffering' with desperate field trips to new towns like Zoetermeer where 'there was nothing to see, absolutely nothing'.[14] Striking is the disappointment at the intellectual captainship of Weeber, disqualified by Neutelings as 'an adequate station manager'.[15] The architectural profession as taught in Delft felt like an intellectual fishbowl.

In this situation, Koolhaas did not merely introduce a set of new ideas, he also established a practical role model for the 1980s. Koolhaas never complained. In the world of OMA, there was no space for worries about difficult clients, philistine contractors, building regs, specs and constructions detail. Koolhaas found his way seemingly easy and was careful not to contradict this reputation. Negotiation[16] and a 'merciless good cheer'[17] became the self-evident weapons of a new architect's practice and problems seemed to bounce back on his ironic elasticity.

This was confirmed by projects like the design study for the conversion of the Arnhem Panopticon prison, commissioned by the Dutch government in 1979. Koolhaas' design report was analytical, well written and lucid. Koolhaas had no office, but was reported to have a good presence and to be able to talk. He asked a fee that was considered to be way too low by the client representatives, but produced an enormous volume of neatly drawn perspectives, plans, sections and puzzling diagrams. The prison design illustrated Koolhaas ability to idealise the architectural problem itself, in this case the Panopticon principle. In fact, based on a basic understanding of the building type, Koolhaas proposed to replace the central control that had originated from the solitary confinement with an *empty* centre overlooked by prisoners, *living* in enlightened groups as the ethos of the 1970s demanded. Koolhaas freely discussed loose facts like the monumental properties of the architecture, its semiotic and ideological values and its typological possibilities. Ultimately, the *dismantled* Panopticon is placed upon a cruciform new set of corridors below ground a new ideological basement like a *historic relic*.[18] Such rhetoric was appealing to Dutch students and young architects at every level. Finally something real happened.

Marketing of Failure

The prison was never built and neither were a range of other early OMA schemes. The designs that did make it to the construction site in the 1980s were anxiously awaited.

Many publications, most notably OMA's first retrospective book SMLXL, make us believe that the Dance Theatre in The Hague, the Kunsthal in Rotterdam, and the villa Dall' Ava in Paris are the first built works of the paper architect Koolhaas. This is inaccurate for OMA had built a number of schemes well before that. In the 1980s, a police station in Almere, a twin tower housing estate in Groningen, a bus terminal in Rotterdam and IJ-Plein social housing district in Amsterdam were realised. All these designs were excluded from SMLXL. The Byzantium Building in Amsterdam was included, but merely as the setting of a comic strip revealing the philistine nature of the developers and contractors involved. We see outrageous clients disqualifying the technology of the building with the untranslatable term 'Kut details' and hear the resident say 'We didn't ask them for the interior . . . I hear they are impossible'.[19] No photographs or drawings were printed. The Byzantium story in SMLXL is ostentatious in its attempt to compensate for the poor reception of the first generation of OMA edifices.

There was one exception: IJ-Plein. This estate quite rapidly became an icon for a new elan in social housing design. The scheme (re-)introduced a range of novelties of different nature: an insulated render facade, the urban villa, landscape design as an emancipated architectural category, traditional apartment typologies with front doors at street level and ingenious internal staircase arrangements. In design terms, the scheme established a sharp discontinuity with previous norms in volume house building. IJ-Plein was an acceptable and desirable type of modernity. The scheme was immediately adopted in urban design and architecture practice as well as in teaching. Elementary studies of Leupen were published prior to completion, followed by a more elaborate documentation of the scheme a few years later.[20]

The architectural development of the IJ-Plein master plan was supervised by OMA (but for the most part designed by local architects and commissioned by clients that insisted on ordinary brick facades). IJ-Plein contained the promise of a design-led future in Dutch house building, while simultaneously absorbing the practical assets post-war volume building had generated for the construction industry and it had an enormous impact on housing specialists. If OMA has ever made a scheme that was impersonal enough for it to be copied, it was IJ-plein. However, the status of the scheme in the international context was less vibrant. IBA Berlin was dominating the discourse in housing. And the shining white aluminium panels of Richard Meier and his modernist virtuosity stood for everything the profession believed in.

SMLXL repositioned OMA's work and set an agenda suitable for the international design world. The remarketing of earlier disappointments was of strategic importance. This marketing of failure is not just evident in SMLXL in the sense that it was selective in the choice of buildings that were included; the book established also for the first time a coquetry regarding imperfection and improvisation. So, we do not only find computer or quasi computer drawings, but also scribbled brief fax instructions for a bus pavilion, and handwritten remarks on the prints upon the general arrangement drawings of Villa Dall' Ava.[21] It is not important whether these pages in SMLXL are staged or not or whether their message is confirmed by Koolhaas' actual behaviour in his studio. What counts is the message: the relativity of the architectural end product and the self-confidence of the architect to show his disinterest in the end product. Paradoxically, this cultivation of imperfection reinforces the position of the architect. In a world without measures and standards the architect can easily claim his assets.

'There is no success like failure', Bob Dylan sang, 'but failure is no success at all'.

Consensus

And then there are the peculiarities of construction practice in the Dutch polder. Two are worth mentioning here. First, there is a strong bias towards consensus-based co-operation. In contrast to the Anglo-Saxon business world there is limited opportunity for case law. In addition to the already solid legal framework – based on Roman law – much regulation is drawn up between branch organisations and the government. As a result there is a weak claim culture. The reflex is to sort out conflicts by compromise. The size of the country is a natural self-regulatory factor: conflicts quickly inflate in scale in a small country and may wreck reputations for a lifetime. There is no second chance for architects, contractors or clients who have seriously failed.

Second, the Dutch procurement of projects is quite specific in its definition of responsibilities and liabilities. The standard contracts between client and builder transfer the liability for the performance of the project in its entity to the builder. Additionally, the contractor is obliged to guarantee the performance of the project in its entity for a substantial period and has to offer a back-to-back guarantee for the sub-contractors involved. Dutch contractors carry the end responsibility for the technical quality of the building. The liability of the designer is limited. As a result of their legal liabilities, contractors were forced to develop expertise on building technology. The technical design skill within Dutch contracting companies, compared to that of, for instance UK builders, is therefore substantial.

The classic role of the architect as a building master has slowly evaporated after Second World War and it is often held that this has weakened the position of the architect as a determining force in construction. But that needs to be nuanced. It should be noted for instance that this situation also is the background for a continuous and easy penetration of younger and foreign practices in the architects' market. Experience and reputations are relative assets for clients when there is always a contractor to take over the liabilities. Furthermore, the large contribution to the technical development and management of the construction process reduces the effort of the architect substantially and allows him to concentrate on the typological and spatial development and aesthetics of their scheme. Architect's fees are relatively low, but the project administration and related management is not extensive. Again, this works in favour of smaller and younger practices.

It is inevitable that all this stimulates a strong industrial vernacular. Construction components in the Netherlands are standardised to a high degree. It is virtually impossible for architects to design bespoke building components and structures. Buildings present themselves as assembled catalogue products on what could be characterised as a *serviced frame*. Structures and services have their own logic. They are determined by an authorless, shared know-how. At the level of this serviced frame, building methodology escapes any architectural control. Typically, construction is an additive process. It is not exclusively a Dutch modus operandi, but reversely the Dutch industry is not capable of switching to more integrated design approaches. Architects like, say Peter Zumthor or Tadao Ando, would be unlikely to flourish in Dutch conditions. Dutch industrial vernacular at the level of the *serviced frame* is extremely refractory.

Projects are *born naked* in which action limited typological or spatial manipulation is possible.[22] The newborns are then dressed up according to the demands of the day. Dutch architectural design, also that of the famous and *experimental* variety, focus on spaces, typology and skin materials, but not on the issues that may be located between. The tactile exuberance characteristic of Koolhaas' turbo-modernism is a celebration of this situation, much rather than a victory over it. It is a survival strategy.

Playing Man

Clearly Rem Koolhaas is a homo ludens, a playing and playful man who has considered any suitable professional category as an object of play. Koolhaas' profession is a rational game with ideology, positions, reputations, success and failures of others and the architect himself and the conception and making of buildings itself is a game as well. There is little news here perhaps, as others have understood it as a Dali-like critical paranoia.

However, Koolhaas' carefully constructed metropolitan image, does not contradict the fact that he remains a Dutch boy. It is tempting to swap the international perspective and look at Koolhaas from a regional perspective. One then sees Koolhaas as the grandson of an Amsterdam architect, as the architectural successor of the other playing, no Dutchman, Constant Nieuwenhuis, as the inheritor of Dutch experimental improvisation a la Rietveld, as a salesman and entrepreneur. There is also the Koolhaas who in his early career has profited from the accessibility of the Dutch architectural market and the architect who not only ridiculed local construction practice, but also extensively profited from it in his first realised works – and on the international stage. He is the Hollywood star that was once supported by the vast Dutch cultural grant network and who introduced the awareness of negotiation within the making of architecture.[23] There is the Koolhaas who was so frantic about the tension between the moralism of Van Eyck and the brutal rationalism of Weeber, but apparently reconciled these contradicting positions in the Dutch discourse. And then there is the architect building individualised masterpieces with an awareness of a shift in the role and responsibilities of the architect, simultaneously riding the waves of Dutch industrial vernacular.

Looking at Koolhaas as a polder boy helps to explain the limited volume of his realised work abroad. International business life is incomparably more antagonistic than the Dutch business world. Dutch architects, like their counterparts in the construction industry, are badly prepared and equipped for the demands that are common on the international playing field. Dutch diplomacy is not always appreciated and effective.

While Koolhaas is perhaps not a typical Dutch architect – whatever that may be – there is much evidence that he is the product of his home country. The playing man is a spectacular, but not the only option within Dutch architecture, although in terms of publicity it is a domineering one. Indeed, Koolhaas and his colleagues prevent themselves from establishing firmly in practice, also in the Netherlands. The lack of counter pressure against the construction industry's monopoly of the serviced frame turns the architect into a reliable partner, but has paradoxically eroded his expertise and possible input further. Whether the judo attitude Koolhaas so eagerly adopted and advocated is a reason or a symptom, it is safe to say that it has gained popularity amongst clients and decision makers in recent years: the architect is hired to *design-in* the weird surface, well isolated from crucial structural and logistic components of buildings. Dutch playing architects are thus well suitable for the festival architecture of a recent generation of embassies, world-expos, city centre malls, train terminals and an occasional housing project, but are as yet not acceptable in less spectacular areas where integration matters.

A painful example is the redevelopment of Amsterdam Museumplein and the restoration and extension of the surrounding museums. Being regarded as a pivotal, but complicated urban task, it is mainly designed by Portuguese, Spanish, Danish and Japanese architects. Only the supermarket and the underground parking garage are left to Dutch firms. Is it a coincidence that their input is restricted to *shopping* and *infrastructure*, two key Koolhaas themes?

Germany – (Un)edited Architecture; *Wettbewerbe Aktuell*

8

Torsten Schmiedeknecht

Introduction

Wettbewerbe Aktuell makes a competition entry into an original architectural achievement.[1]

Architect Ramona Buxbaum

The work shown in *Wettbewerbe Aktuell* is of a decent standard but is rarely ever spectacular. You don't win design competitions with spectacular projects in this country – a successful project needs to be able to reach a consensus between a lot of different people.[2]

Architect Dorothee Stürmer

The best schemes never win.[3]

Prof Johann Eisele

Germany has a unique procurement system for publicly funded architecture. For the decades following the Second World War every town hall, kindergarten, school, hospital, etc. was commissioned via, mostly anonymous, architecture competitions. In 1971, Thomas Hoffmann-Kuhnt, then a student and working as an architectural assistant in an office frequently participating in design competitions, had an idea that subsequently transformed the dissemination of information about competitions throughout the country. He founded the journal *Wettbewerbe Aktuell* to publish results and drawings of prize winning schemes from architecture competitions all over Germany, chronicling details such as the type of competition, the building type, the names of the jurors, the prize money and prize winners.

Between July 1971 and December 2004, *Wettbewerbe Aktuell* has published the results of 2467 architecture competitions in total. Its first 34 volumes present the largest coherent collection of drawings of un-built design ideas in contemporary German architecture.

The journal currently has a distribution of 13,500 copies per issue and is read widely within the architectural profession and among architecture students in Germany. Over the years *Wettbewerbe Aktuell* has become a kind of reference catalogue of German architects who regularly participate in competitions. Every month the results of about six competitions are documented and published in detail by *Wettbewerbe Aktuell*. The journal is structured into three main parts: advertising of competitions to be launched; detailed documentation of competition results and a section showing built projects that resulted from earlier competitions (this section – *Wettbewerbe weiterverfolgt* – was introduced in the mid-1990s). In addition to this, the successful applicant's schemes (that usually includes 1st, 2nd, 3rd, 4th and 5th place and a number of commendations) of about 10 competitions are documented on a maximum of two pages each, mainly presenting model photographs.

The detailed documentation of a competition usually consists of two parts. Each competition opens with a title page containing the factual information on the competition: client, geographical area for eligible participants, professionals eligible (i.e. architects in self-employment, employment, public service employment, landscape architects, etc.), number of participants, date of jury, jurors and prize-winners, a brief text containing background information on the competition's purpose and a summary of the schedule of accommodation, followed by the recommendation of the jury as to which scheme should be awarded the commission. The second part of the documentation consists of the publication of the drawings and model photographs – usually about one or two A4 pages per scheme – of the awarded projects, plus the jury's statement on each project.

The journal has its own reference system ordered by functional building type. Each page is punch holed, suggesting that the reader could establish their own library by filing the competitions according to the publisher's reference codes (also corresponding with and summarised in an annual contents list).

Wettbewerbe Aktuell is solely dedicated to the publication of competition related information and does not publish any other material. This essay attempts to investigate and illustrate how the publication contributes to the culture of publicly funded architecture in Germany by disseminating ideas and information in very particular ways, and how it thus might be affecting the continued production of the built environment and the architectural discourse in the country. Between July 2003 and September 2004 I interviewed nine architects all of whom had studied architecture in Germany and six of whom are currently working as practising architects and are regularly participating in architectural (design) competitions.[4] The practising architects were critical and not entirely convinced regarding the measure of influence the journal might have on their own design or competition practice, and the main credit given to the journal by the architects was that in their view it made the process of procurement by design competition more transparent. To the contrary, a city planner, a representative of the *Architekten- and Stadtplanerkammer Hessen*[5] as well as the founder and editor of *Wettbewerbe Aktuell* all believed that the journal could or did have an impact on design practice and thus the development of publicly funded architecture.

Wettbewerbe Aktuell provides the material, like no other journal or forum, not only for a national discourse around publicly funded building projects but also for a discourse around a vast number of un-built contemporary architectural schemes.

Given its readership it could be said that no members club or other kind of architectural organisation could achieve this level of communication between architects about their work.

This essay will assess the influence of *Wettbewerbe Aktuell* by considering the following questions:

1. What does *Wettbewerbe Aktuell* offer ordinary practising architects and newly established design practices?
2. Does the competition system itself lead to a tendency towards design by consensus or does it provide the entrance platform for the potential super-star? How are either of these possibilities reflected in or supported by *Wettbewerbe Aktuell*?
3. What does a competition actually do? Does it produce stars? Does it prevent very bad architecture? Does it promote good architecture? Does it prevent very good architecture? How does a possible promotion of a *high*

level middle ground fit into the contemporary profession's obsession with publicity?

4. In what way does the catalogue style of *Wettbewerbe Aktuell* help architects?

5. What are the effects of the very particular competition format and drawing style and its reproduction in *Wettbewerbe Aktuell*?

6. What are the effects of *Wettbewerbe Aktuell*'s specific editorial control and what are the dependencies between owner, publisher, editor and architects?

Instigating and Maintaining an Architectural Discourse

Through *Wettbewerbe Aktuell* the German competition system is elevated into a competition culture, a forum where people can actively follow and compare what is being done in other parts of the country.[6]

Prof Max Bächer

Wettbewerbe Aktuell elevates an architect's contribution to a design competition – which really in the first place is always simply a bid for a commission – into an independent architectural feat.[7]

Architect Peter Karle

Despite the journal's highly specialised subject area aimed at very specific audiences and its general unsuitability for the coffee table, it is the average German architect's undeniable desire to see their work published in *Wettbewerbe Aktuell*.

Between the 1960s and 1990s Germany probably had the most thriving architectural competition scene in Europe, if not in the world.[8] It is in this context, where open design competitions had for decades provided young practices with a chance to compete with and to beat the architectural establishment and where architects with no previous building experience of their own could get commissions for buildings worth millions of Deutsch Marks/Euros, that the relevance of *Wettbewerbe Aktuell* may be acknowledged.

It is suggested that, due to its specific focus on competitions, the journal could help to build reputations for architects by far exceeding the renown that a practice might be able to attribute to its built work. In addition, *Wettbewerbe Aktuell* offers the ordinary – building – architect a chance to extend their role, and understanding of what they do, beyond that of providing a service to a client. Un-built project work is presented and thus located in the realm of an on-going architectural discourse; the skill of design is focused upon – over all the other complications, compromises and struggles that architects have to deal with in every other aspect of their work. The *application process* competition is elevated by *Wettbewerbe Aktuell* to an independent contribution to the architectural debate and, by putting them into the public realm, awards competition schemes value beyond the acquisitive role they have for the authors. Thus *Wettbewerbe Aktuell* lends the status of a perceptible achievement to a competition scheme and hence a project which is published in the journal might become more noteworthy for the architect, possibly registering in its own project number in the architects' archive, whether resulting in a building or not. Accordingly, most architects regard competitions as independent projects – elevating them from providing a service into undertaking a more artistic feat – and one interviewee thought that it was interesting that most architectural monographs are called something like 'buildings and projects' when really they should be titled 'buildings and applications for building projects' for most un-built projects are really an application of some kind.

Up to the early 1990s there was a tendency for a number of *usual suspects* to win prizes; they would appear in *Wettbewerbe Aktuell* on a regular basis, sometimes to a degree that they had nothing nearly as impressive to show in their portfolio of built projects. One side effect of these practices' continual appearance in *Wettbewerbe Aktuell* was that of *perpetual breeding* where the most talented designers would sift through copies of *Wettbewerbe Aktuell* and apply to the most successful competition practices for jobs. It can be presumed that the work of some of these practices had a tendency to dominate the scene and to have a real influence on other architects' competition practice – both regarding the architecture as much as the presentation technique. However, because of changes in the competition system and the currently difficult economic climate for architects – it is now common practice to select participants of a competition via a lottery or to invite a number of hand picked firms, be it large commercial practices for specific briefs or *international stars* to deliver signature designs – it seems to be impossible for most firms specialised in competitions to have a run of successful contests and subsequent publications in *Wettbewerbe Aktuell*. Hence the market where an office could have previously impacted on the competition scene and built a career from there seems to have ceased to exist for most.

For example, in the early 1980s the reputation of one practice, Eisele & Fritz from Darmstadt, was built mainly on their successful – and at times spectacular – competition entries (and, but to a lesser degree, on a number of built individual dwellings published in *Domus* and *L'Architecture D'Aujourd'Hui*). The impact that the practice had however was through its publications in *Wettbewerbe Aktuell*, where they also featured twice on the front cover. *Wettbewerbe Aktuell* was the main means of communication through which Eisele & Fritz exerted a greater influence on the scene than vice versa, evident in the number of schemes in competitions subsequent to their successes, were competitors tried to copy both their architecture and presentation style.[9]

Are Competitions the Epitome of Design-by-Consensus or the Platform for the Entrance of the Super-Star?

Wettbewerbe Aktuell has a similar function to Hello magazine for it satisfies one's curiosity with regards to who does what, who has become an *Also Ran*, who is having a Come-Back etc. One should not underestimate the emotional dimension of the competition scene where competitions can provide a *mental safety exit* for architects. The emotional set up of an architect is a rather important factor in their design ability. The design competition is one of the few places where architects are not accountable towards anyone, do not have to explain anything and, in principle, can do what they like.[10]

Prof Nicolas Fritz

It is important to think about the task at hand and to find plausible solutions that are also easy to communicate later on between the client and the different user groups and lobbies. In such a system, an architecture that talks about extreme authorship, or a signature architecture, will always have difficulties to win competitions.[11]

Architect Ramona Buxbaum

Competitions might be mistaken by some as a continuation of the way one used to work at university. The danger for young offices is that they don't possess enough background knowledge about the whole competition system and about how juries in design competitions operate. How important it is to reach a consensus in the jury and thus how a project needs to be able to appeal to this consensus. Thus young people might be very disappointed not to get rewarded in a competition with the same kind of work that would have gained them maybe a distinction at architecture school.[12]

Architect Peter Karle

Wettbewerbe Aktuell sets up an interesting conundrum: while on the one hand the journal helps to maintain an architectural status quo based on the idea of consensus, it simultaneously encourages the desire in architects to be recognised for their individual achievements. The former could be interpreted as being in the tradition of German model of democracy and the desire not to stand out caused by a post war national trauma while the latter is a consequence of a growing celebrity culture in all areas of contemporary western society.

In the above quotation Fritz refers to a backdrop to architectural activity that is rarely discussed: the curiosity of architects with regards to *who does what*. The title of this section is polarised; perhaps one of the things that *Wettbewerbe Aktuell* actually does is to inform architects of the shades of activity inbetween superstardom and invisibility. In other countries without a journal like *Wettbewerbe Aktuell* this middle ground of design activity might be less visible, or if, then in journals with a less heavy emphasis on design. In this context the section *Wettbewerbe weiterverfolgt* in which the publishers show completed buildings resulting from won competitions becomes particularly interesting for it is showing buildings that are not always representing the kind of architecture that would find its way into mainstream journals such as *Bauwelt, Arch+* or *Deutsche Bauzeitung*.

One hypothesis about the role of *Wettbewerbe Aktuell* is that whatever effect competitions may have, the journal importantly magnifies the mechanics of the competition system. One interviewee likened the journal to 'throwing iron filings across a magnetic field and thus making more transparent the particular method of procurement that a competition presents'.

The journal provides a significant insight into the relationship between jurors, architects and architectures. This is not to suggest that there are or were active *leaks* between competitors and jurors but it is intriguing to follow that particular architects seem to do particularly well in competitions with particular members or chairmen of juries. With a tool like *Wettbewerbe Aktuell* at hand one is obviously tempted to assess one's chances or to contemplate whether or in what kind of way to enter a contest, by finding out who was on the jury and to scrutinise what type of work they could favour. In turn this is the case for clients wishing to launch competitions and who are looking for jurors, or in the case of an invited competition, needing to select participants. Juries, whether in open or invited competitions, generally consist of members of the profession and a number of representatives of the client which for public buildings would include politicians, civil servants and a high ranking member of the institution commissioning the project. The German competitions directive (GRW) stipulates that registered architects have to have a majority of at least one person on the panel.[13]

Due to the range of representatives that make up the jury panel, the German competition system seldom allows for eccentricities and can generally be seen as being unsuitable for a spectacular approach to architecture. One of the interviewees claimed that only in very rare cases did competitions in Germany produce or generate an architecture that could be described as trend setting or forward looking. As an exception from this rule he quoted the design for the 1972 Olympic Stadium in Munich by Behnisch and Frei Otto. In addition, the – presumed – willingness of jurors to make concessions in order to push their own favourite scheme to the top may result in the awarding of 2nd or 3rd prizes to qualitatively questionable schemes. *Wettbewerbe Aktuell* has no filter to prevent publication of these schemes.[14]

The *Safety First* Phenomenon – Conformism and Breaks with Conformism

The quality of architecture in Germany has increased in the last twenty years. I am not referring to the highlights here but to the general standard, the middle ground. One would have to investigate how far publications generally have contributed to this phenomenon but I would imagine that *Wettbewerbe Aktuell* has played some role in this development.[15]

Prof Johann Eisele

It is easy to imagine that the editor of *Wettbewerbe Aktuell* did not anticipate the success nor the impact that his initial idea would eventually have. However, despite there being no scientific proof, one can only speculate how the German competition scene would have developed without the journal. It was assumed by one interviewee that the journal has a similar effect on competitions as other mass media have on their target audience, encouraging conformism amongst the architectural fraternity leading to a kind of *safety first* approach in competition design. This assumption was in some way confirmed in another interview with the suggestion that the dissemination of knowledge in *Wettbewerbe Aktuell* takes place on different levels: first, on a graphic level where architects can study how to draw what, second, on a typological level and third, on a *how do I win first prize* level appealing to a kind of *how can I improve myself as a successful or an inventive designer* attitude. What is problematic here is that graphics can be copied, typology can be learned, but convincing formal concepts are to a certain degree dependent on the individual's talent, engagement and possibly experience.

While all three levels presumably play a role in the readers' subconscious decision to buy the journal, the *safety first* attitude rooted in the former two levels might also prevent to some degree the rise of a star system by counteracting the desire to produce extreme architectures for competition entries.

Without a publication like *Wettbewerbe Aktuell* architects would, presumably, operate in more of a vacuum, possibly trying to reinvent the wheel in their pursuit of originality every time they enter a competition. This could have a number of effects, one of which is that competition design would take its inspiration from built architectures rather than from published competition schemes – and thus drawings – and another that a more eccentric type of architecture might emerge in Germany.

In the interviews there were a number of suggestions that competitions have changed in a way that it seems is no longer possible to go for a strong idea and to then draw up a scheme in diagrammatic fashion in one weekend. *Wettbewerbe Aktuell*, if indeed it encourages conformism in participants might have played some role in this shift. A tendency to conform could be followed by a reduction of the solutions explored for the same brief and hence more schemes of the same type would compete with each other which in turn would force architects to pay more attention to detail, at least on a planning level. One of the interviewees' description of their approach to a recent Bank competition as 'weighing up between three or four standard solutions and a number of extreme solutions no one would think of' illustrates how *Wettbewerbe Aktuell* might impact on such a scenario. While the argument can hardly be that *Wettbewerbe Aktuell* produces the standard solutions it undoubtedly sets them in the public realm and reveals them to a broader audience of architects. This might then perpetuate the limitation to an approved number of standard solutions in subsequent competitions. Similarly, however, in the rare case where *extreme* and supposedly *avant-garde* projects are published – for example, Libeskind's Jewish Museum in Berlin – there will automatically follow a host of projects trying to take advantage of the moment. The argument here is that while the drawings of the Jewish Museum were published prior to construction in just about every journal, one should not underestimate the impact its publication in *Wettbewerbe Aktuell* probably had, where the scheme could be viewed amongst its competitors and in the midst of a series of other competitions. Surely, for any one who fancied work à la Libeskind this was the sign they all had been waiting for and the beginning of a brief escalation of all sorts of supposedly *radical* architectures.

Emphasis on an Architecture of Form

The journal provides little factual information on the history of a project or on why a specific competition was launched for a specific brief on a specific site.[16] A number of the non-practising professionals interviewed as part of this research did see the lack of material in *Wettbewerbe Aktuell* on the competitions' social, political and cultural development (e.g. necessity and relevance for a community) as problematic, and a possible factor in unhealthily detaching the architect and end user from each other. One suggestion during the interviews was that the information provided portrays architecture, or the architect's way of responding to a brief, first, as a formal exercise and secondly as a series of functional requirements to be fulfilled. Concerning the latter, however, the actual brief or schedule of accommodation is usually presented in abbreviated versions and hence cannot be taken into account when assessing the published schemes as a reader. Since all competition entries are usually being scrutinised for their fulfilment of the brief prior to the actual design jury sessions one must assume however that any scheme published will have included all the requested accommodation. Due to the difficulty of making proper judgements regarding the functionality of the schemes based on the published material and to the lack of more background, social and cultural information about the project the main focus of the reader and participant is certainly shifted towards the formal qualities of the projects.

Wettbewerbe Aktuell as Library/Catalogue/Pattern Book?

Wettbewerbe Aktuell has a textbook character.[17]

Prof Johann Eisele

Architects who have entered many competitions without ever being awarded a prize continue to do so. *Wettbewerbe Aktuell* might play a role here for its lists and tables dwell on the fascination with the competitive side of a contest.[18]

Prof Max Bächer

The focus on a straight forward, non-edited publication format of *Wettbewerbe Aktuell* which has, apart from some fine tuning, virtually stayed the same for 34 years, and the required submission format for competition entries – usually anonymous, not relying on text or annotations but on drawings and models – have over the years built a somewhat reciprocal relationship, manifesting together the visual standards for competition entries.

Wettbewerbe Aktuell is the only journal in Germany allowing a direct comparison between contemporary competition schemes, both regarding the actual design and the graphics (use of line weight, colour, layers, etc.).[19] Perhaps because of the current lack of commissions for architects more practices enter competitions resulting in the fact that there is also an increasing number of novices who will study *Wettbewerbe Aktuell* very carefully with regards to competition graphics. One of the questions that repeatedly arose in the interviews that I undertook was whether or not *Wettbewerbe Aktuell* had become something like an unofficial *DIN* (*Deutsche Industrie Norm*, equivalent to *British Standards*) for competitions. It is indeed remarkable how architects refer to and consult the journal in an almost similar manner to the way they use building regulations or other statutory norms. *Wettbewerbe Aktuell*'s publishing format, the title page per competition, its reference system and the division of projects into, albeit functional, building types combined with the diagrammatic drawings of the projects themselves provide a temptation for the reader to think of the design of competition architecture as a logical operation. The graphics of the title pages and *Wettbewerbe Aktuell*'s general *fact sheet* aesthetics suggest a desire to categorise architects and architectures and, perhaps drawing styles as well.

One of the architects interviewed stated that they used the journal to explain specific drawing styles to their employees but added that they might also scrutinise the publication for precedents when working on building types with which they had no previous experience. In these respects *Wettbewerbe Aktuell* seems to fill a gap in the publishing market, namely that of a collection of drawings of specific building types represented in comparable scale. Thus the journal actually also complements textbooks like the Neufert Data Collection.

As the architect Dorothee Stürmer stated, the quest for originality is not at the centre of the German competition system. *Wettbewerbe Aktuell* is supporting a procedure by which tried, tested and successful standard solutions take on *model* character. It could be the case that whole schemes, plan layouts or sections published in *Wettbewerbe Aktuell* might get recycled by other architects using them for building commissions and reintroducing the found material to the main stream. As long as these built projects are ordinary enough and remain unpublished no-one will realise where the source of the layout was. Perhaps by its existence as an extraordinary extensive data-bank of design solutions for public buildings – in 14 categories, subdivided into 104 sections – *Wettbewerbe Aktuell* encourages the cutting and pasting of borrowed solutions – a contemporary pattern book – thus existing as an invaluable resource for architects.[20]

Drawing Style

The journal makes competition drawings available to an estimated audience of 30,000 architects. Anyone studying *Wettbewerbe Aktuell*, specifically issues from the first two and a half decades, will realise that there had developed something like a *competition drawing convention*, revealing itself in many different ways. Since the use of colour has been allowed in almost all competitions, architects have been provided with another means to make their work recognisable. Looking at, for example, drawings by Guenter Behnisch's office from the late 1970s to the early 1990s it would be hard to conceive how one could draw in a more abstract and diagrammatic manner. Behnisch was tremendously successful and his practice's competition style was copied innumerable times. Presumably Behnisch, a very experienced architect with countless buildings to his name has developed his style over the years and his drawings were a diagrammatic representation of tested architectural ideas. Consider however the effect these kinds of drawings might have had on young and inexperienced practices entering their first competitions. Behnisch's drawings in *Wettbewerbe Aktuell* might in this case well have presented a distraction or rather a temptation to be used as models for their own sake. The drawing style could thus override the content of the ideas it supposedly represents. The advent of computer-aided design (CAD) and the subsequent demand by clients for competition schemes to be developed in more detail might suggest a return to old values where what one drew was what one knew. However, as one interviewee pointed out 'these days you've got all your details in the CAD library and just drop them into the drawings when required'. The interesting question here is whether the fact that architects develop their own drawing techniques and graphics for competitions has an impact on their thinking about space.

Editorial Control

> I would like *Wettbewerbe Aktuell* to be a mirror of contemporary architecture.[21]
>
> Thomas Hoffmann-Kuhnt

The two only mechanisms that the editor of *Wettbewerbe Aktuell* is exercising to control the contents are the choice of the competitions to be published and the choice of the cover.[22] *Wettbewerbe Aktuell's* exclusion of any theoretical comment or debate from its contents could potentially render the journal into an uncritical means of propaganda of the profession's feats. Yet, the exclusion of theory has an interesting side effect, namely that there is no dominant voice. If there is a manifesto to be found within *Wettbewerbe Aktuell* then it is that of the power of drawings, or more explicitly diagrams, over verbal explanations. *Wettbewerbe Aktuell* by default defines the term *concept* as a formal concern.

One problem with the non-editorial approach could be a possible perpetuation of inferior quality through the journal. Despite, or maybe because of, the consensus driven culture of the last decades in architecture competitions in Germany one might hope that the central idea of an architecture competition is to raise general standards. However, not every competition yields desirable results – from both ends of the spectrum – which can be due to the difficulty of the brief or to the lack of strong contenders or also to mistaken decisions by the jury. Hence, if weak competition results are published in *Wettbewerbe Aktuell*, a *bad* example is set which might not instantly be recognisable as such. The problem with this is that the medium carries an inherent authority by way of *if it is in print it must be good.*

Wettbewerbe Aktuell accidentally emphasises a key problem in the competition system for unlike in architecture schools, (hopefully) no distinction will be awarded if the quality is not right. In a competition, the ranking is always relative and on jury day there is only the choice between the submitted projects. Having said that, occasionally several 2nd or 3rd prizes are awarded instead of a 1st prize.

Dependencies in Journalism

In most forms of commercial architectural publication, editors, journalists and architects have established a reciprocal and dependent relationship. While architects happily pursue the publication of their projects in journals, they are often reluctant to accept even a mild form of criticism of their work in publication. Hence the majority of architecture journals are at the mercy of the architects whose work they are featuring regarding the provision of the practices' drawings and photographs. At present few journals have the financial power to pay for their own images. *Wettbewerbe Aktuell*, unlike most other commercial journals in Germany, uses architecture drawings as the key medium to communicate architectural information. The drawings published in *Wettbewerbe Aktuell* are mostly *original* competition drawings and since the journal does not rely on high quality photography provided and paid for by architects it is thus relatively independent of those architects whose work it is publishing (except for the images from the *Wettbewerbe weiterverfolgt* section, and the cover which has been featuring photographs of buildings since 2001 – see below).

139

Excluding any form of editorial criticism on individual projects, the owner, publisher and editor of *Wettbewerbe Aktuell* takes a very low risk of upsetting the vanity of architects – a risk that other journal editors have to constantly weigh up.[23] The absence of written criticism, however, might expose the published projects even more to the reader's unadulterated scrutiny for there is no schmoozing text to go along side the drawings. What you see in *Wettbewerbe Aktuell* is usually what you get and must be taken at face value. The excerpts from the juries' reports are generally written in a rather dry and technical language and since only fragments from the winning schemes' reports are published they – carrying the authority of an award giving body – hardly present a threat to any architect.

Wettbewerbe Aktuell thus, unlike most other journals, to a certain degree expresses the *Vox Populis*, or the common architect's voice on contemporary architecture. However or perhaps because of this, apparently lecturers in German schools of architecture warn against the use of *Wettbewerbe Aktuell* by students precisely because of its lack of editorial control.

Outlook

Any publication's influence is dependent on who is having access to the information and how the individual is processing the material published. However, in *Wettbewerbe Aktuell*'s case the hypothesis might be that over the past thirty years it has encouraged some forms of architecture more than others and hence the readership might have become conditioned into a less diverse group than it otherwise would have been.

Despite the journal's consistent format since 1971 a few changes have been applied to the journal suggesting that the editor is trying to respond to a changing market. *Wettbewerbe weiterverfolgt* was introduced in the nineties; photographs of buildings feature on the title on occasion and a web site is now in existence offering a range of services. Out of these, *Wettbewerbe weiterverfolgt* was named as the one section the interviewed architects were least interested in and which was thought by them to be out of character for the magazine. The practising architects also pointed out that beyond the wish to study the work published in *Wettbewerbe Aktuell* the other important reason to buy the journal, namely the notification and advertising of new competitions has lost its significance due to the availability of such data on the internet on a much more short term basis.

More competitive interviews and less design competitions will no doubt make the editor of *Wettbewerbe Aktuell* think about the content of the journal, which in its current form is very much geared towards architects operating within a healthy and flourishing competition system. As it was pointed out by some of the interviewees, *Wettbewerbe Aktuell* could potentially become more important for authorities as clients if there was more information on the competitions' context or history published.

This essay set out to investigate the influences that *Wettbewerbe Aktuell* might have over publicly funded architecture in Germany. While it is impossible to claim direct influences over emerging styles or specific buildings, the possible effects on working methods of a large number of architects have been considered, suggesting that the journal itself, separately from the competition system may certainly be influencing and indeed helping to create a strand of architectural discourse in Germany. This discourse undoubtedly revolves around architectural form. Prof Eisele's quotation at the start of this piece that 'the best schemes never win' and the editor's ambition for the journal to be a mirror of contemporary architecture reflect the journal's importance and relevance for the ordinary architect rather than for the limelight seeking starchitect. The journal itself, with its catalogue style and reference system, thus supports the consensus driven competition culture in Germany, by magnifying the competition system as a vehicle to maintain a relatively high standard middle ground architecture. *Wettbewerbe Aktuell* encourages discourse and exchange between architects, while at the same time the journal has to make relatively few concessions to its readership.

The author would very much like to thank the interviewees for their participation in his research.

Spain – The Fame Game

9

Javier Sánchez Merina and Halldóra Arnadóttir

Who in Spain doesn't know the extraordinary work of the Catalan architect Gaudí? He has practically been heralded as a saint. But the Spanish public also recognises buildings by contemporary architects like Rafael Moneo and Santiago Calatrava and their built work and personalities frequently appear on news and television programmes such as *The Praise of Light*, a recent TV series that showed buildings analysed by their own authors – as much as in National newspapers like *El País*, *El Mundo* or *ABC*.[1]

In addition to National papers and TV, numerable magazines such as *Arquitecturas Bis*, *El Croquis*, *AV*, *Pasajes*, *Tectónica*, *OnDiseño*; publishing houses like Gustavo Gili (GG), Actar, Tusquets, Tanais, Arquilecturas (COAATMU), magazines published by each of the regional Architectural Associations like *Quaderns* (Catalonia), *Arquitectura* (Madrid), *Documentos de Arquitectura* (Oriental Andalusia), *ViA Arquitectura* (Valencia Region), *Catálogos de Arquitectura* (Murcia), *Fidas* (Seville), *Oeste* (Extremadura) . . . 19 magazines in total, disseminate the work of (some) Spanish architects throughout the country.

I. Background

Spanish architecture has won international acclaim relatively recently through the work of architects like Antoni Gaudí, Santiago Calatrava and Ricardo Bofill.[2]

This is due to the fact that Fascism detained the development of the *Modern Movement* from flourishing under the Republic and largely isolated Spain from the critical debates taking place in rest of Europe. Spanish architecture was later to appear on the international scene than, for instance, its Italian counterpart. Although never as coherent as Fascist architecture in Italy, the architecture commissioned by the state in the 1940s, when not merely occupied with the pragmatics of reconstruction, pursued an expression that was grandiose, 'profoundly Spanish', and intended to contradict the country's technical and economic poverty.

The few architects who sought to combat this climate in the 1950s and tried to continue in the tradition of GATEPAC (the Spanish affiliate of CIAM and primary exponent of rationalism from 1930 to 1936, when it was outlawed) did so under inauspicious conditions. However, they acquired pioneer status for the succeeding generation by resisting the official route of monumentality and sentimentality. Foremost among them was the Catalan architect José Antonio Coderch de Sentmenat whose work was singled out by Alberto Sartoris and the Italian architect and editor of *Domus*, Gio Ponti, at a meeting in Barcelona in 1949 as a unique achievement. This was also at a time when architects like Coderch himself and Miguel Milá extended their professional practice into furniture design as they considered the general market in need of a greater choice. Coderch's thoughts called upon the importance of respecting popular tradition. In 1961 he wrote an article titled 'It's Not Geniuses

We Need Now' for *Domus* and argued that the country needed a greater number of good architects who were able to design buildings that were rooted in the *place*, in the Mediterranean tradition. In order to reinforce his argument, Coderch recalled 'An old and famous American architect (if my memory serves me well) said to another who was much younger and was asking for his advice: "Open your eyes wide and look; it is much easier than you think" '.[3] As a promoter of Mediterranean architecture, Gio Ponti published the works of Coderch in *Domus*, so propagating this modest, regionalist, line.

The economic prosperity that had arrived in Europe in the 1950s did not reach Spain until the early 1960s when mass tourism entered the country and when Franco responded to the economic crisis by establishing a new program aimed at stabilising the economy while replacing a number of political appointees with specialist technicians. These changes, opening Spain to industrial development, went hand in hand with the relaxation of censorship in the cultural domain, encouraging democratisation and effectively neutralising the long-standing leftist opposition to the dictatorship. For architects, a profession whose ranks were still small, this meant major new opportunities to work, for example, in the case of Miguel Fisac whose research into concrete and his numerous patents were put into practice in a number of extraordinary churches, civic and private buildings and who wrote hundreds of articles in newspapers and appeared frequently on television. By the mid-1960s, especially in Madrid, architects only a few years out of school were building whole sectors of the city, and the favourable conditions were transforming both the profession and the schools into prosperous and increasingly outward-looking institutions. Simultaneously there was a lot of pressure on architects and the building industry to respond to the demands of mass tourism on the Mediterranean coast. The architect Javier Sáenz Oiza, the key figure in the Madrid School of architecture and author of reference buildings like *Torres Blancas* or *Banco de Bilbao* in Madrid, warned against this and insisted on the importance of architecture to be rooted in the place. He argued that for the tourists, the house was completely secondary. They sought the sun, sea and sun lotion. Inevitably the coast would be divorced from its traditions and character; and, as a consequence of the speed of construction, the coastline would not look tomorrow as it did yesterday. Lamentably, there did not seem to be any time to reflect upon traditions or customs to build onto or to place things in context.

With the tied strings of dictatorship being loosened, architects began to have an individual voice in shaping the urban fabric. Their degree of renown would therefore increase via their private houses as much as through the civic buildings. Different from many other countries in Europe, the Spanish architect also embodies the figure of the civil engineer and therefore the issue of construction has traditionally been considered to be extremely important and it has been used as a tool to measure the quality of the architect. Architects gained fame at home and abroad primarily through their built architecture.

II. Situating the Architect in the Social Setting

Spanish law provides architects with the monopoly to design and build architecture. Only architects have legal rights to submit drawings to the planning committee and they alone can sign and provide insurance for the projects. The different Associations of Architects in every region, known as *Colegio de Arquitectos*, supervise and manage this procedure. This monopoly gives architects an incredible amount of control and power over the built environment, whether the client is a public or private.

In order to try and raise the quality of architecture, most of the Associations organise competitions for new civic buildings to be built and arrange biannual prizes for the best completed buildings in the region. In this way, great opportunities appear for young architects to win commissions for public buildings and newcomers are able to compete with more experienced architects on equal grounds and free of any geographical limitations. The jury for these competitions consists of political figures and architects representing the *Colegio de Arquitectos* and it is becoming common practice to include the editor of a magazine or an architectural columnists, hence a person who is directly in contact with the media and therefore supposedly familiar with the latest developments in architecture. Still, the Spanish architectural scene has not been about making a star-system in the conventional sense, it has rather tried to create what it believes to be good quality buildings to be recognised and appreciated by the general public. Within this context, the prizes of architecture organised by the Architectural Associations do not merely benefit the architect inside his circle, but offer him a greater reputation and attract clients, ranging from people in their twenties commissioning a single house to city mayors concerned with the redevelopment of parts of their city.

Intertwined in the structure of society, architects have a unique opportunity to approach the public. In Barcelona, *Foment de les Arts Decoratives* (FAD) was already founded in 1903 to promote design, architecture and image. This private, non-profit-making cultural organisation became the first association of decorative arts in Spain, dating from the same period of the *Arts & Crafts* in England or the German *Werkbund*. To fulfil its aims, the organisation organises competitions and cultural activities and works closely with institutions and organisations that have an interest in creative pursuits of whatever kind. Under the presidency of the practising architect Juli Capella, *FAD* is now one of the most prestigious prizes in Spain, drawing its members from different parts of the country.[4]

III. National Magazines, a Nucleus for Creating Fame

The editorial boards of the large number of regional magazines belonging to the respective *Colegios de Arquitectos* are constantly revising their positions, hence their line of thought and their influence are not necessarily consistent. To the contrary, magazines such as *AV Monographs* or *Arquitectura Viva* – edited by Luis Fernández Galiano – and *El Croquis* – edited by Richard C. Levene and Fernando Márquez Cecilia – were born out of a perceived need to react to the then present situation of urban architecture in the 1980s. Other magazines followed, like *DiseñoInterior* and *OnDiseño* – which focused on design and interior design – *Pasajes* that reported latest news about international architecture, and *Fisuras*, which was edited and owned by the same architect, Federico Soriano. The editors of most of these magazines are architects who focus their professional activities on what we might call 'editing the city'. The magazines are, according to their own account, explicit in spreading sophisticated ideas on architecture and design across different sectors of society.

In the first issue of *AV Monographs* in 1985, the magazine explicitly stipulated its aims and commitment towards establishing a dialogue about housing. It expressed its concerns about the state of housing, which it saw as having lost its links with society. *AV* committed itself to encourage a continuous reflection and dialogue and to stimulate a discussion about housing in the schools of architecture and in the cabinet rooms of politicians.

On the other hand *El Croquis*, for example, made it explicit from its very first issue in 1982 that the magazine wanted to fill existing gaps left by the publishing industry and to focus on construction details as an essential part of a – built – architectural project and to trace the development from the first conceptual ideas to the project's completion on site. Furthermore, they wanted to make a link between students of architecture and the profession by recounting what was happening in the schools. Every issue included a final project from a selected student, in addition to sections on the international, critique, works and interiors. The emphasis was put on showing projects and built work rather than following an ideology through the written word. The first monograph on a Spanish architect was dedicated to the then young architects Enric Miralles and Carme Pinós in the issue no 49/50.[5]

IV. The Value of Being Famous

Many of the Spanish architects who are established in the publishing world, like Santiago Calatrava, were selected to shape the Expo in Seville 92. The urban master plan and numerous buildings for the Forum 2004 in Barcelona were designed by such outstanding national figures as Oscar Tusquets (who owns his own editorial), Josep Lluís Mateo, Elías Torres, Alejandro Zaera, with young local architecture offices organising exhibition spaces and ephemeral architecture. Similarly, architects such as Rafael Moneo, Luis Moreno Mansilla y Emilio Tuñón, Juan Navarro Baldeweg, Cruz y Ortiz and Ricardo Bofill are all among those included in Madrid's bid for the 2012 Olympics.

Despite not being able to agree on the nature of what a modern monument should be, mayors, architects and critics all seem to share a view of the political and economic benefit of the creation of new icons. 'The megastars are political weapons with which elections can be won', pointed out Oscar Tusquets. Where new icons are needed, architects as stars seem to be a necessity. It is no longer solely a matter of leaving a mark behind, nor to build facilities in the spirit of the age of modernity, it is also necessary to announce and boast.

The architecture critic, Anatxu Zabalbeascoa, in her article on famous architects in *El País* argued that for many mayors, Santiago Calatrava who runs offices in Zurich and Paris, is among the favourites. He seems to be a secure choice guaranteeing public praise. There are few cities in Spain that have not been decorated with a monument by a Calatrava. He has designed airports and bridges in Barcelona, Bilbao, Mérida, San Sebastian, Sevilla, Tenerife, Murcia and Valencia where he also designed the immense complex called the *City of Science and Arts*. Recognition of his fame is also evident by the commission to design a transport terminal in Zone Cero in New York. Zabalbeascoa claims that mayors consider Calatrava to be *safer* than, for example, Alejandro Zaera, who with his wife Farshid Moussavi won the international competition for a harbour terminal in Yokohama. Zaera, investigating and proposing a new kind of urban landscapes in his work, has taken a leading role among the most promising Spanish architects after the sudden death of Enric Miralles in 2000. Zaera believes that outstanding buildings – however one might define this – could encourage citizens to take more interest in their city.[6]

Alberto Campo Baeza has recently expressed his doubts about the benefits of becoming famous. He insists: 'I think there is a difficult point in the equilibrium in relation to fame because if one falls into its arms or into the hands of money the creative power gets dissolved. A writer who writes five books a year does not write with the same quality as another who writes one. In the field of creation there also exists fast food. It's the Ken Follet type of architecture by architects working on 30 projects simultaneously'.[7]

Yet what about the increasing general interest in architecture among the public? Doubting the truth of that hypothesis, Alberto Campo Baeza pointed out that people are generally more concerned with the price of a kilo of pears. This is surprising, for especially in Spain it is possible to hire the best architect for the same fee as any other and hence 'good' architecture is potentially available to everyone. As Sáenz de Oíza's points out: 'good architecture, the one we value as good, is really not considered as such by the man in the street'.[8]

The question that remains open is who determines fame. Óscar Tusquets believes that there were only a set number of architects who could maintain such standing.[9] Only if one of the famous leaves the seat, can another step in. Traditionally, the quality of the work would determine success, but today visibility takes precedence. New stars seen as capable of creating urban icons are also the ones who promote them. Those who are not prepared to take part in this fervent play are being kept out. Rafael Moneo, the only Spanish architect who has received the Pritzker Prize, being the exception. Moneo does not move at ease when in the newspapers and avoids the cameras. Perhaps he does not need more promotion, but there are few or maybe none like him, being able to get important commissions without making a lot of noise.

Architects move in certain architectural circles created by affiliation and respect towards each other. This in turn ensures a trust of not stepping onto each other's toes. Belonging to such a circle, the architect still feels the need to be different, to propose a line of thought that is recognised in his own architecture, but the circle is important. It brings a readily packaged and publishable body of work to any editor. An editor follows the production of different circles (or even creates one around him) and publishes the work he identifies with.

V. Editing the City

It has been argued in these reflections that, at the end of the day, the editors of the various national magazines are those who have the real power to 'edit the city'. Although deprived of editorials disseminating a consistent line of thought, editors are faithful in their magazines to a kind of architecture that they belief could benefit the city – or their magazine. They write in newspapers and are also commissioned to teach at schools of architecture. Furthermore, beyond what can happen in other countries, due the Spanish tradition of organizing competitions for the design of civic buildings, and since editors are asked to sit on juries for these architectural competitions, they become the key figures in selecting the architects who will be published and those who will be commissioned for important and lucrative jobs.

Young architects can benefit from this situation as they can be supported even though they have no built work to show if their thoughts are powerful enough. The role of the editors is therefore extremely sensitive, in spotting new talents on the way to recognition and to encourage those who are on the way to fame. To be caught by the eye of the magazine editors or architectural columnists is therefore the channel that leads architects to fame. On the other hand, and in the same line of thought as that of Óscar Tusquets about the limited amount of architects who can gain fame, it is acknowledged by many editors that their readers can only memorise a few names. It is interesting to realize that new names are not promoted until there is a vacant position. This attitude is contrary to the one proposed by Coderch who was concerned with trying to raise the quality of post-war architecture in Spain. Analysing the most recent publications one can claim: it's geniuses we need now . . .

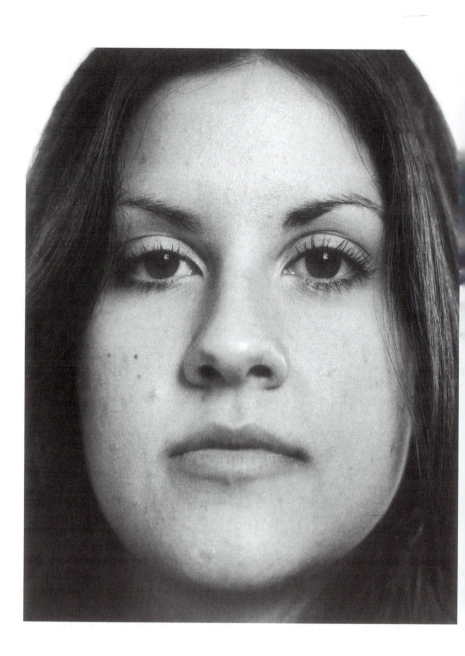

USA – Ground Zero: 1,776 ft into Thin Air

10

Markus Miessen

I believe that architecture is not reducible to any particular climate of opinion. No abstract theory, game of forms, application of technology or pragmatics is sufficient to communicate the fact that architecture is a movement beyond the material. It is length, height, and width, but also the depth of aspiration and memory.[1]

This essay is a short introduction to the adventures of an architect (Daniel Libeskind) and the city of his dreams (New York).

Born in Lodz (Poland) in 1946, Libeskind's family immigrated, first to the new state of Israel, where Libeskind's musical talents were recognised alongside those of Daniel Barenboim. A gifted musician, he studied music in Israel on the America–Israel Cultural Foundation Scholarship and performed frequently as a virtuoso pianist. Becoming American citizen in 1965, a natural performer, he started to play professionally at New York's Carnegie Hall, but soon after abandoned a promising career and enrolled on a course in architecture at the Cooper Union in Manhattan.

According to Libeskind, one day, he bumped into somebody on a street in New York who introduced him to Joseph Rykwert. Something very radical was happening at the University of Essex: a new course had been introduced that was not about to polish the professional skills of architects but rather challenge their understanding of space and its implications. Graduating from Cooper Union in 1970, instead of joining a conventional office, he joined the post-graduate degree in History and Theory of Architecture at the School of Comparative Studies at Essex University in 1972. It was here that he met Dalibor Vesely who, today, is professor at the Department of Architecture at Cambridge.

In 1978, Libeskind moved on to become director of the Department of Architecture at Cranbrook Academy of Art. Running his own school of architecture, he lent to architectural education his unique approach, promoting deep questioning as to what architecture does and why we need it. He would pursue these questions in later years when he was teaching at Harvard and UCLA.

After years of drawing, the content of which bemused almost everybody, the *Chamber Works* series was exhibited in 1983. Libeskind understands these series of drawings as enquiries and meditations, produced with pen and ink. Using the most traditional method, they were not drawn to represent a hypothetical problem, but – in Libeskind's sense of the world – questions concerning the relationship between an act of thinking and the act of building.

In 1986 Libeskind founded the so-called *Architecture Intermundium* in Milan, a private, non-profit institute for architecture and urbanism.

This period proved to be most beneficial for him, also being introduced to the world of European architectural discourse both in Italy and Britain including being a Unit

Master at London's Architectural Association (AA). An important centre of architectural debate, the AA introduced him to people such as Nigel Coates, Bernhard Tschumi and Zaha Hadid. Gossip labelled him 'a genius'.

With a series of competition entries in the late 1980s, seemingly haunted by the Jewish experience of the holocaust, he managed to win the architectural competition for the Jewish Museum Berlin in 1989. It would force him to move to Berlin in 1990. With the Jewish Museum opening to the public some 10 years later, Libeskind finally ascended into architecture's hall of fame.

Bearing that in mind, alongside any commercial drive, he participated not only in numerous competitions concerning terror and pogrom, but finally in that for the rebuilding of Ground Zero in 2002, which he won.

Daniel Libeskind is presently living in New York.

The Beginning of the End: *You've got to have Faith*

'Even if we skip the whole bunch of conceptual nonsense, it's still a bloody ugly tower'. I turned around. The person sitting behind me was referring to the very lines I had just started to wonder about. Trashing my morning copy of *The Guardian* (I was about to leave at the next stop) an early bus ride on the number 24 towards Centre Point was turning in to something of a revelation.

Back in the Berlin days, the first time I met Daniel Libeskind was at his studio in Charlottenburg. He entered the room in order to check on some news concerning the extension of London's Victoria and Albert Museum. Charismatically shy, he wouldn't trust most of us. But saying that, aren't we all a little bit anxious sometimes? And we don't have to worry about winning and paying the wages. If it wasn't for the sake of supplemental superstar-imagery, I couldn't care less. He would only talk to the people he knew well, and hardly ever without consulting his wife. That is to say that she pretty much ran the show. After 9 months, I found myself thinking whether or not he actually noticed some of the people in the office. Nina would. She was the real employer. Daniel was mostly interested in the models, which – lucky me – I wasn't responsible for. A couple of times, I remember, he looked at me and smiled.

Today, Daniel Libeskind smiles a lot, preferably into the wide-angle lenses of TV productions, obnoxious faces of local politicians, and out from the glossy covers of magazines.

Learning from Berlin: *Between the Lines of Benjamin, a Strategy*

A 10-year project, the extension of the Berlin museum – better known as the Jewish Museum Berlin – had allowed Libeskind to prove that his remote drawing exercises were in fact usable in terms of constructing architectural space. Arriving in Berlin with a custom-made visa from the Senate, he started working on a proposal which would become one of Germany's most important and talked about buildings of the 1990s. Contradicting to familiar concepts of order and conventional systems of measurements, the layout was deliberately branded by associative images. To cynics within architecture, they may never have had more gravitas than the fairy-tale of a wordy magician, but the process was intriguing, the interior being composed as part of a concept of voids, as Libeskind calls them. These voids, physical in one sense, yet echoing the speculations the French poststructuralist Jacques Derrida in another, are, in fact, breathtaking, patronising and oppressing at the same time, locking the visitor into space, into the space of the holocaust. He also began to worry about window details.

Not only was the building a great success, it also presented Daniel Libeskind as a man capable of dealing with a brief loaded with political implications as well as the memory of Third Reich terror. His way of dealing with such issues was to become his trademark. Project titles such as *The Book and the Wall*, *L'Chai'm: To Life* and *The Eye and the Wing* were to follow. However, alongside the trademark there was another reality, that is to say that this style of representation would only allow for a very particular reading of his work, that, for most of us, meant that Libeskind, was the architect of the memorial.

After 9/11, and a competition concerning the future of the site, Libeskind managed to convince the final jury. He finally won the battle over the future of the Hudson River Basin, presenting a scheme loaded with political stamina: *non de salute desperare*.

A Helpful Associate: *Hey, Architecture is Business*

Following the media sensations of the architectural competition for Ground Zero, one easily starts to suffer from frustration realising that – in the real world – architecture is business. Here the projected image of Daniel Libeskind – the role model he consciously advocates – and the way in which he participates in the media circus, might not be exactly compatible.

In the current debate one can trace Libeskind's underlying habit of dwelling in the echo of his public statements, presenting himself as the liberator who is interested in an open debate and consequently a critical analysis of his work.

The city of New York was in the unique situation to allow for an urban statement, beyond self-interest, namely to represent New York's open and vibrant mind-set. On the other hand, commercial interests were never far away.

But then something happened. In fact, it was far beyond anyone's expectations. Larry Silverstein, the owner of the site, asked David Childs, senior partner at Skidmore, Owings & Merrill, to oversee the entire project. Childs is an architect who builds. And he builds a lot. At the moment, he is controlling four major projects that will shape the new face of Manhattan, designs, which are hailed by investors but violently objected to by the architectural community.

David Childs and Larry Silverstein managed to reduce Libeskind's role in the equation to that of the producer of metaphors. The only remaining parts from the original Libeskind design being the location and size of the so-called *Freedom Tower*. Since Childs was to oversee the detailed design-work, Libeskind faced a situation in which his proposal – which had already been described as 'emotionally manipulative and close to nostalgia and kitsch'[2] – has been taken over by someone who couldn't care less about his architecture and well known for commercial success. In a recently published book,[3] Libeskind uncovers a personal narrative of the events and gives his own account of what he calls the forced marriage to David Childs. He is fairly patronising about it.

Libeskind returned to his argument that controversy and diverse discussion are both vital elements within the realm of democracy: 'discussion is part of a civic process. If people don't discuss a building, they don't really care about it. Architects have to be ethical'.[4] Then it seems rather surprising that one of the mechanisms he utilised in order to critically deal with the primary civic process was the following:

Dear All,

Herbert Muschamp (Architecture Critic, NYTimes) wrote a vicious and close to liabelous letter in the New York Times yesterday (see link: http://www.nytimes.com/2003/02/06/arts/design/06DESI.html). We have been advised by "people in the know", many of them journalists, to start a write-in campaign to the letters to the editor department of the *New York Times* (letters@nytimes.com). With this in mind we would be very appreciative if you could find a few moments to write an E-mail letter which might sound as follows, of course these sample letters are just to give you an indication of what should be their contents . . .

(1) I have been a long time reader of the *New York Times* and have always enjoyed reading about architecture. Yesterday's article by Muschamp is over the top. He is just not reliable anymore. Please get rid of this guy.

(2) I am not an architect but I follow architecture articles written in your newspaper for many years. I read with dismay (or increasing anger) Herbert Muschamp's article yesterday about the two World Trade centre schemes. Mr. Muschamp seems no longer to be a critic but rather a campaigner! His letter was off the wall. I will not be reading architecture articles again.

(3) Muschamp's article especially about Libeskind was incoherent and almost crazy (too much over the top,

beyond normal judgement). I will not be reading him for a long time.

(4) This time Muschamp went too far. Why is he still writing for the *New York Times*! Your paper deserves a serious journalist.

Again thank you for your support. The more people who write the more effective this will be.

Everyone play nice now![5]

Libeskind officially salutes the public debate. But since then his allies, with the help of the toolkit supplied, have tried to do everything to shut down opponents and possible critiques of his proposal,[6] Libeskind's formally charged propositions expose architecture's fragility in terms of democratic representation.

Democracy's reality on Ground Zero has been exposed to the notion that we are free to decide as long as we make the right choice. As Zizek observes; 'at a fundamental level . . . the new media deprive the subject radically of the knowledge of what he wants: they address a thoroughly malleable subject who has constantly to be told what he wants'.[7] As a citizen I might find myself resentful. After all, how does the public get involved? And is it possible (or even necessary) to involve, or even evoke, the public in the first place?

The Beautiful Project

As Libeskind points out, the role of ethics in architecture is central.[8] But it's difficult to believe Libeskind's testimonies since the office has been exceptionally active in trying to eliminate external criticism as well as attempting to jeopardise Muschamp's professional future at the *New York Times*. One feels obliged to elaborate on the notion that he is in favour of free speech, but only as long as it supports his internal politics.

If we now decide to reduce Ground Zero's heritage to a formal project with complimentary Western morale, let's simply be real about it and talk about its formal aspects only. Some might merely call it a *beautiful project*, a formal exercise within the prevailing notion of the previous ideological system. Let's not argue about whether it generates new layers of memory, whether it creates a climate of participatory involvement. There are corporate interests blurring the screen between the general public and the gentleman in black arguing his way through layers of complexities, which confuse the proudly proclaimed public participation. When it comes down to it, even an emotionally charged competition has to deal with square meters and whether or not it economically makes sense for the investor. This is precisely what has successfully been put out of sight within the Libeskind debate. So lets be honest: as in any other business environment, stylistic shifts in architecture are market driven. And hence talking spirit, faith and belief might be nothing more than prosthetic.

But Daniel Libeskind asserts that his design has a democratic impact on the city, yet as we have seen, trying to critically discuss Libeskind's proposal we run in to problems, rather as Vicky Richardson comments, 'all this seemed to prove Muschamp's point, that the danger of Libeskind's approach is that it returns us to a quasi-religious, pre-Enlightenment condition where reason is replaced by emotion and where criticism itself can be condemned as offensive'.[9]

One could argue that we are being confronted with a 'utopia of form'[10] as a way of embracing disorder by imposing order. If Ground Zero's formal experiment would have been promoted for what it is, one would at least have been able to rethink its meaning, an architecture for the sake of an aesteticised part of the city, an architecture promoting freedom from value. Architecture's cultural contribution should have been positioned precisely in this gap: the ability to analyse and overcome the existing political cliché. But unfortunately, Libeskind seems to be stuck within the social and intellectual calamity of representing atrocity, and it's an atrocity that is happening right now.

The determinacy with which Libeskind describes his proposal as a symbol of freedom does become worrying:

> I went to look at the site, . . . to listen to its voices . . . The great slurry walls are an engineering wonder designed to hold back the Hudson River. They stood the unimaginable trauma of the destruction, and stood as eloquent as the constitution itself, asserting the durability of democracy, and the value of individual life.[11]

Daniel Libeskind's citation on the value of individual life might not only be read in terms of tolerance, but its very opposite, that is to say prejudicial narrative. One has to bare in mind that the problem is not to render value, but precisely in its negating context, in its inability to be universal: it draws a line and excludes while trying to manifest its own regime of truth. If Daniel Libeskind claims to tackle democratic issues, it would be interesting to know how.

'The world will never be the same again'. How could we possibly disagree? But then, if I'm striking up an imaginary conversation with the New York director Jim Jarmusch, he might tell you to 'shut the fuck up'. It's the same old world. Yes, there have been 3000 casualties in

New York, but 30,000 in Sudan the same month. Does it make a difference? In the end, the tragedy is of a different kind: we won't stop. Like Sisyphus, repeatedly struggling uphill, we keep on falling back into previous ideologies, only to suffer from our own action. But, dissimilar to Sisyphus' punishment, we are in control of breeding it. Just as Koolhaas concludes: 'the winning architect, an immigrant, movingly recounts his first encounter with liberty but avoids what he left behind: Stalinist Poland, in '57. (. . .) New York will be marked by a massive representation of hurt that projects only the overbearing self-pity of the powerful. Instead of the confident beginning of the next chapter, it captures the stumped fundamentalism of the superpower. Call it closure'.[12]

In this context, the young genius simply descends in to a figure of mawkish sentimentality.

The Pop Star: *Even Bad Publicity is Good for You*

Libeskind's media squadron is already focusing onto *Time* Magazine and *Rolling Stone*. All they seem to worry about is whether Mick Jagger will be the first to order a *Vespa* with some Libeskind graphics on it. Libeskind successfully manages to reapply his formal language, which he developed some 20 years ago; whether he builds for the Berlin Senate, some private art collector, or the city of New York after an atrocity. Fair enough if its sells.

According to Libeskind, he had abhorrence to conventional architectural offices. As he says, the exhilarating aspect of his trajectory is that its goals are unknown and its ends indeterminable and uncertain. What do we gain from these statements? What is the underlying message? It somehow seems that Libeskind knows how to act.

169

Presenting himself as an architectural intellectual, however, locked into the most arcane kind of private professional discourse, the staging of his public performance reads as the combination of populism and the ability to do the job. He has been in touch with almost everyone; with the city, the survivors and the victim's families. And he started to discuss even the most trashy, pop-cultural issues with the New York Times style page. So that in the end, all it needed to convince the Americans was a serious injection of morale and a bit of *1980's architecture goes FormZ* turned vertical into the New York skyline; with a complimentary Photoshop sky for instant post-trauma optimism.

The Media: *How to Sort out Your Tools*

Neither concentrating on deciphering architectural nor urban issues, Libeskind's proposal is based on media and marketing strategies, the architecture of image. There is – of course – nothing wrong with that. You can do all sorts of architecture: some seem to be fascinated by detail, others wonder about the city. Architects talk about circulation and programme, cyberspace and Foucault. It's only that sometimes one longs for a little more decency.

I am wondering about the architecture and the words around it. Highly fascinated I am witnessing Libeskind's strategy working so well, which seems to be the instant answer on a purely emotional competition: a north-American public debate. *Time* magazine did not only present him like a pop star, but a creator, the saviour that was desperately awaited by the public.

At a cost of 1.5 billion Dollars, Libeskind's formal proposal for Ground Zero offers something original indeed. It doesn't aim for functional problem solving, although it pretends to do something exciting for the city; it caters for a media strategy of the highest order. A strategy that was so successful that its success tells us something about the change within architectural production: it's not only the superficial formal languages that have changed entirely, but even more importantly, the tools to get them across. In his proposal, he is part and parcel of the show. Rather than simply being the designer, the invisible monarch of all labour, he emerges as the ultimate mediator between the public and the design. Architecture and imaginative narrative are being intertwined in order to make them inseparable. This process allows for a relative reality, a system that the German architectural critic Olaf Winkler calls a self-referential reference: there is no church without a priest.

Libeskind's project has become 'the Libeskind Project'; the meta-physical production process of delivering something meaningless.

After the Gold Rush: *Law-cases and a Dopey Consultancy Agreement*

While Libeskind currently re-claims that 'you've got to have faith', we learn that – apart from Ground Zero – he has master-planning commissions for projects in Hong Kong, Seoul, Milan, Denver, San Francisco, Bern and Tel Aviv: an impressive collection of an approaching architectural oeuvre. It's a long road and on its way, you may be better off on the right side of the fence. For the very reason that every now and then, things might go wrong. Sometimes, the reality of an architect who talks about truth, belief and memory, turns into the realisation that in fact reality consists of hard cash and media coverage. Embittered about the fact that some of Libeskind's new 'employers' wouldn't pay, the odyssey of freedom turned into yet another battlefield, a lawsuit against Silverstein: *843,750$ worth. Let's go high court, darling!* He, who managed to direct the media, is now in charge of the future within the constraints of a consultant.

A bit later, the Lower Manhattan Development Corporation announced the selection of Gehry Partners LLP as architects for the cultural complex on the World Trade Centre site. Gehry's office will now work on a schematic design on two buildings that will be part of Libeskind's masterplan. And – believe it or not – after Libeskind had proven to the architectural extravaganza how to deal with the American public, not even Gehry could resist: 'When I was interviewed for the Signature Theatre and the Joyce Theatre, I was taken to the window to look at the site from above and tears came to my eyes'.[13]

Have we all gone completely mad?

Dostoyevski once said: 'why do we have a mind if not to get our way?' One wonders about the moment of realisation in which this very way turns out to be a dead-end and is overruled. Contemplating on his recent success in *The Guardian*, Libeskind successfully skipped the dead-end, which – in his case – is the annexation of responsibilities. His living nightmares, David Childs and SOM, have started to distract his thoughts, culminating in a condition in which they had to come in to make the *freedom tower* work.

But whatever the argument, Libeskind remains optimistic, stating that 'faith moves mountains'. What he calls the 'rebirth of Lower Manhattan' is effectively being presented as the result of his current state, that 'I am living on adrenaline'. He claims that he is in the privileged position to enjoy a great view of Ground Zero from his new office on New York's Rector Street, which constantly reminds him of what he is doing. If you are thinking between those lines, there is obviously nothing corny in designing a building, which is 1776 ft tall (the date folks, the date!), a materialised interpretation as saccharin as *The Last of the Mohicans*. These days 'there is such a strong spirit here'; on top of the international interest in the site and its physical becoming, the focus has turned onto the man in black, who presents us with an ego that is able to deal with both the mass media and public presentations. And he loves it. The only thing he is not so keen of is the indecency of journalists wondering about his cowboy boots and black specs, his leather jumpers and Woody Allen appearance. That's the kind of hell you have to go through. People will be writing about your boots. I could imagine worse. But even if I couldn't, I am sure that I could do with faith. And with Libeskind, spirit comes for free.

When the sun sets down on New York, there is one man standing in front of an architectural model, which is indicative for the Western concept of freedom we have arrived at in the Twenty-first century. He smiles and yet, there seems to be an underlying worry. Not that he wouldn't be talked about, but maybe about the possibility of not being taken serious any more: 'you have to be prepared to be beaten up a little. This shouldn't shake your faith. And, even then, you can always punch back'.[14]

Libeskind's media-strategy tripped over its own wordy narrative, that is to say the stoic suggestion of returning to pre-enlightened vision. After decades of enlightened cultural debate, we are being re-introduced to moral truisms, which – in an age of trans-sexual emancipation – appear to be fairly outdated. Libeskind's pre-enlightened vision is returning to a model of the city in which religion is once again part of the public realm. It has become a mirror-image of the contemporary American understanding of freedom. But since the pre-enlightened condition is the very state that we criticise as soon as we get into conversations about the potential enemy, we should pursue – with the same rigour – our own argument, applying to ourselves the standards we apply to theirs and in fact – if we were serious about it – more stringent ones. Instead, we are being presented with a spatial manifestation of *Iraqi Freedom*, the architectural equivalent to the smart bomb. In a time in which people retreat back into pseudo-religious categories, in which the world is once again being painted into black and white, we are witnessing the emergence of a man, who appears strategically in vulgar western terms as the saviour from all evil, exposing yet another layer of truism. This time, it is the architect talking; the problem's name is God.

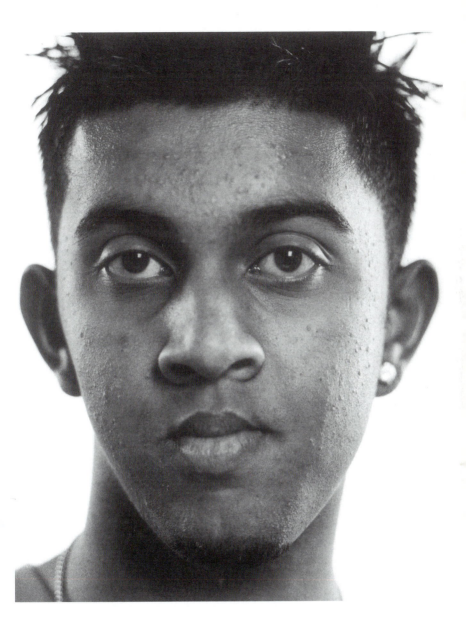

Part III

CONDUITS

Editors – *Architectural Design* in the 1970s and 1980s

11

Ryan McCrudden and Mat Witts

Architects' careers can rise and fall by the coverage they receive in journals. A journals' potential to influence the architectural profession is of great interest, but some are more successful than others, and some are in more control of their own success. The editor of an architectural journal is in the enviable position of having a regular forum to comment on the world of architecture. Editors have the means to talk to those involved and those establishing themselves in architecture. If we assume that architects and students read journals, and they are somehow inspired by what they see in them, then how does this influence transfer from the editor as an individual to the market they aim at, and the buildings we inhabit?

In order to set a basis for our investigations in to editors we have looked at 'architectural journals'. This is to say journals which are marketed specifically at architects and other members of the construction industry. This excludes publications such as *Blueprint, Icon* and *Wallpaper**, which although read by some architects have a broader target audience. To further refine our investigation in to how an editor can be influential we have identified two distinct types of architectural journal; the *reporting* and the *representative*. Each of these plays their own specific roles in the architectural profession.

Reporting Journals

A reporting journal is more likely to see itself as challenging and exposing the state of the architectural profession. This is predominately focusing on its country of origin and the work of that country's practitioners at home and abroad.

A handful of journals will find their way in to 90% of the architectural practices in the United Kingdom: *Architect's Journal, Building, RIBA Journal* and *Building Design* to name the most notable. These examples all deal predominately with industry news and gossip, though the latter two have the advantage of being supplied to every architect in the country registered with the RIBA and ARB, respectively. The circulations of reporting journals are less prone to the fluctuations of those with an alternative agenda which is not based on reporting to the profession.

Representative Journals

A representative journal will broadcast an architectural agenda, paying closer attention to defining the current architectural epoch or discovering where its future may lie. These types of journal tend to split the profession ideologically and rely on subscription to its message, as well as the publication. It is uncommon for most practices to subscribe to a wide range of these magazines; therefore the quandary that some journals of this nature fall in to is one of constantly trying to stay ahead of the game.

Architectural Design (AD) and the *Architectural Review* (AR), which profess a more innovative approach to architectural journalism, are British examples. These journals represent the architect and architecture they publish and perhaps have a wider international market than reporting journals.

The Space Between

Whatever appears in the representative journals as avant-garde will eventually appear in the reporting journals as the norm. This takes the notion of the 'noted and ignored'[1] to the realm of architectural journalism. For every architect that considers themselves avant-garde, there are hundreds that produce the ordinary buildings that make up the bulk of the built environment. This is true of architectural journalism in terms of the representative and the reporting journal, although admittedly on a smaller scale. As a consequence, architectural reporting does not suffer from the same fickle, if self inflicted, nature which representative journalism endures. After all, good or bad, there will always be something to report.

We have identified seven factors of importance to an architectural journal all of which will affect both the representative and reporting journal. These are: Reputation, Publisher, Content, Market, Style, Editor's background and Contributors.

Reputation

A journal may change any number of factors over its lifetime but there will always be a consistent thread that cements its reputation. This thread will manifest itself differently in representative and reporting journals. In the 1960s veteran industry journal *The Builder* changed its name to *Building*. Re-branding broadened its market to include those who would have been discouraged by the implications of its previous name.

Where a reporting journal will rely on its consistent content to establish its reputation, a representative journal will often rely on its name or initials because its content is more likely to be controlled by contemporary trends. In the case of *AD*, each reincarnation of the past 40 years has borne the same initials but whimsically realigned its content with each new editor's interests. Consequently the process of naming a magazine to some is as important as the content. For Haig Beck, ex-editor and part owner of *AD*, the need for a good acronym is paramount. His current journal UME is based on nothing more than its letters' compositional effectiveness, and even more arbitrarily it spells emu backwards.[2]

Publishers Support

A publisher can be at any one time the most important player in a journals direction but for the main they take a laissez-faire approach. The relationship between publisher and journal is simple; if the journal is profitable the publisher is happy, if the journal is unprofitable the publisher is unhappy. The publisher's influence over a journal is fundamentally unrivalled; it controls the life and death of a journal. On a marginally less dramatic level, the publisher chooses the editor, how much money they have to spend and how much the journal retails at. A decision made on any of these fundamental factors will have wide ranging effects on the content, style and market of a journal. If a publisher drastically cuts the budget of a magazine then it may be forced to shift its target market and consequently its content and direction. However, it is important to note that the publisher will enforce change but not necessarily inform its manifestation. That is ultimately the job of the editor.

Content

A journal's content is directly linked to the editor. This is especially true of the representative journal. A reporting journal has no qualms about publishing something it finds undesirable, as it aspires to objectivity. This makes its content less reliant on the editor's personal taste. It is open to discussion whether this type of journals can be truly critical. Reliance on advertising and product placement may alter a journals content and editorial stance. For example, manufacturers and suppliers will often take out several page adverts if their product is heavily featured in a building study. Additionally many journals require architects to supply photos of their latest projects to avoid the expense of employing an architectural photographer. It is therefore unlikely that a reviewer will criticize a building or product because the journal is financially dependent on an architect or supplier's future support.

A representative journal quite often revolves around a theme; its nature is not investigative in the same way as the reporting journal. Its content is often geared toward provoking thought rather than influence by example. As it is topic driven, it often involves the inclusion of varying contributors. This can have an effect on the continuity of a journal, something which the editor must be in complete control of to allow the content to be read together as a journal, and not a series of books.

The content of representative journals must in some way appear relevant to the reader. Some reporting journals can rely on what is essentially industry gossip to grab the readers' attention, but representative journals must appeal to popular feeling in order to sustain interest and therefore influence. The ability to consistently do this requires an editor who can spot a trend and objectively portray it, what could be called a *passive* approach. Or it takes someone with the passion to pursue something they believe in and have fortune on their side so that it captures the imagination of the readers, a more *aggressive* approach.

Market

In general a reporting journal is marketed towards practicing architects and anyone who likes a bit of gossip. A student might read a reporting journal to see what they are letting themselves in for, or to learn by example how to detail a 20-m glass wall. It could be said that these types of journal function like a catalogue; they contain a plethora of useful and always tangible examples. The market of a representative journal is not so easy to classify. To Andreas Papadakis his former journal *AD* acted as an 'encyclopaedia', though in his own words 'not as boring'.[3] An encyclopaedia contains definitive descriptions of its content. To some architects, academics and students this could be influential. This marks the difference between the two journal types. Just as it is mainly academics that contribute to the representative journal it is academics and their institutions that buy it. Academics are inextricably linked with students, and what student, or architect for that matter, does not like a glossy publication full of seductive architectural images?

Style

The style of a journal is no doubt linked to its content, depending on the editors approach one may become dominant over the other. In some cases, notably *AD* in the mid-1970s, style has been governed by financial restrictions, though gradual improvements in print quality and desktop publishing have lessened this as a concern. Now proportion and quality of the images and text are more relevant; even the format, thickness and eye catching performance of the cover are stylistic considerations. The style of a magazine will sometimes be the primary way in which it communicates its message. This is something which differentiates a journal from a book, even if the packaging might blur the boundary at times.

Editors Background

The editor is the one person who has most influence and control over the architectural journal today. Once the publisher has made the primary decisions, the editors have a platform on which to build their vision. The editor is entrusted with the reputation of the magazine and can go about producing the journal in a passive or aggressive way. This does not assume that one approach is better than any other, just that the editor is the only individual with the power and authority to use the magazine to pursue their own agenda or to give others a voice. From looking at individual editors it is clear that once their overall supremacy is questioned by someone else they will leave, regardless of whether their approach is passive or aggressive. Furthermore, they will inevitably pursue their interests in future publications they are involved in. This brings the idea of an editor's background to the forefront of the discussion, in relation to how they drive a journal's content. Which school did they graduate from and when? Who are their known associates? How did the individual break in to journalism? This is without questioning what kind of architecture it is that they prefer.

Regular Contributors

One of the simplest ways the editor can impose his own agenda on a journal is through the careful selection of regular contributors. Regular contributors can be found in all mainstream and architectural journalism. They provide continuity between sequential issues of a journal and their reputation can be used to add weight to statements made by the editor or other authors who are not as well known. Their fame or in some cases notoriety can be used to generate interest in a publication, especially if they are covering a running debate or regularly providing obnoxious opinions.

The use of contributors solely to provide running opinions is usually limited to the mainstream press and reporting journals, this is because they tend to be more reliant on industry gossip than representative journals. As well as employing regular columnists to provide opinions the *Architect's Journal* invites a big name architect to provide a series of weekly comments on the events of the day. Currently Simon Alford provides a considered, careful opinion, before him Will Alsop made irreverent observations on architecture. The editor of *AJ* chose these contributors because their fame within the architectural world guarantees interest in their opinions, thus hopefully increasing sales of the magazine.

Representative journals use regular contributors in a different way. Assuming an editor chooses who writes in his or her journal, a well-known figure that shares their interests and opinions can be used to reinforce a journal's message and status as cutting edge. Charles Jencks' long-term involvement with *AD* provides an insight into how representative journals use regular contributors. His distinctive writing style and opinionated texts have featured regularly in *AD* since the late 1970s. When he started writing for the magazine he was close friend of then editor Haig Beck, having both graduated from the Architectural Association (AA) in the same year.[4] A significant overlap of architectural interests meant that Beck regularly turned to Jencks for a critique or an opinion on a variety of subjects, providing exposure for Jencks' writings. In turn, as Jencks personal fame grew he was used to generated interest in *AD* and provided gravitas to any issue that he contributed to. Similarly *AD* has an editorial board (formerly known as consultants) that consists of respected academics and celebrity architects. Their names alone are enough to give respectability to the journal even though they only meet once a year and rarely contribute.

These six factors bring us back to the conclusion that the editor is the one person in journalism with enough personal influence to affect the architecture we see. The editor will react to the journal's reputation, study its market, follow the publisher's guidelines, and set its content and the style it delivers it in. The representative journal type bears most significance in terms of influence when all of the aforementioned factors are laid bare next to each other. They speak to current and future architects, they mark the beginning and end of whole architectural movements and influence the content of all other types of representation; from the reporting journal to the glossy monograph books commissioned by architects.

Case Study: *AD*

To explore the role of the editor in influencing the architectural profession, from students to architects, we have decided to use a case study. We chose *AD*, mainly due to its current condition. It is a journal with an established reputation, yet has changed publishing hands four times in the last 40 years. Additionally its style is almost book-like, but has the regularity and recurring features of a journal.

Most importantly, since 1973 AD has had six different editors each promoting their own personal agenda. Between 1973 and 1980 the journal's circulation rose from 1,500 to 10,000.[5] It continued to rise through out the 1980s, reaching 12,000 in 1992.[6] What was it that *AD*'s editors did with the reputation, content and style of the journal to make it appeal to its market in the 1970s and 1980s?

A Brief History of Control

In 1975, *AD*'s long-term editor Monica Pidgeon left and took control of the RIBA Journal. Her technical editor Martin Spring and a regular columnist Haig Beck took up Editorial duties. Shortly after their take over the magazine's publishers the Standard Catalogue Company decided to drop *AD*. *AD*'s staff were offered the chance to buy the magazine. Spring and Beck, wary of their lack of publishing knowledge but unwilling to let the magazine slip from their grasp, contacted the established architectural publisher Andreas Papadakis and collectively they paid £30,000 for *AD*. They became joint owners of the magazine with Papadakis owning 52% of the shares.[7]

Editorial differences saw Spring relinquish editorial control towards the end of 1976. In mid-1977 he was forced out of *AD*, handing his shares in the magazine to Papadakis.

He is currently architectural editor for '*Building*'. Papadakis now owned the vast majority of the magazine and was able to force Beck into signing over his shares.[8] By the end of 1977 Papadakis was financer and publisher of *AD*, and Beck was left in control of the magazine's editorial direction.

AD's popularity increased; by 1979 the journal's subscription had grown from 1,500 to nearly 10,000. Papadakis was keen for the journal to follow its theoretical route. Beck, however, wanted AD to cover more built architecture. That year he left *AD* and formed UIA International Architect. This left Papadakis in the unprecedented position of owner, financer and editor of AD, allowing him total creative freedom over its content and format. He remained as editor and publisher until he sold Academy Editions (his publishing company) to the German publisher VCH in 1990 and remained as editor until falling out with the company in 1992. When Papadakis left *AD*s circulation was 12,000.[9]

Martin Spring (1973–1977)

Martin Spring replaced Peter Murray as technical editor of *AD* in 1973. Although Monica Pidgeon had been nominal editor of *AD* since the end of the Second World War, her technical editors controlled the magazines direction and format. Under Spring's leadership, the journal continued to move in the direction that it had successfully adopted during the late 1960s. Murray and his predecessor Robin Middleton had faithfully covered the green movement. Having studied architecture during this era, Spring was inevitably influenced by the changes in lifestyles and attitude that had occurred within it. As editor he continued to advance *AD's* investigations of green, social and alternative building issues, moving away from strictly technological solutions towards embracing alternative lifestyles.

As a journalist he believes that an architectural journal should report on what is happening in architecture and construction. He saw investigation as essential for any journalist and therefore journal.[10] When a journal strays away from investigations, and moves into promoting its own ideas or backing a stylistic or ideological camp, it becomes a promotional tool, not a journal. In this respect *AD* in the 1980s became a form of vanity publishing. Architect profiles and monographs, such as those appearing in *AD*, had more in common with book publishing than journalism. *AD* in the late 1970s was becoming less critical and moved away from what he saw as the cutting edge of investigative journalism.

In many respects his tenure as editor can be seen as a smooth continuation of the Middleton/Murray era, working with and updating the issues they had brought to the fore in the decade before he joined *AD*. Under his control *AD* concentrated on several themes: New town developments, alternative lifestyles such as self-build projects and analysis of the successes and failings of green techniques. Spring retained the magazines 1960s format unchanged, relying more on text than images to put forward an argument. If an issue of *AD* had a theme, it was usually kept toward the back of the journal behind a current affairs round up. *AD* was then a monthly publication, a demanding printing schedule that allowed individual journals to be physically thin when compared with the bimonthly coffee table tomes published by Papadakis during the 1980s.

Initially, Springs *AD* talked to students, academics and environmentally conscious architects. During his period of control, however, he failed to move with his readership and

AD lost touch with their interests. Form based, theoretically loaded architecture was becoming fashionable. Ideological and form making developments had led to a more visually aware generation of students that were not so interested in the green and social issues that *AD* was reporting on. Papadakis viewed environmentally conscious design as a journalistic non-runner.[11] Green technologies were not developing as fast as *AD* would wish and its shelf life, as a subject, was limited. The increased popularity of *AD* after Beck changed its direction and format illustrates that Spring had neglected *AD's* traditional readership.

Spring did not overtly back any single architect, focusing instead on the issues that he thought were important. He was not an influential editor because he lost contact with the people *AD* traditionally talked to, namely students. His refusal to move *AD* with the times diminished his ability to influence the architectural scene in anyway. Furthermore, his desire to report on construction trends left him out of his field and depth in the representative journal that *AD* had become. He did not see editing as a means to influence, merely a method of reporting and could therefore be argued to be editor of the wrong journal.

Haig Beck (1975–1979)

Haig Beck began writing for *AD* in 1975 after graduating from the AA in London. He produced a regular 'Letter from London' column that provided a roundup of London based architectural gossip with the apparent intent of rousing controversy. When Monica Pidgeon left later that year he was invited to become associate editor by Martin Spring. It quickly became obvious that their outlooks and opinions of what direction to take *AD* in differed greatly and for a year they edited alternate issues. This period allowed AD to shift its readership. Its long-term readers who were interested in alternative technologies and lifestyles were catered for whilst, at the same time, the magazine was able to court the new generation of architecture students.

Beck's editorial style was heavily influenced by the London architectural scene which, in his opinion, orbited the AA.[12] Having recently graduated from the school he was interested in the debates and theories that were becoming part of the school's lecture series and teaching programme. It did not take long for these influences to filter through into his journals. Like Spring, Beck used his issues of AD to report on events in architecture. However, he moved AD away from green issues and instead focused heavily on the theoretical and form-making developments that were taking place internationally and in London at the time. He used lectures, seminars and exhibitions as the basis for several issues of AD. Beck's friends from the AA were Charles Jencks, Rem Koolhaus, and Leon Krier, with Zaha Hadid 'on the periphery'.[13] This is not a bad library of contacts for man with undoubted ambition.

Robin Middleton had experimented with the use of thematic issues in the 1960s. Beck took the format adapting it to suit his own editorial interests. The result was AD profiles. Whole issues were devoted to a single architect or theme. This also saw AD becoming a bi-monthly publication due to the 'expansion' of the content. As the format developed, AD profiles started to rely on guest editors. Experts in their fields, they were given almost free reign to present a synopsis of a topic or theme. Many were plucked from the AA's staff and guest lecturers, and from Beck's friends and acquaintances. At the same time AD produced several retrospectives of pre-modernist architecture based on exhibitions and seminars. These allowed *AD* to investigate and legitimise the use of semiotics in architecture, an issue that was hotly debated at the time.

When he took over as sole editor, Beck had *AD* redesigned. The 1960s scruffy newsprint look was replaced by a slick and glossy journal, heavily laden with illustrative drawings and photographs. The first new format issue was a retrospective of Arata Isosaki, both its presentation and content announced his editorial stance, confirming *ADs* interests in eclectic and conceptual design processes.

A measure of *ADs* position in, and perhaps influence over, the British architectural scene at this time is the amount of articles it published that went on to become significant texts. Several key works by fashionable architectural theorists were first aired by *AD*. An embryonic version of Rem Koolhaaus' *Delirious New York*[14] started life as part of an *AD* profile and Charles Jencks' highly successful *The Language of Post-Modern Architecture* was expanded from his 1977 *AD* article *Arata Isozaki and Radical Eclecticism*.[15]

Beck's key readership during his time with *AD* was undoubtedly architecture students. During the 1960s and 1970s the journal had been forced to speak to students by the budget and print quality cuts imposed on it by its then owner The Standard Catalogue Company. Beck continued the *AD* tradition of covering issues that students were interested in, his close links with the AA meant he had an enormous potential to test the water. Any improvements in circulation were due in part to his understanding of their interests, though perhaps it was more fortuitous than that. His *AD* talked to an audience who were hungry for new architectural twists and because of this eclectic approach to subject selection, *AD* was successful. Perhaps deliberately, *AD* launched some illustrious careers and movements in the late 1970s. However, the editor's eclecticism and the journal's role as vessel for other people's theories limited Beck's personal influence. This only serves to highlight that Beck, by his own admission,[16] did not really have an opinion of architectural journalism and what it should do. Working with an established format and using each issue as 'a fabulous high level tutorial with the best people in the world', in an interview with Haig Beck, he agreed he was not changing the world. He was following a discourse he saw as shifting within the realms of architectural theory.[17]

Beck's departure highlights an interesting twist in the relationship between a journal's editor and publisher. When Beck wanted to change the journal's direction he was overruled by Papadakis who as controller of *AD*s purse strings was unsurprisingly unwilling to ' . . . kill the goose that laid the golden egg?'[18] Unable to take *AD* in the direction he wanted to Beck went on to produce a journal that allowed him to comment on architecture as he wanted to. Though Beck's personal dislike for Papadakis was clear, it is also arguable that as a businessman Papadakis was right. The magazines success had been built around its shift in content, the time was not right to shift this again. Beck viewed *AD* as a vessel to further his own knowledge and expected it to evolve with him. By the time of his departure, Beck had established his opinion of what architectural journalism should be which can be seen in UME, an attractive and deliberately low key journal.

Andreas Papadakis (1979–1993)

Papadakis, unlike Spring and Beck was not trained as an architect, his academic background being in science and philosophy. He became involved in publishing in the late

1960s, choosing architecture and design because he saw it as a commercially promising field. He owned a specialist architectural bookshop in Central London, one of only a handful that existed anywhere in the world at the time. This outlet allowed him to gauge the interests of students and architects, enabling him to gear the books he published, and later *AD*, towards what was in vogue. By the time he became editor *AD* was geared towards students more than practicing architects. As such his background made him perfectly placed to judge which issues would be important to them.

Papadakis grew to see *AD* as a mouthpiece, viewing the position of editor as 'the best job'[19] in architectural magazine publishing. He believed that to function critically a journal had to have an opinion.[20] He continued to use the *AD* Profile format that had made the journal popular, but used it to push his own preferences. Under his control, *AD* became less eclectic and more focused than it had been under Beck. Guest editors were still employed to present topics but there were several key changes in the way they were used. Beck had seen editing *AD* as a series of tutorials and used guest editors to explain subjects to himself as much as to *AD*s readers whereas Papadakis exercised more control over the process. He chose guest editors whose opinions and tastes complemented his own.[21] In this way he guaranteed a certain bias in the content of *AD*. Handing the control of *AD*s content to guest editors meant that he rarely had to contribute himself. This allowed him not to give his personal opinions on architecture and gave him the scope to realign his tastes with the fashions of the day.

By the time Papadakis gained total control of *AD* the journal had become heavily reliant on the editor's contacts. Beck had repeatedly used an extended network of contributors, often linked to the AA. Papadakis however appears to have enjoyed a more glamorous circle of acquaintances. He was able to call upon academics and respected architects from around the world to put their weight behind the movements and arguments his journal promoted.[22]

AD at the start of the 1980s promoted classicism and post-modernism more than any other British journal. Papadakis used Beck's historical retrospectives to present Classicism as part of the greater evolution of architecture. Figures like Robert Stern, Demetri Porphyrios, and the Krier brothers edited issues. Some guest editors used *AD* to promote the works of specific architects; it was not unusual for an issue to be a one-man polemic. Other guest-editors provided a round up of projects that interested them, illustrating the latest formal developments in their field.

Gradually *AD* increased its reliance on paper architecture and building photographs. Text was kept to a minimum and was used to complement ever more elaborate images, an indication of the editor's own preferences.[23] This can be seen partially as a response to *AD*s young market, but it illustrates the importance placed by Papadakis on the development of architectural styles.[24] The promotion of style had become central to many debates in the mid-1980s and architecture students had become visually adept and image hungry. Stylistic experimentation was fundamental to the architects and projects published during Papadakis' 10 years in control, James Stirling being a prime example of his kind of architect.

Papadakis' initial interest in post-modernism stemmed from its desire to question the accepted wisdom of the time.[25] Deconstruction also displayed a similar interest in pushing back the boundaries of what was being built. Many of the leading lights of the Deconstruction movement were first published by *AD* as post-modern. Peter Eisenman featured consistently throughout the 1980s, initially under the ever-expanding post-modern umbrella, only being labelled as a 'Decon' architect in the mid-1980s.

By the mid-1980s AD had changed drastically, so much so that it had become unrecognisable from the AD Papadakis had first become involved in. It lost the relative objectivity it had thrived on under Spring and Beck and was more like a coffee table book than a reporting journal. Each issue put forward an argument but there was no debate within the journal. It no longer tried to be influential by taking a provocative stand point on an issue, instead it relied on its ability to publish drawings that were easy for students and architects to imitate. To some extents this transformation had been started by Beck when he introduced the AD Profiles series but it was Papadakis that truly perfected the process. Each issue aimed to showcase the best examples of a particular style and they were inevitably biased and single-minded. There was an obvious editorial preference for post-modernism and classicism but each issue tackled a different subject. This approach becomes easier to understand when you consider that Papadakis saw each issue of AD as an instalment in an ever-growing encyclopaedia.[26] This meant that an issue did not have to be impartial because a later issue would give the opposing angle or promote another style.

As well as editing and publishing AD, Papadakis continued to produce books through his publishing company Academy Editions. However, publishing was not his only avenue of expression; by the mid-1980s he had organised a successful series of symposia. Leading architects were invited to debate topics and the results were published as issues of AD, at first unedited. Although the subject of the seminars varied, many of the debates degraded into stylistic arguments.[27]

His use of seminars and lectures as the basis for issues of *AD* was not new; Monica Pidgeon had used the format in the 1950s and 1960s as had Beck when he was editor, but the relationship between the seminar and the journal had changed drastically. Beck was never responsible for setting up the debates he reported on. Papadakis, through his publishing company Academy Editions, controlled the topics of the debates and the participants. Reporting on these seminars and exhibitions became another way of promoting his interests.

Like Spring and Beck before him, Papadakis' *AD* was read mainly by students. As an editor and publisher he wanted to be influential and saw students as the most impressionable architectural group.[28] His use of big name architects shows an understanding of the fickle nature of students. Under his leadership *AD* provided massive exposure for several key architects. He used his position as editor and publisher of AD to build an international network of celebrity architects and theoreticians, using their opinions to create notoriety for himself within the architectural community.

Papadakis believed that his opinion was more relevant than others, a condition many editors suffer from. This initially proved a successful approach, though one mans vision will inevitably lose touch with its audience. As financer and editor of AD Papadakis' position of control was unique in architectural journalism. When he sold Academy Editions to VCH he lost control of what he saw and to some extent still sees as 'his journal'.[29] Despite AD accounting for only a tiny fraction of Academy's' income, he had lost his voice.

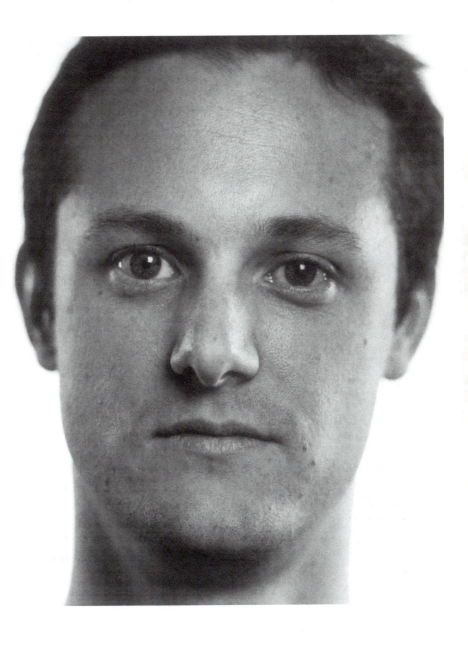

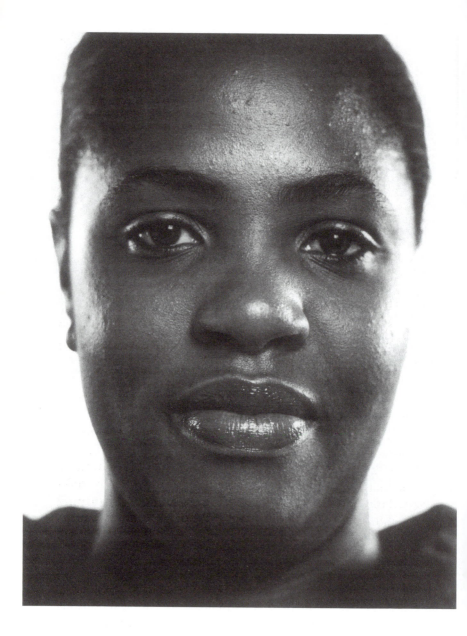

It's not About the Work! 12

Laura Iloniemi

Architects are keen for recognition. They work, sure, for commercial reasons but much of what they do is driven by a need to express some sort of artistry as well as need to feel valued for a contribution to society as a whole. This type of civic recognition does not come easy. This is partly because the general public is not particularly interested in the types of discussion, often rather academic or scholarly in nature, which really tackle design issues.

In the media at large, there is little room for the level of analysis of buildings that would gratify architects. Instead, the media is compelled to cover the latest trends, what is considered to be fashionable, and the architect who looks good on paper be it as a personality or through a grasping graphic presence. This explains why it is not unusual to architects to feel that the most interesting or worthy work does not get enough exposure. But, the truth is, It's not about the work . . .

Sure, good work helps and there are enough intelligent critics out there to try and vouch for it, but other things come into play too. It is clear, for example, that if a project is by a certain flavour-of-the-month practice, it will have an easier time enticing good press than if it were by a relatively unknown entity. No doubt the same scheme could be presented as the work of a super star, award-winning practice, or as that of a hum-drum commercial one, and the former would get the oooh-ing and aaah-ing amongst the architectural fraternity whereas the latter would be approached with great suspicion. The same applies to the art world. Who would come out and denounce big painters' works? Even mediocre paintings merit wall space in retrospectives of blockbuster artists.

When does good work alone make a case for itself? This is evident when looking at the media profile of practices that are neither exhibitionistic nor seeking attention. These sorts of practices rely on the consistency of high design standards. Year after year, they produce well-detailed, well-considered and well-resolved buildings. Year after year, they present their work in a highly professional manner with good renderings and photographs. Such practices may win prestigious awards as a result of their efforts. This adds to their credibility; as might their institutional connections with schools of architecture, or, having become influential figures in the field as a whole. Teaching and publishing are also widely accepted as excellent introductions for a practice into the world of endorsing one's stance in the profession.

When does good work go amiss and never reach the opinion makers? This sad scenario tends to happen to badly managed practices unable to deliver information to relevant persons or bodies on time. They do not produce text or images that put their ideas clearly and in a good light. Basically, their lack of ability to articulate concisely those aspects of their work that might attract positive publicity never takes place. This is due either to an absence of skill in communications or to a paucity of time given to getting favourable messages across about the work of the practice.

Architects have a real difficulty in understanding why – despite their design teams working on what they might rate as extremely interesting projects – no-one is out there supporting them. Often, it is as though they feel publicity is owed to them. Architects, however, do not own the media in any way, not even the trade media. No journalist has to conscientiously take a project on board. Nor do editors have to give architects the opportunity to fact-check copy or publish their project descriptions. The press, with a very few exceptions, is not there to give architects a voice. It is there, at its best, to discuss and put into a wider context what architects are doing. The architects most apt at media relations understand this and do not bore journalists with their internal way of describing things, but, instead, engage members of the press by reflecting on how their work might be relevant in broader debates.

One of the reasons for a divide in what editors and readers want from the media and what architects want is caused by designers' fetish to record projects and that in great detail. Architects, in particular, have little control of how their buildings will be presented in the future, after the owners have taken over and the occupants moved in with their own furniture and ways of life. Photographs allow architects to 'control' the image of their buildings, as do words. Of course, an editor may not be motivated by the notion of describing a building in the architect's terms even in a trade journal building study. Yet, it is not unusual for an architect to try and impose such control over a publication, if not directly, then by suggesting writers close to the practice or supplying photos that a publisher could not otherwise afford. It has been said, that the architectural press will never truly be free editorially until the publishers can afford to commission the type of photography they would like to use on the pages of their magazine. There is certainly truth in this.

Inability to communicate and to see the wider picture because of a desire to control are the two most common causes for not making it in media terms. Lack of charisma and all sorts of insecurities do not help. One needs to be very aware of the press and what makes them tick. One also needs to be self-aware and realistic about how one is seen. An architect may not be that great a designer, but by being honest about the practice's ambitions – to perhaps do better work in the future – this architect will gain the respect of the media far quicker than by trying to convince it of the supposed brilliance of the design team's work. Self-criticism is good in this way. It can also hinder, if one never feels a project is ready enough to publish or is too protective about the information that accompanies a building. Yes, ideally, information needs to be very good but this will not matter much if the timing is wrong.

The most experienced self-publicists are those who have learned to relax. They do not get over-excited by every bit of media be it good or bad. They see exposure as a long-term process and do not read into it personally. They are generous in giving straight-forward opinions that are welcomed by journalists so used to hearing platitudes made to stick to party lines or to be 'on message'. If firmly adhering to a policy on speaking about an issue, one should at least spice it up with humour or balance it out with some personal point of view that does not compromise the topic at hand.

Architects tend to be very cautious when it comes to speaking their minds in the press. They are often afraid of upsetting clients and losing their patronage. This has created an atmosphere where it is perhaps too easy to gain points with the media by doing the opposite: by being an *enfant terrible* daring to step out of line in the otherwise polite company of the profession. On the other hand, it may suffice to produce the first wacky or off-the-wall book that borrows from other creative industries in its street credibility. Or, to say the odd four-letter-word in public and, particularly, when receiving an official accolade. The actions of such rebellious architects can be quite contradictory. Accepting the support of the establishment, yet, in the next breath trying to be seen to be above it. Similar incongruencies may apply in criticising commercial business while gladly seeking and holding onto commercial clients. Little is made of such discrepancies; instead the adolescent temperament of the media encourages it.

The *enfant terrible* posturing exists not only in architecture of course but, in fashion, fine art and even catering. It was perhaps started off by rock-n-roll and Hollywood mavericks. Other creative industries tried to create similar iconic personae and have succeeded. Architecture is just following suit on this score. Unusual personae who will 'be individualistic': through this behaviour formula are the 'big personality' stereotypes coveted by magazines and newspapers alike today. It is as though our world is perceived as dull and boring if straight and honourable and somehow fascinating and dynamic if a bit naughty and disgraceful.

Loud seems universally good. In other words, not only the creators but their creations are preferred at maximum volume. The culture of the media icon goes hand in hand with a culture of iconic statement buildings. It is not unusual for loud people make loud things either. In the United Kingdom, especially, refinement in architecture has been out of headlines recently. Writers struggle with how to explain subtlety or justify its uniqueness for meriting coverage. The one-liner, however, is immediate and, if far from unique now, is still a big hit. Icons too are interpreted or understood as such if they are voluminous; the symbolic intricacies, or actual content of icons, are rarely understood by those who use the originally Greek term. Perhaps the term is best understood as iconoclasm and has thus become popular as something controversial.

Together with icons, we are seeing an increasing amount of design that is generated by a media culture of people liking childish things. There appears to be a desire amongst adults to defy responsibility by being teenage for as long as possible or resorting to the comforts of bratty or baby culture. A bit of craziness is considered good, or, happy: fun colours and soft, friendly shapes. Telly-tubby buildings that spark up a city into an amusement park like a joy ride. Let your hair down; come as you are. All this again as the antithesis of joyless adult design associated with dignified seriousness or drab, dull, contrived, or too formal an environment.

The phenomenon of the *enfant terrible* is not that far from that of the clown. In design terms too, it can be more akin with a toy land intended to entertain. The potential of any scheme to entertain raises its media potential as well. Editors are often too lazy or blind to distinguish between entertainment value and actual design merit. With the media ever further moving into the arena of entertainment this is not surprising. One wonders whether too many journalists, or architects for that matter, are frustrated scriptwriters or performers.

Today, trade magazines, too, are following the urge to entertain. It is believed that this is a route to more successful publications in terms of circulation and advertising revenue as a result. Could it be that the media in and of itself has given rise to a society in which it is acceptable to judge and comment on the media's terms. The media has increasingly self-generated media personalities, like commentators, the focus of their coverage. They seek the opinions of these media figures on a wide variety of issues that fall outside their expertise. Mediocre columnists write about their lives as though they were worth a biography.

Historically, the media has existed partly to counter-balance and challenge the establishment. Could it be that for the media to gain its current status, it has relied on an almost free for all in breaking of traditional values? Anything extraordinary no matter how gratuitous or daft seems OK in terms of attracting media attention. Architects who design wild buildings too expensive or structurally outré to ever actually get built generate coverage because they have produced *an iconic* image. Publicists know that tricks like inviting celebrities who have little else but their media persona to contribute to an awards ceremony give it endless mileage. Get a bear to cross an average bridge at its opening and attention is guaranteed. It is largely about entertainment value of stories.

Hooks for architectural stories are all too often the types of things you would expect to see in The Guinness Book of World Records, world's tallest building, for example, thus bearing a theme that owing to its sheer simplicity of concept and visual ease of presentation captivates editors over and over again. Other *hooks* are provided by exhibitions, talks, book launches that somehow make things topical and worth writing about as though publications had a responsibility to record what all the museums were showing. For writers, this creates an environment in which it is increasingly difficult to pitch original stories. Whilst their editors demand *exclusivity*, they also wonder why their correspondents don't pile on to a specially laid out PR package tour to the opening of a museum that *everyone* is covering.

The architect who is not building the latest landmark museum with a promise to regenerate an entire city, or who does not have a solo exhibition in the pipeline, has to find a way of promoting the practice's work without such immediate hooks. His task is not easy. His main hope is to get a handful of influential members of the press to support his work because they find it worthwhile or are somehow charmed by the architect. The trade media may help sway an architect's reputation in such a way that it gains the support of a national correspondent or other opinion leaders as can the high profile of a satisfied client.

With all this fuss about publicity, how important is it really? Huge numbers of practices thrive commercially with barely any. They can thrive far better than smaller, hungry practices with oodles of coverage about say a sole practitioner's own self-designed home. As was said earlier, 'Architects are keen for recognition. They work, sure, for commercial reasons but much of what they do is driven by a need to feel valued for a civic contribution to society as a whole'. Partners of highly commercial practices can feel this need too to be valued beyond their turnover. Publicity is perhaps not as important for business reasons as it is for reasons of ego. This makes the entire topic of publicity all the more uncomfortable. Which publicist has not heard their client claim that their only motivating factor to be published is to get more work. Seldom this is true. The type of publicity that practitioners seek and the way that they do it tends to prove such hard-nosed attitudes about publicity false.

A recent article in *Newsweek* deals with this phenomenon of vanity publicity well. It starts, 'Gwyneth Paltrow is not a movie star. Neither is Nicole Kidman, if stardom is based exclusively on box office grosses . . . And Demi Moore's "comeback", it turns out, existed only on the cover of *People*'; 'Never has star power been harder to define than it is today. As late as the mid-1980s, an actor's media popularity was a solid indicator of his public appeal'.

The article goes onto describe how certain celebrity stories make more money for the publications than they do for the films and by-products that the big names are attached to commercially. The author cites Eddie Murphy, who does almost no print interviews for his films or cover profiles, as the fourth in the ranking of stars by career in US box offices in billions. Whereas Jennifer Aniston who ranks top by appearances on US magazine covers (2003), 'can't "open" a movie by bringing in ticket sales on the first weekend . . .'. The articles concludes that Tom Hanks who is ranked second for stars by career in US box offices cannot '. . . get the cover of US Weekly to save his life'.

No architect is anywhere close to having the profile if the above-mentioned Hollywood names who truly ARE household names much like Rolex or Nokia are. Nonetheless, the publicity profiles of such film stars does put things into perspective. Could an architect – short of Frank Lloyd Wright or Philip Johnson – ever make it on the cover of something like US Weekly, or The Economist? What is the monetary value of architects' coverage. Or, is it a case of getting to do buildings with more kudos – something that cannot be measured in currencies. The publicity seeking architect is often like the refined actor or actress who seeks to do the art films, to work for perhaps

less pay to be on board a team with a respected director . . . or in their case, commissioning body.

Perhaps all creatives have this in common: the need to be
valued for what they leave behind. As a second runner-up to
this type of recognition, there is fame which also has the
attraction of some level of immortality. A lot of famous
people end up trying their hand at something to try and
get recognition through. The publicists who work with
these sensitive types should be attuned to this dichotomy
between professional and personal goals. The distinctions
are predominantly not very clear, and certainly not clear in
the way many creatives lead their lives.

No, It's not about the work. It's more about creating characters for the media from within and out there to play with,
about fabricating dreams and selling these, about selling
art and culture, about ego and a strong desire, whether
merited or not, for recognition. Surprisingly, media aside,
it's not really so much about dollars and cents. No wonder,
people shy away from talking about publicity and wanting
it. Looking at it like this, it appears to be more shameful
than making money.

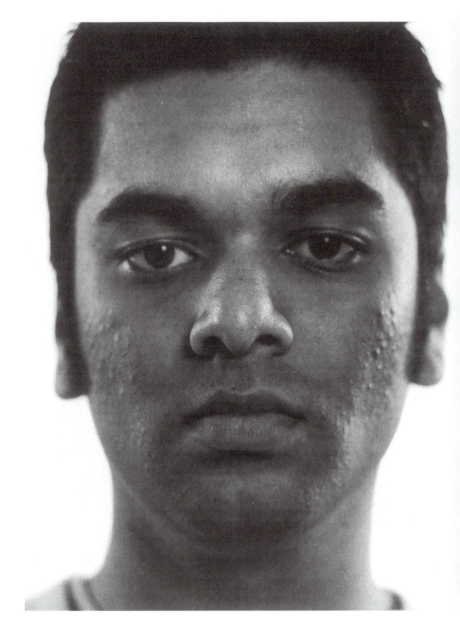

All The Kings Men

Judith Farren-Bradley

13

Other essays have looked at how the architect and patron have worked together over time and territory, to provide the conditions necessary for the creation of architecture. The aim of the following two chapters is to look at how the effect of two or more architects coming together, to form an association of like-minded persons, has impacted upon this relationship and whether the development of architecture as a profession has helped or hindered architecture and the practice of architecture. This chapter will look at why and how architects came together and how they used their collective position to influence the social and political environment in which they operated.

All professions are conspiracies against the laity.[1] When Adam Smith, in his famous work '*An Inquiry into the Nature and Causes of the Wealth of Nations*', wrote:

> People of the same trade seldom meet together, but the conversation ends in a conspiracy against the public, or in some diversion to raise prices.[2]

Smith was not referring to the learned professions. But ever since this statement was written, it has been difficult for many and impossible for some, to see further than this description. However, he did address his thoughts to professions and his observations are none the less interesting and relevant for the passage of time. Smith added:

> Most of the arts and professions in a state, [says by far the most illustrious philosopher and historian of the present age,] are of such a nature that, while they promote the interests of the society, they are also useful or agreeable to some individuals; and in that case, the constant rule of the magistrate, except perhaps on the first introduction of any art, is to leave the profession to itself, and trust its encouragement to the individuals who reap the benefit of it.[3]

Today the title *architect* and the concept of the architectural profession are synonymous. However, the title *architect*, was not commonly used to describe the activities of someone who is 'a designer who prepares plans for buildings'[4] prior to the seventeenth century. Even then, the titles *architect* and *surveyor* were interchangeable. Christopher Wren, the architect most often cited in public polls as the best known in Britain,[5] held the title of Surveyor to the Kings Works.

The creation of an architectural profession is the product of the nineteenth century. Before looking specifically at the often tense relationship between the individual who practices, or is in some other way concerned with architecture as a discipline, and the collective body, who are described as constituting the profession of architecture, it is necessary to look briefly at past and current concepts of a profession.

A number of studies suggest that a profession can be recognised as having all or most of the following attributes:

- possession of an identifiable and circumscribed body of knowledge;
- recognition by society, that this body of knowledge, when applied, is of significance to society and individuals;
- an acceptance by society that the body of knowledge is so specialised that only those in possession of it can define it, control standards in relation to its use and make judgements about those who use it;
- an acceptance by the those who hold and apply this knowledge that they will act with integrity and undertake to enter into a voluntary relationship of service towards individuals and society as a whole, agreeing to act in accordance with ethical codes and standards, over and above those defined by general legislation or standard commercial practice.

As Adam Smith observed 220 years before, *the professional* enters into a reciprocal agreement with society. No profession can exist or operate without this agreement. The *professional* tends to have to undergo long and laborious education processes, accept higher levels of liability and make judgements where incomplete, ill defined or contested facts exist. In return, they expect a higher status and higher than average remuneration.[6]

When Carl. M. Sagers was considering the state of the professions in 1997, he noted, that the terms 'professional' and 'profession' have become less well defined:

The dry cleaners, the insurance agents, the real estate brokers, the automotive mechanics, all think of themselves as professionals. It is downright undemocratic to deny any American citizen the right to call him or herself a professional.[7]

The professionalisation of everyone is the title of an important study of professions by Wilensky.[8] This phenomena is particularly interesting since it is taking effect at the same time that all the established professions consider themselves under siege from the forces of free-market enterprise.

Along with the basic attributes of a profession, there are identifiable subsequent characteristics. In order to define and control the boundaries of its knowledge, all professions restrict membership by some means. This is usually done by defining the level of performance required for entry to the profession, and for this, criteria have to be set and the means of assessing compliance created. Most professions have a combination of criteria for entry including past performance, the acquisition of certain academic awards or other forms of certification and/or the creation of a standardised and regulated educational process.

The Aristocracy of Rank or Talent[9]

If the mark of a consummate professional is an ability to act independently and 'exercise discretion wisely',[10] it is not difficult to see that the creation of professional body might be difficult but is also ultimately useful. However, in the case of design professionals, many of whom consider themselves to be artists rather than responsive professionals, the relationship between individuals and the body corporate is often tense.

From its inception as a professional body in England in 1834, the Institute of British Architects (IBA) has had something of a problem in creating and maintaining collegiate control over its independently minded membership. It has spent not inconsiderable amounts of time and in some cases money, defending itself from those who were excluded from its ranks by personal choice or failure to conform to prescribed standards for entry. In recent years it has spent, even more time and money defending its right to exercise such control. As previously stated, one of the characteristics of a profession is how it controls entry to its ranks. Another is how it deals with non conformity within its ranks. The history of the architectural profession in Britain is no exception to this.

The professional body is often caricatured as the refuge for the mediocre and those who enthusiastically embrace *compliance culture*. If we accept the lineage drawn for the inception of the Royal Institute of British Architects (RIBA), this is far from the truth. On the 20th of October 1791, in the Thatched House Tavern in London, the Architects Club was started by four (now recognised as eminent) architects, who had already earned considerable prestige. They were James Wyatt, Henry Holland, George Dance and Samuel Pepys Cockerell. At the initial meeting, 11 other architects were elected to join the club, amongst these were Sir John Soane, Sir William Chambers and Robert Adam. Those deemed eligible but resident outside London were made honorary members.[11]

Less than a decade later in 1806, a more focussed organisation was started called the London Architectural Society (LAS). This appears to have been something of a reaction to the former as it expressly stated, 'among institutions so liberally established in this City there is not one calculated for the encouragement of architecture. The feeble protection afforded by the Royal Academy (RA) can hardly be deemed an exception'.[12] Membership was exceptionally demanding and failure to attend more than two meetings, incurred a fine. In addition, the LAS demanded of its members the regular production of original designs and essays. Failure to provide the required work to order, incurring a fine of five shillings. Its meetings were fortnightly and much of its energy seems to have been devoted to the self-improvement of its membership and the publication of the designs and essays. This society did not attract a wide membership and in 1831, the Architectural Society was formed with the express ambition to set up a British School of Architecture with professorships, a library, museum and periodic exhibitions.[13] The membership criteria, for this society was less exclusive than for the Architects Club. It was open to anyone who had 'studied the profession of architecture in the office of an Architect for five years',[14] provided of course that they had the ability to pay an annual fee of three guineas.

The direct predecessor of the RIBA was, according to Gotch, born in the Freemasons Tavern in London in January 1834.[15] It was called the Society of British Architects (SBA).

By the following June, the future of the SBA was discussed in a meeting to which 'established and well-known' architects were invited. These included Charles Barry and Decimus Burton. There was clearly a recognition that without the association of well known and well established practitioners, the new society would founder. At this meeting, the name Institute of British Architects (IBA) was proposed and a committee formed to agree its aims. By the end of 1834, the IBA had a council and members and the aims were announced. These included 'the acquirement of architectural knowledge, ... the promotion of different branches of science associated connected therein ... and establishing an uniformity and respectability of practice in the profession'.[16]

The IBA hoped to have Sir John Soane as its first President, however as a Royal Academician he was unable to join any other 'society of artists'. The position of first president was filled by Philip, Earl de Grey, a non-architect but a nobleman who lent gravitas and status to the newly formed Institute. Soane's principles of professional ethics and professional practice were however closely followed in the initial codes of conduct. The acquisition of the Royal Charter raised the public profile of the Institute. But it was engaged in activities to promote itself to the public even before this. In 1836 it produced the first volume of *Transactions*, in which it suggested a suitably dramatic and poetic description of its birth:

> ...with the most cordial desire to forward the true interests of art by seconding the endeavours of that distinguished body [the RA] in adopting every genuine means likely to promote its advancement, our 'Institute' burst into existence.[17]

The early years of the RIBA were, according to Gotch, concerned with the consolidation of the Institute and dealing with matters of importance to its Membership. It is interesting to note that some of the items of business mentioned as exercising the Membership and council have appeared with monotonous regularity over the next 170 years. One of these is the problem with architectural competitions, where collegiate solidarity met individual personal ambition!

The RIBA used the judging and awarding of prizes, as a means of establishing standards, encouraging individual architects, and associating the institute with great works of architecture. The Royal Gold Medal was instituted as a prize for the 'encouragement of young architects' and a brief for new premises for the Institute itself, was duly set. Regrettably, the standard of entries was considered too low, as all the entries failed to take into account the cost limit imposed as part of the conditions.[18] The Gold Medal was not awarded, and in order to avoid future embarrassment, as the medal had been donated by Prince Albert, it was agreed that it would be awarded to older, established architects in recognition of their contribution to the architectural profession. The first recipient was Charles Robert Cockerell, the son of one of the founding members of the Architects Club and the architect of the Ashmolean Museum as well as many other notable buildings. He became the first architect President of the RIBA in 1860, the year in which the word Royal was added to the name of the Institute. It was not unusual for a President of the RIBA to receive the Royal Gold Medal.

The link between the profession, aristocracy and politics is not a recent occurrence. Sir William Tite, who was twice President of the RIBA between 1861 and 1870, was simultaneously Member of Parliament for Bath, a magistrate and chairman of several City companies. He was sufficiently well connected to have had the following exchange with the then Prince of Wales recorded, 'I inherited a fortune, I married a fortune, and I have made a fortune'. To which the Prince is reputed to have replied, 'Lucky man'.[19] As now, the possession of a private fortune and friends in high places is helpful in establishing a healthy private practice.[20]

All's Fair in Love, War and Architectural Competitions

The use of architectural competitions to secure the design of major British public buildings, predates the formation of the RIBA by some 60 years. These competitions were truly *open.* Anyone could enter them and more importantly for the architects of the day, anyone could judge them. In a lament as to the state of such competitions, Soane is quoted as remarking of the typical 'committee of taste' or judging panel for public competitions:

> ... such persons are no more fitted to correct the public taste and to instruct the architect, than the presumptuous and ignorant pedant was to school Hannibal in the art of war.[21]

Despite these reservations, Soane was one of the few architects of note to enter such competitions and won the commission for the Bank of England as the result of a competition. Whilst some architects might protest that their work was ill served by the operation of unregulated competitions, other architects were not averse to using the lack of regulation to their advantage. The outcome of competitions such as that for the Royal Exchange in Dublin, were certainly influenced by the lobbying of interested parties. Unsolicited modifications to competition entries were offered, on receipt of inside information[22] and in some cases judges were not averse to inducements whether in terms of flattery or hard cash.

In 1838, the RIBA commissioned, 'a report to consider the subject of Public Competitions for Architectural Designs'. In it the competition system was described as possessing, 'great and manifold evils', a rather strong use of language. However, its conclusion was to continue to recommend the use of professional advisors, although it was not minded to limit this role to other architects but included and in some ways preferred, those who might offer specific and technical rather than artistic advice.

The competition for the design of the Royal Exchange, set in 1839 was one of the first public competitions to use the system of professional advisors, recommended by the IBA. Three eminent architects, Smirke, Barry and Hardwick were invited to be the professional assessors. Barry excused himself on the grounds of lack of available time, and Gwilt, a founder member of the Institute took his place.

Despite clear conditions for the entries, which included the price limit of £150,000, the assessors considered that none of the entries which met the conditions, were acceptable and some were 'unbuildable'. They however short-listed five of these designs but also short-listed three designs which they considered far superior, but which exceeded the cost limit. The lay selection committee then chose one of five schemes, which had been within the cost limit and duly awarded the prizes for 1st, 2nd and 3rd place. The winner turned out to be the work of Sydney Smirke, the younger brother and pupil of Robert Smirke, one of the assessors. The lay committee then announced that despite awarding the prizes, they would not be building any of the projects and asked the professional assessors to base a design on the best of the submissions received. Surprisingly, Hardwick and Gwilt initially agreed but when Robert Smirke refused, not on the basis of filial loyalty, but on the basis that it was an impossible task, the other two also withdrew.

The lay committee then proposed to draw up a list of potential architects, which included a few of the original competitors and several, who had not entered the competition, including Sir William Tite. Tite was selected but was then confronted with the proposal that he should work up the previous eight schemes with the committee's surveyor, George Smith. Tite refused, but Smith continued anyway and a scheme was selected which had been submitted under the name Henry B. Richardson but was in fact the work of C.R. Cockerell, the Professor of Architecture at the RA and future president of the RIBA. Whilst Cockerell was supposed to be working on his scheme, the committee invited a further five architects to enter a limited competition. These architects were none other than the original professional assessors, including Barry who had been too busy and Tite, the newcomer. All refused except Tite and so he was set in competition with Cockerell.

A more ridiculous and chaotic set of proceedings could scarcely have been imagined. The aim of bringing the competition system under some form of regulation had proved impossible and the architectural profession and the commissioning clients had made matters worse. As a final chapter in this sorry tale, Tite and Cockerell submitted their designs. Tite limited himself to the competition restrictions of only drawings but Cockerell considered that his scheme could not be fully appreciated without a model. However, the model he built was too large to be transported and so the lay committee was invited to his studio. Following discussion, it transpired that they had all in fact visited his studio to view the model as individuals and so they deemed a further visit unnecessary. When the final vote went to Tite, Cockerell objected on the basis that the committee had not revisited his model. He wrote a letter of complaint to the Lords of the Treasury citing the irregular behaviour of the committee, who were duly summoned to appear to explain their behaviour. Few emerged from this competition with credit, but Tite emerged with the commission!

At intervals throughout the nineteenth century and to the present day, the profession as body corporate, has wrestled with the issue of architectural competitions. In 1907, the RIBA was much exercised with the terms of the competition for the new headquarters for the London County Council (LCC). Again there had been an inability to resolve the demand from younger and less well-known members of the profession for an open competition, with the aspirations of the LCC for a high quality building from an eminent and experienced architect. By this time however, a further complication had been added. As the influence of the state acting as a client increased, the RIBA recommended that all town councils should appoint an Official Architect. Their role would be to oversee the letting of architectural work to other architects and to advise the elected councillors and officers of the council on matters relating to architecture and urban design. Thus were the first Official Architects appointed as public servants, responsible for large offices of architects, surveyors and draughtsmen.

The LCC competition for a County Hall was devised as a two-stage competition with the first stage open and the second stage limited to a few designs selected from the first stage and other designs submitted by an invited list of eight eminent architects. The text of the conditions, as passed by the LCC were published in the Chronicle Section of the *RIBA Journal* on 9 February 1907 and included the statement that two assessors for the first stage would be R. Norman Shaw RA, a prominent member of the Memorialists and W.E. Riley FRIBA, the Official Architect to the LCC. These would be joined in the second stage by an assessor nominated by the second stage competitors themselves, providing that any individual so elected, could vouch that they had not be an entrant in the first stage of the competition.

In November 1906, a resolution had been brought before RIBA Council by H.W. Wills, that:

> The RIBA considers it unadvisable in the interests of architecture that public officials should act as architects for public buildings.[23]

A second resolution requested that a survey of the sums paid to Official Architects and their offices be carried out with a view to comparing them against the fees charged by independent private practitioners. The object being to demonstrate that it was more cost effective to use the private sector, thus preventing vast amounts of public work from being completed 'in house' removing work from the wider profession.

RIBA Council discussions were reported verbatim in the *RIBA Journal*, and make for interesting reading, especially as they read like eloquent versions of the arguments rehearsed on innumerable occasions in architectural debate since. On this occasion, W.E. Riley, the Superintending Architect of Metropolitan Buildings and Architect of the LCC, had offered an amendment to the resolution, namely that it should read:

> The RIBA considers it unadvisable in the interests of architecture that public officials should act as architects for public buildings *unless they have had an architectural training.*

This amendment he stated, was in the 'four walls of the Charter', being in support of Art and not man, whereas the initial resolution, 'was not intended wholly in the interests of Art but in the interests of man as well'. He concluded by directing the attention of the Council to the two busts in the corner of the room. One being of Inigo Jones and the other, Christopher Wren, stating they were 'probably the greatest officials who ever lived'.

Although the amended resolution was the one carried, it seems that Riley had not convinced all the Council members.

The general terms of the LCC competition had been published in the *Builder* magazine in July 1906. The final terms and detailed conditions, had then been published in the RIBA journal, in the following February. The competition conditions stated that following the selection of the winning scheme, Riley, as Official Architect to the LCC would have 'discretionary power' over the scheme, 'in all matters relating to internal economy, building construction and stability'. For this and other services, the successful architect and the Official Architect would be required to split the 5% fee, with Riley receiving 0.5% for his services.

An initial objection to the terms of the competition had been raised in the January. This maintained that the two stage format, disadvantaged the first stage competitors and privileged the eight eminent architects who were allowed to enter the second stage directly. They would have several months longer to complete their entries and had a much higher chance of success. The first stage competitors also had a much higher chance of losing their entry fee. After discussion, these objections were dismissed but the rest of the competition conditions were checked against the RIBA Examination rules or the Codes of Conduct.

In April 1907, a group of 12 members summoned the RIBA Council to a Special Meeting to consider the conditions and instructions of the County Hall competition and the consequences for any members who were in the process of entering it. In 1898, the RIBA had set up the permanent Competitions Committee to assess whether competitions met its requirements. In 1903, a resolution had been passed stating that if a competition did not meet the requirements, 'Members taking part shall be adjudged guilty of unprofessional conduct and the Council shall take such steps in the matter as they may think proper.'[24] Notification of non-compliant competitions would be placed in the *Journal*, thus precluding the membership from entering.

James Gibson, the spokesman for the members who called the special meeting, maintained that the LCC competition conditions contained clear breaches of the RIBA competition regulations, and these revolved around the position of W.E. Riley as an assessor for both stages of the competition and also the future *joint* architect for the project. His position as the latter was based on the statement as to his discretionary powers over the scheme and his receipt of part of the fee. In his address to Council, Gibson also pointed out that of the architects invited to enter the second stage, five were currently Council members and a sixth had been a member, at the time of agreeing to enter. As a result of this, Gibson and three other members of Council, had resigned in protest and he asked Council to vote on a resolution that until the terms and conditions of the County Hall competition were revised, all members should be prohibited from entering, and that this prohibition should be published in the journal of the RIBA.

The debate was fierce. Collcutt, the President was clearly incensed and Riley considered he had to make a personal statement, to refute the implications made as to his integrity. He made an impassioned plea for the resolution to be withdrawn and for Council to 'go heartily into the competition'. Professor Beresford Pite appealed to Gibson to withdraw the resolution. Other members offered placatory alternative resolutions with phrases such as 'That this Institute regrets that the terms of the competition are not satisfactory, but . . .'. However, these were rejected.

When asked by Alfred Cross, one of the 12, why in this instance Council was departing from 'ordinary regulations', Colcutt stated:

> There must be exceptions to every rule. The London County Hall was an exceptional case altogether and there was ample justification for treating it in an exceptional manner.[25]

The Gibson's resolution was defeated by 50 votes to 29.

Beating the Bounds

If the arguments related to architectural competitions took place in the heart of the profession, the most fiercely contested zone is at the boundary and more particularly about the form of the gateway into the profession. As previously stated, one of the necessary conditions to the creation and maintenance of a profession is the ability to define and control its membership. The suggestion to make entry to the RIBA dependant upon examination, came from outside its ranks in a prize winning essay by James Knowles, submitted to the Architectural Association (AA) in 1853.[26] This paper saw entry by examination as both a means of securing the appropriate level of skill and knowledge required for architectural practice and a way of increasing the social status and prestige of the RIBA and its membership as a whole. J.W. Papworth suggested to the RIBA that a Board of Education should be instituted to hold examinations and issue diplomas. A Memorial from the AA, supported by its President Alfred Bailey[27] called for the establishment of an examination. Bailey added that:

> they felt that to be of any use to them, the examination must be severe, adding that it should be, No disgrace to a man . . . to get 'plucked' even two or three times.[28]

A committee was subsequently formed in 1860, under the chairmanship of Papworth, its membership including John Ruskin, T.L. Donaldson and a non-architect patron, Beresford-Hope.

From 1863, until the present day, The RIBA has had a continuing and often difficult relationship with architectural education and the assessment of suitability for entry to the professional body. For many years the examination remained voluntary, and was little used. In 1882 an obligatory examination was instituted, but it was not until it was proposed to link this to a Registration Bill in 1889, restricting the title *architect* to those passing the examinations, that significant dissent was heard. The initial proposal failed, but a new lobby group calling itself the Society of Architects had been formed and it actively pursued the idea of a Registration Act. Its membership was mainly disaffected young Associate members of the RIBA. Only Fellows of the institute could vote, and so the younger members considered their views were not being represented in RIBA policies.

In 1891, another Bill was proposed, supported by the Society of Architects. But a group of eminent architects and artists were appalled at the prospect and took their objection to the public arena, with the well-known copy of their *Memorial to the RIBA*, being published in *The Times* and endorsed by 70 eminent signatories. This is often portrayed as a battle between some of the most famous Arts and Crafts architects of the day and the stolid ranks of the profession, as represented by the RIBA. In fact, the RIBA opposed the proposed Bill and lobbied MPs to that effect.[29] Twenty-four of the 70 Memorialists were members of the RIBA, a further 22 were architects but non-members. The remaining 24 were artists and patrons, including William Morris and Herbert Marshall.

Despite the furore caused by the Memorialists, which resulted in the now famous publication of *Architecture: A Profession or an Art'*, a volume of 13 essays, edited by Norman Shaw and T.G. Jackson,[30] only seven or eight of the members of the RIBA resigned over the issue.[31] The Bill was not successful, and architectural education developed on the basis of the three tier examination system which remains in modified form, to this day.[32] By 1903, several of the Memorialists, including Lethaby and Blomfield, made a further presentation to RIBA Council, lamenting the state of architectural education. They maintained that neither pupillage nor a school-based education was the answer, instead they suggested a combination of both, with the addition of building craft skills. In 1904, the Board of Education was appointed, including at least six of the Memorialists. Under the RIBA Presidency of Aston Webb (1902–1904) and then Belcher (1904–1906), many more of the Memorialists joined or rejoined the RIBA, including Lethaby, Ricardo, Lutyens, Macartney and W.E. Prior.' From the early years of the twentieth century, RIBA Council and its various committees and boards have wrestled with architectural education and the issue of a Registration Act. The fact that these topics remain not only relevant, but as burning issues, is a testament to their centrality to the profession of architecture. But there have always been those who have presented a challenge to the profession by apparently demonstrating all the outward attributes of an architect but who have not met the explicit, formal requirements for admission. For these persons, the profession has reserved 'exceptional' measures whilst demonstrating a degree of ambivalence towards their success.

By 1922, the Visiting Board system for schools had been instituted. The transformation from vehement critic to lauded champion of the profession, has continued over the years. Many who spent their early years antagonistic to the profession have been content to accept its approbation in later years. Feisty student members have become energetic officers of the profession and radicals find themselves serving on committees and defending the RIBA and its policies against more insidious proposals.

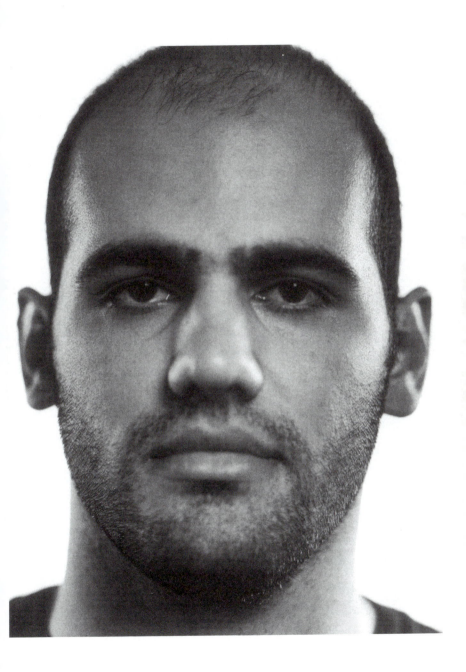

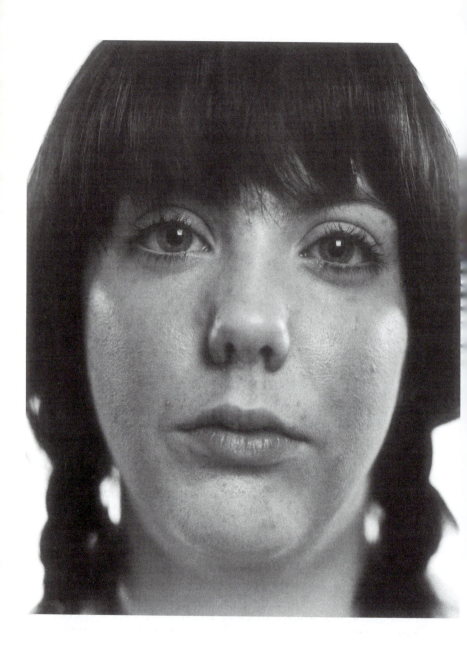

All The Kings Men and a Few Women

14

Judith Farren-Bradley

How has the fact that architects came together and the use of their collective position affected their relationships with each other, including those who practised architecture but were not registered as architects? This essay will look at how the professional body, in this case the professional institute, the Royal Institute of British Architects (RIBA), and the professional regulatory body formerly the Architects Registration Council of the United Kingdom (ARCUK) and now the Architects Registration Board (ARB), relate to the individual. In particular, how they attempt to accommodate and promote professional autonomy and the cause of the *architect* singular, whilst devising structures and processes to maintain control over standards and codes of behaviour for the profession plural.

In any history of the architectural profession there have been those who, for a variety of reasons have stood outside the architectural profession whilst being deeply concerned with architecture as a discipline. The most obvious of these have been the eminent academicians, theorists and critics, who may or may not have engaged in some part of what is accepted as architectural education, but have for a variety of reasons seen fit not to complete the process to the point of registration. From 1931 to 1997, the protection of the title *architect*, had been the remit of the statutory body, ARCUK. This responsibility now lies with the ARB. Whether or not the protection of title, without the protection of activity is sensible, or whether any kind of protection for the activity of making architecture is appropriate, is not the focus of this essay. The Architects Acts of 1931–1969, and it successor Act of 1997, have added a procedural and legal basis to any discussion of what it means to be an architect in the United Kingdom.

Few architects will find their names and their activities mentioned in the national broadsheets, and even fewer will find their names and deeds recorded in Hansard, the official record of Parliament. However, in 1996, a young, female designer of buildings managed both.

An Architect by any Other Name

Gabriele Bramante came to the attention of the public and the profession within a relatively short space of time. She was commissioned to design a new building for the Citizens Advice Bureau in Chessington, Surrey. The building was profiled in several architectural magazines and came to particular prominence by winning the BBC Design Award for Architecture, and three other awards. Bramante, it was reported, had not only designed and overseen the construction of the project, but had also acted as a fundraiser and project manager. Bramante had sourced donations for the project in cash and in kind, and had also gained sponsorship for the project from media sources.

Bramante's main claim to fame prior to the construction of the Citizens Advice Bureau, was as a writer. She had contributed to a book on Foster's, Willis Faber Dumas Building and written for other magazines. She had completed her first degree at Kingston Polytechnic School of Architecture, had travelled to Japan and had then won a scholarship to Harvard University to the Masters programme in Architecture. She had been published in June 1992, as establishing a 'new medical design consuiltancy' and was stated in an article in the *Times* of 29th August 1996 as having previously designed toilets in St George's Hospital Tooting and completed refurbishment work for a housing association.

The success and public profile of young women operating in the field of architecture, would have been a splendid opportunity for the profession to celebrate. However, there were two problems. By this time The Architects Act 1931–1969, prescribing the terms for registration in the United Kingdom, had been in force for over 60 years and was *policed* by the Architects Registration Council. There had been a less than happy relationship between it and the RIBA, which still considered itself to be the most appropriate body to regulate and educate the profession. At the time of Bramante's success there was considerable interest in the operations of ARCUK and the Architects Act 1931–1969, as the Warne report published in 1993, had proposed the abolition of the protection of title for architects and the RIBA had been forced by its membership to lobby for its retention.[1]

By 1996, The Housing, Grants and Regeneration Bill, was in its final stages in Parliament. This enabling Act, contained many measures which were exercising the attention of the profession, including the proposed demise of ARCUK and the creation of the ARB, with a lay majority of eight to seven on the Board itself. As part of its progress through the House of Lords, Lord Rogers of Quarry Bank, former Director General of the RIBA, had spoken in its favour, citing that it offered not so much protection for the profession but protection for the public. This concept was received by a spirited repost from the Earl of Caithness 'What a load of rubbish!', Caithness then went on to say:

> Many of my own designs have had to be rescued from the hands of architects by quantity surveyors and others in the profession. There are too many buildings in this country, too many ideas and too much money has been lost as a result of bad workmanship by architects that others have luckily been able to rescue or, in many cases, not.[2]

The parliamentary debates, and the plethora of articles in the architectural and construction press, had certainly momentarily raised the profile of profession. Another matter of concern was the progress of the Cardiff Opera House competition, which had been won by another young female *architect*, Zaha Hadid, whose winning proposals were meeting considerable resistance from the commissioning clients and much of the popular press.

On 29th July 1996, the *Times* published a small article by Diana Thorp, under the Home News section, stating that The Citizens Advice Bureau, as clients to Bramante's Chessington scheme, had refused to allow the project to be entered for the RIBA Stirling Prize.[3] This, it reported, was despite Ms Bramante offering to split the £20,000 prize money 50/50, if it won. It suggested that the less than cordial relations between, designer and client had in some part been caused by an event some months earlier. Ms Bramante and two friends had gone to the Citizens Advice Bureau in the early hours of the morning, prior to its being opened in May 1996, by the Princess Royal. Their purpose had been to remove two 6-m high cypresses, which had been planted in front of the building, and replace them with two Polish silver birch trees, in accordance with Bramante's original specification. Other matters which had confirmed the unwillingness of the clients to allow the project to be entered into another competition, were that since it had achieved some degree of notoriety, they had been inundated with architecture students asking questions and had been required to 'entertain' several sets of competition judges.

The architectural press, repeated the tale of the trees. In Building Design, Scorpio quoted Bramante, from an article in the *Independent*, and by this time the offending trees had grown to 7 m. The author applauded Bramante, for taking direct action, 'to prevent aesthetically-incorrect crimes being perpetrated'.[4] The *Architects' Journal* presented a more measured piece, which included comments from Mark Welling, then chairman of the CAB, as to the technical problems with the building and the 'difficult relationship', with the designer. He stated that Ms Bramante needed 'to accept that the building was completed and opened in March', and that the publicity was now affecting the ability of CAB and its voluntary employees to carry out their charitable work.

Bramante's eagerness for publicity for the project, related to the way she had arranged sponsorship for its construction. Many of the building material suppliers, who had donated products, had apparently done so on the basis that the project would be extensively publicised. The AJ gave the final cost of the building as being £350,000, of which CAB had paid £200,000 including architect's fees. Welling stated that this was three times the original budget.

The detail and timing of the following events are known only to those directly involved. Suffice to say, two weeks later the AJ printed the following:

Unqualified Gabriele Bramante has been fined £2000 plus £700 costs for describing herself as an architect on correspondence to the Chessington Citizens Advice Bureau.[5]

In his comment section, Martin Pawley was less restrained. In a piece in which he admitted that he too was 'unqualified' in the ARCUK sense, he lambasted the actions of the CAB and ARCUK and echoed comments attributed to Bramante herself in the earlier article, that:

The occupiers of the building got more and more fed up with Bramante's fame and the growing stream of visitors the building attracted after each wave of prize winning and consequent publicity.

He concluded by saying:

In the end, such dustups never do any harm to the reputation of an architect. They only show us what a splendid thing a real architectural reputation is.[6]

On the following day, BD offered a front page piece under the headline:

Bramante will fight conviction.[7]

Pawley's piece had also drawn attention to the fact that Zaha Hadid, who was being heavily supported by the architectural press, eminent members of the profession and the RIBA, for the way her winning scheme for Cardiff had been dismissed, was also 'not on the ARCUK register'. Under the Architects Act, she was therefore not entitled to use the title architect, which she herself had never done. However, sections of the press and public had been referring to her as an architect. On the same page as Pawley's piece about Bramante, a letter was published from Mira Bar-Hillel, referring to the way the profession had jumped to the defence of a non-RIBA member (Hadid) but had not seen fit to be as energetic in its support for the ousting of an RIBA member on the scheme for Paternoster Square. Bar-Hillel concluded:

> Not for the first time, I find the acrid stench of architectural hypocrisy quite nauseating.

A month later, Bar-Hillel, had another letter published in BD. On this occasion he made reference explicitly to the case of Ms Bramante. The tone of the brief letter can be judged from this extract:

> Of course she (Bramante) is an architect! Why, she has all the essential attributes: supreme arrogance, intolerance of any criticism and a healthy contempt for both clients and users of her buildings.[8]

Another letter from Stephen Buzas, reserved its criticism for ARCUK and the RIBA (although the RIBA had been sensibly quiet in relation to Ms Bramante). He accused both of abandoning their:

> . . . function of high-priest-like guarding (of) the holy grail of the profession.[9]

It is important to note that the case against Bramante was overturned in September 1996, due to a failure of ARCUK to notify Bramante of the legal action, rendering her incapable of offering a defence. ARCUK was disbanded in 1997, to be replaced by ARB and despite suggesting that it would reopen the case against Bramante, ARB finally abandoned it in September 1997. Following the initial action by ARCUK, Bramante, had asked how she could prove her qualifications were equivalent to those required for registration. Both Bramante and Hadid were subsequently entered onto Register of Architects, under ARBs period of jurisdiction. Both are therefore fully entitled to call themselves *architect*.

As a postscript to the above, The RIBA Journal, which had been circumspect to say the least about the Bramante debacle, included her as 39th in its 'Top 40 women in architecture', as compiled by Will Callaghan, in October 1996. Zaha Hadid, is 2nd, and a young ex-student Council member, Leonie Milliner, now RIBA Director of Education, was cited 11th. Of the other 37, three were or have become Heads of Schools of Architecture, one contested the RIBA presidency after appearing in one of the first television series showing an architect at work, and another was President of the RIAS. Just over half are now on the register of architects.

As for the mention in Hansard, this came on 14th February 1997. Mr Dennis MacShane, MP for Rotherham led an Adjournment debate offering, 'a brief moment to consider the state of architecture in our country'.

The opening speech was witty, and promoted the use of architectural competitions, stating that in some cases these should be limited by upper age limit, to provide opportunities for the younger members of the profession. He even, mischievously suggested, the creation of an *Ofarch* to regulate the quality of architectural production.

Sir Patrick Cormack MP for South Staffordshire, contributed to the debate, referring to the commissioning of Portcullis House by Hopkins as an example of enlightened government patronage. The Minister of State for the Department of National Heritage, Mr. Iain Sproat, had been invited by MacShane to take part. He too was keen to debate the topic and hoped the Government whip would find time, 'for us to have a good, in-depth and detailed debate on this truly important subject (architecture)'.

He went on to defend the government policy of procurement through PFI and in relation to the extended use of architectural competitions, whilst acknowledging their value in bringing forward new talent, he stated:

> However, they are expensive in abortive effort and are not always appropriate. Sadly, they also have a record of intemperate accusations and recriminations.

and noting the increased public interest in architecture, attributing it in some part to the intervention of the Prince of Wales in the 1980s. He did, however, comment on the increased attention given to architecture, in the media. It was in this connection that Ms Bramante found herself mentioned in the same paragraph as proposals by Norman Foster and Daniel Liebeskind.[10]

Plus ca change

The profession has always had something of a problem engaging with the public. It has for centuries bemoaned the fact that the public does not understand architecture or architects and appears to have a limited interest in current architectural debates. In a similar way, when individual architects (or non-architects) acquire a degree of notoriety, whether it is within the profession or in the larger public forum, it finds it somewhat destabilising and struggles to both applaud the individual and to uphold the contribution of its less famous members.

The RIBA Code of Conduct, and until 1997 the ARCUK Code of Conduct and Discipline, have always concerned themselves with four main issues:

- that architects should not mislead the public
- that architects should be clear about the terms of their engagement with their clients

- that architects should have proper regard for the interests of the wider community
- that architects should identify and remove themselves from any situations where their integrity is in question.

The detailed interpretation of these principles has been modified to account for changes in custom, practice and the law, over time. Hence the abandoning of restrictions on advertising, the charging of minimum fees and more recently even the publication of recommended fees. One way of reading the shifting relationship between the profession and society would be through the amendments to these documents. Until its substantive revision in 1984, the RIBA Code of Conduct can be seen as an evolution and series of adjustments. In the post 1986 versions, the main change came in Principle 3, which concerned the way members should promote themselves. Prior to 1984 this read:

A member shall rely only on ability and achievement as the basis for his advancement. It also contained the following explanatory note, written under Principle 3.6, a member is permitted to exhibit his name outside his office and on buildings in the course of construction, alteration or extension, provided that such exhibition of his name is done unostentatiously.

In earlier versions there had even been a stipulation that *lettering* on signboards should be no more than two inches high.

After 1986, a series of amendments reduced the specificity of the explanatory notes and began to reflect the more hostile commercial climate of the day. It has been suggested that if one were to plot the major changes to the Code of Conduct against the graph of the economic cycle, most would coincide with recessions or be a reaction forced by government or legal edict.

In late 2004, the Code of Professional Conduct was substantially revised, coming into effect on 1st January 2005. Principle 3 now makes no explicit restriction on self promotion. However, of the Guidance Notes provided, Note 3, concerning Advertising, remains the most prescriptive.

The new RIBA Code is far less detailed than its predecessors, and members are exhorted to be:

> guide by its spirit as well as its precise and express terms.

Reading it through, one may still detect a general encouragement toward a sober and measured response to all professional activities. Despite being able to transform whole areas of cities, being showered with honours, being invited to advise governments and sit on international juries for internationally important projects, the architect should remain a consummate professional. It seems the chartered architect should not seek greatness and fame for its own sake, but may accept greatness and fame if it is thrust upon them. That is, of course, always providing that this does not contravene Note 1.3 under *Principle 1 – Honesty and Integrity*.

> Members should not be party to any statement which they know to be untrue, misleading, unfair to others or contrary to their own professional knowledge.

So, if you are truly great, accurately great, fairly great and you know you are great – the world can know – that is official!

Part IV

PORTRAITS

The Portraits

15

Julie Cook and Paul Davies

The photographic element of this book comprises the complete cohort of full time, first year students of architecture at London South Bank University, shot by Julie Cook on their second day at the university, the 28th September 2004.

South Bank is an inner London university that attracts students from a wide range of cultural and ethnic backgrounds. The architecture division started life in the Brixton School of Building, and has maintained a tradition of opportunity for all within a highly stratified higher education sector in the United Kingdom.

The Brixton School of Building was opened by London County Council in 1904. It was a response to a localised concentration of building trades across Camberwell and Lambeth, with the intension of augmenting existing talent with classes in stone carving, plasters' modelling, drawing for the building trade, chemistry and physics of building materials, land surveying and levelling. By 1912, 5-year courses were available in all trade subjects with the addition of general building, quantity surveying, architecture, and structural engineering. With the post war boom in all sectors, the school grew rapidly, becoming part of the Polytechnic of the South Bank in 1970, and moving to a new purpose built concrete building on the Wandsworth Road as a Faculty of the Built Environment in 1972.

South Bank Polytechnic became South Bank University in 1992. Competition within the new university sector lead to it's re-branding as London South Bank University in 2003, when the Wandsworth Road building was sold, and the architecture division moved in to various accommodations across an revamped Elephant and Castle campus in a fresh rationalisation exercise where architecture sits within a faculty of Engineering, Science and the Built Environment in a School of Architecture and Design, whose subjects include Industrial design, Computing design, Product Design, Special Effects, Computing Design and Design for Sports.

This history speaks volumes about the trajectory of architecture within higher education over the last 100 years in the United Kingdom. Nevertheless, the architecture division received both the full 4-year recognition from the RIBA[1] and praise for *excellence* in teaching and learning from the QAA[2] in 2003/4.

The hegemony of white, middle class, males in architecture has long been an issue, even inside the profession. Even after a century of attempts to broaden access to both architectural education and the profession, these students will still be amongst those who will face the biggest of battles. On the one hand, perhaps there are already too many architects. There is the possibility that there will be a backward step to a protectionism not based on these students ability to study, learn and work hard, or communicate well or work well in a team, but on those recurrent questions of wealth and taste; those values which prevailed over 100 years ago, where architecture was best thought of as a gentleman's hobby. On the other hand architectural education in the United Kingdom is uncomfortably polarised. Peter Cook, professor of architecture at The Bartlett, UCL, has only recently stated 'there are only two schools of architecture in the UK . . . and maybe two others trying'.[3] He means of course, that the only true path lies through the portals of either the Bartlett or the AA. The rest of us appear to be wasting our time. He means the avant-garde, he means the passionate, he means the architecture most people simply can't understand.

The photographic portrait has only existed for about 150 years. The portrait, which was once a rare and occasional event, commissioned, as you would do a painting for personal use or to demonstrate wealth and position, is now common place. Portraits are no longer a personal affair but are placed in the public domain, especially for the famous or those who want to be. Portraits are regularly commissioned by magazines, advertising, fashion, image libraries, in a process that hugely influences the end representation. Photographers may be given a background on the subject and instructions on style, perhaps issued by a PR Agency, and they will often be expected to show something of this person that reflects them as a *professional*. Meanwhile picture libraries don't want facial hair, tatoos, people who look unhappy, or who are not the right size. Advertisers and fashion have work boards that pre-plan the social, political and personal beliefs they want to project. Hair and makeup artists patch up the subjects, and the more famous the subject is, the more attention they receive. In post-production, there is usually retouching: hair, skin, whole heads, expressions are manipulated, so that the final portrait may be barely recognisable from the original model. Male and femaleness is accentuated in this process, towards some ideal we somehow collectively respond to, but has little to do with how we actually look.[4]

These days even buildings need model releases.

Black suit, heavy glasses, conservative, sensible, serious and arrogant, yes arrogant, hard, male, white. This is the cliché that comes to mind when we think of *architect*. Perhaps this is dated, something unfortunate stemming from the portrayal of Howard Rourk in *The Fountainhead*, but it is also unfortunately enduring. Returning from watching Louis Kahn in the film *My Architect*, it is still there, the heroic, even tragic figure, struggling against the odds. We are not sure that even the age of postmodernity has changed that.

Even when we look at our second years they look somehow different. Older, yes, but also there is something that they have lost, or is it something they have gained, we can see them growing into architects. Something has already changed in them as they attain a certain attitude and confidence. These first years on the other hand look different: friendly if a little nervous. They are certainly innocent of what lies ahead.

The students were given their instructions for the portraits: they must look directly into the camera and not smile. The portraits are intended to allow them to be seen in equal light: they have been shot in the same format, on the same background, in the same lighting at the same angle, as neutral as possible – black and white. They were asked not to adjust their hair or make-up. The close up angle is to cut out as much of their clothing as possible and cut in slightly on the face and hair. The focus of the camera is on their eyes, eyes that address the viewer as directly as possible.

We wonder how many will get through and qualify. It will take them at least 5 more years. A few had not even made the second day, and some we would hardly see again. But this day is the beginning for them, perhaps becoming architects, perhaps, becoming famous,[5] perhaps . . .

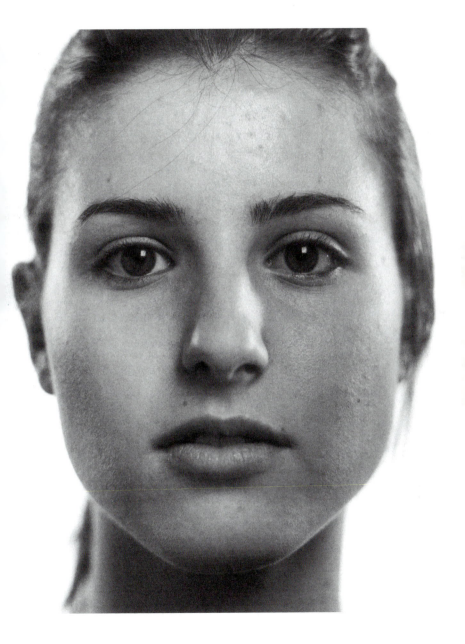

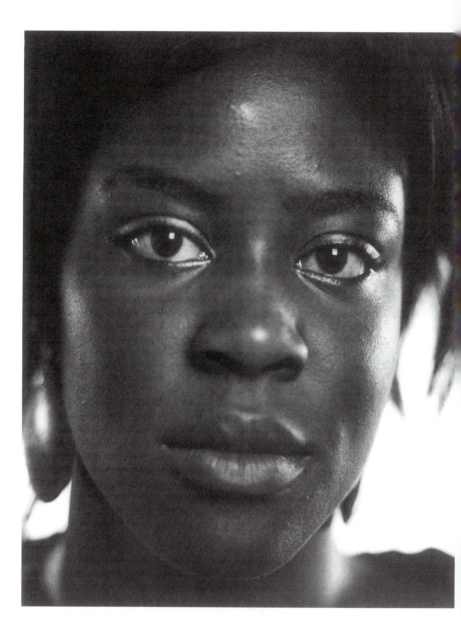

Art, Architecture, Artists and Architects

16

Edward Winters

Everybody knows that the dice are loaded

Everybody rolls with their fingers crossed

Everybody knows the war is over

Everybody knows the good guys lost[1]

I

Let it be simply assumed that Architecture is an art; and an important one at that. It is a very special art in that it occupies a particular position within the fabric of the community into which it is woven. The question that I shall attempt to answer here is best articulated in two parts: What is the particular role that Architecture plays in our lives; and how does an understanding of that role constrain our conception of those who design and build our environment? In this essay I would like to consider the nature of recently emerging public art in order to cast light on our twice folded question. I shall, that is, hope to illuminate the nature of architecture, seen as a public art, and then move on to say how that publicity constrains the notion of what the architect does; or should do. I shall aim to take us from fairly easily acceptable premises to a conclusion that is normative and which is, therefore, regulatory in our conception of the practice of the art of architecture.

II

> and all the lousy little poets
> coming round
> trying to sound like Charlie Manson
> . . .
> *(and the white man dancin')*[2]

Art, as it has come to be seen during the modern period, is the province in which genius shines through. The notion of genius, however, is both difficult to grasp and, in consequence, is notoriously difficult to attribute. It is a notion that gained much currency in the Romantic era, but which has creditable intellectual foundations in the philosophy of art as that was developed within Aesthetics by Immanuael Kant.[3] Genius, according to Kant, is that facility an artist has to make original works, such that it is as if Nature speaks through her. The art of a genius arrives as second nature; fit to be the standard that other artists, less gifted, might take as their template. It is entirely mysterious, since genius cannot be taught – it can only be imitated by those who lack it. However, it can be seen and recognised by anyone with sufficiently developed sensitivities. There is, as might be imagined, much more to be said upon this issue. I raise it only to give the flavour of what Kant had to say and to introduce it in a way that immediately demonstrates how that notion has seeped into our culture – and to remind ourselves of how modern a notion it is. It ought to be remembered, however, that whilst Kant thought that *originality* is the mark of genius, he warned us that nonsense too bears the mark of originality.[4]

It is now fairly easy to see how it is that the common imagination thinks of the artist as a remote figure, sloping around the dark edges of society – troubled, dislocated and verging on insanity. The common imagination looks for eccentric, wayward, rebellious individuals, uncompromising in their expression of a divine gift that poor mortals can only glimpse; and can barely grasp. Van Gogh is almost everyone's favourite genius, lopping off his ear to give to his friend Paul; and wandering off to the asylum, there to paint bright brushy paintings whilst scrounging a living from his more respectable brother. Whilst Kant provides an almost impenetrable account of fine art and genius, Kirk Douglas hams it up in Vincente Minnelli's and George Cukor's *Lust For Life*. No doubt it is Kirk Douglas's van Gogh that has, at least in part, shaped our modern sense of the artist as genius. I think it likely more people have watched *Lust For Life* than have read Kant's *Critique of Judgement*. So the sentimental sickly romantic version of what constitutes the life of a painter has crept into the popular representation of art and artists.

It is through some such spectacle that we see the Young British Art pack. We see them in light of this easy corruption of Kant's efforts to delineate the artistic temperament. Tracey Emin is surely just what the media wanted; and what the media purveyed to a malleable public. If Tony Hancock's *Rebel* was a pastiche of Existentialist notions of artistic genius, then Tracey Emin is a contemporary pastiche of Hancock; perhaps a less amusing pastiche than Hancock – less intelligent than the man from 23 Railway Cuttings, East Cheam; and certainly less perceptive. Easy celebrity is the common ambition of contemporary artists. Art students everywhere put out their portentous wares in the hope that Saatchi – or whoever the new weather-makers are in the art world – will come along and buy up their shows providing them with instant fame and fortune; just for as long as each of these conditions might be eked out.[5]

It is heart-rending to walk round the final shows of fine art schools in the decadent western world; heart-rending if not sickening. All is now focused upon the concept and its expression of a barely developed personality – for it is the personality that now takes centre stage in the contemporary art world. It is through personality that the aspirant art student hopes to become a celebrity.

The collapse of theory in the humanities is, perhaps, the result of the collapse of Marxism in the eastern bloc. What is left in the art schools is a fairly self-inflated set of enthusiasms that might be collected together under the banner rubric 'Marxism Lite'[6] – a loose rag-bag of complaints on behalf of the so called 'disenfranchised'. Nothing, however, remains of the intense political argumentation that had art students struggling to imbue their work with ideas in the mid-twentieth century. What we have now are post-Thatcherite individuals looking for *careers in art*. (A phrase that would once have been utterly unpalatable.)

III

Here is your crown
And your seal and rings;
And here is your love
For all things.

Here is your cart
And your cardboard and piss;
And here is your love
For all this.

May everyone live,
and may everyone die.
Hello my love,
and my love, Goodbye.[7]

There is nothing more pitiable than looking at the work of an artist who has no talent and who is not in the process of developing any critical competence. This is especially true if that artist is transparently attempting to pass off the work as if it is touched by troubled genius. The emptiness is conspicuous. Backed by tendentious conceptual posturing, that emptiness has the overwhelming effect of making the dispirited observer swoon with nausea. Let us move from the Fine Arts to Architecture, where this celebrity culture is currently being imported.

Architecture, we might feel, should be polite. Recently at a research seminar Penny Florence remarked that there is an interesting gaze that belongs to the work of art.[8] Furthering her point she suggested that this is not the gaze we have come to understand as belonging to the virtual spectator, the gaze organised by the artist and occupied by the spectator as she takes up an attitude toward the work of art in front of her. The gaze that Florence referred to is to be identified with the work of art as *it* strikes an attitude toward the spectator. Despite the fact that Florence was talking about the fine arts, I was immediately struck by how useful this notion might be in our consideration of architecture. It is something to think of ourselves as being fixed by the gaze of works of art. In architectural works we feel the building and our place within it, orientating ourselves toward it and taking our behavioural cues from the building's embrace. It is no accident that totalitarian regimes produce works of architecture which are demeaning of the individual and which produce awed silence in those whose lives are engulfed within them. Polite architecture, by contrast, does not impose itself upon the spectator, but rather suggests itself as a venue for life's pleasurable pursuit. I have nothing to say here about what style of architecture best recommends itself as ministering to our serious pursuits. Indeed, I believe that good contemporary architecture, making use of modern cheaply available materials can put us at our ease – just as the smell of wax polish in the rich wooden interiors of university libraries can put us in the mood for reading and thinking. My point here, is not to argue for the supremacy of this or that architectural trend, but rather to argue in favour of the phenomenon that architecture can make us feel at home. In doing this we are to think of architecture as polite in the same way that the polite host puts his guests at ease and provides them with a sense of being at home.

Architecture has the function of providing us with a sense of belonging in this world – the world of human endeavour. I am inclined to think that some of the buildings of Frank Ghery manage to make us feel at home in our modernity. However, there are architects who singularly fail in doing this and I believe that Daniel Libeskind is one such example. In order to see what is meant by the notion of home and how that fits with the nature of architecture, I would like now to turn our attention to public art.

Set against the individualism and expressive genius of the tormented artist; and imbued with the value of a *sensus communis*, the public art movement has developed into a way of making art that relies upon the community's shared values. Civic sculpture in the form of statuary of the great and the good has been replaced by public art that serves to unite the community in its expression of communally held values. A fairly straightforward example is Maya Ying Lin's *Vietnam Veteran's Memorial*, 1982.[9] There is nothing of the artist expressed in this piece. Rather, the artist has undertaken a job on behalf of the community for which the piece is a monument. The artist here is to be seen as a public servant, using her talent and her expertise in bringing about a work of art for a public place of remembrance. It is instructive to notice how differently we are required to look at and appreciate this work when comparing it to van Gogh's *Wheat Field Under Threatening Skies*, 1890 (his last melodramatic picture before suicide removed him). Maya Ying Lin was a post-graduate architecture student at Yale University when she won the competition to realise the memorial. It is in this spirit that I think that public art and its appreciation is to be seen as the model for architecture and its appreciation. Architects should regard themselves as highly talented, educated and sensitive artists in the service of a wide public into whose lives their work is to be placed. No such form of creative endeavour could have been properly required of van Gogh.

IV

> It's coming to America first
> The cradle of the best and of the worst
> . . .
> Democracy is coming
> To the USA[10]

If architecture is best understood in terms of its role in our lives, rather than being seen as the expression of some eccentric impulse passed through the artist by nature herself, we can dispense with the work of architects that do not attend to our lives and the pursuits with which they are constituted. Just as public art is a corrective to the notion of genius and its latest mutation in the character of celebrity, so the constraint upon our understanding architecture as the shaping of an environment for a community should suitably limit the ways in which architects have come to see themselves as expressionists and increasingly as celebrities.

If this argument is persuasive, then there is something of vital importance that has yet to be developed. I shall now make some introductory remarks in the hope that what is sketched here will provide the basis for a further project. For what is at stake is the nature of democracy. If we look at the way that our culture has developed over the past 5–10 years we shall have reason to worry about the present cult of the celebrity and we shall have cause to resist its many temptations.

The demise of art and architectural criticism has come about as a result of a contemporary loss of faith in critical standards as that has emerged from postmodernist thinking. Roland Barthes's '*The Death of the Author*' and '*From Work to Text*' are now required reading in cultural and visual studies. Their legacy, however, is a democratisation of the reading of works of art and therefore, on the view rehearsed here, a move away from the idea that there can be anything like objective criticism. To attempt to argue that the appreciation of art takes time and requires the development of sensitivity is immediately to run the risk of being sidelined as elitist; and hence, anti-democratic.

However, I think this move has been made too quickly. Why should we think that the man who knows nothing of western architecture might have anything interesting to say about its works? The mistake is in thinking that any thought upon architecture (or art more broadly) has to be as valuable as any other. But this is not democracy of taste: rather it is taste by *referendum*. In confusing these two notions we run the risk of heading for disaster.[11]

Similarly with aesthetics: we need a consensus that hangs together as a body of reasonable criticism if we are to feel secure in the judgements that we make about works of art. The *sensus communis* of a people's aesthetic sensibility will be strengthened not by taking into account any and every opinion, whether carefully worked out or casually thrown in. Instead it shall rely upon a body of well-informed, sensitive, developed and persuasive descriptions of works of art that encourages our looking at works this way rather than that. It takes both time and effort to develop ways and means of looking at art. There is nothing intrinsically elitist about this. It takes time and effort to become sensitive to the nuances of personality; or to the niceties of football. Yet in neither case would we think it elitist for someone to spend time developing their appreciation of such nuances and niceties. Agreement in our judgements is, at least in part, what binds us together and provides us with a sense of home. The equivalent of aesthetic *referenda* promotes the dislocation of art from society – and threatens to render meaningless judgements that attribute value to works of art. The democratisation of judgement, by contrast, permits the consolidation of judgement according to sensitive and reasoned criticism.

V

> Give me back the Berlin Wall
> give me Stalin and St Paul
> Give me Christ
> or give me Hiroshima[12]

In this final section of the essay, I return to the notion of genius and original nonsense; and then move on to write what I hope is a piece of architectural criticism. If what I say is persuasive, then the reader will come to look at the building under descriptions with which she can agree in experience. The point is not to tell someone what to think about a work of art, but to persuade them that this is a perceptive way of considering the work under view. Thus the description under which the work is seen is, at least in part, *constitutive* of the experience undergone. This, then, is the mark of successful criticism: that the spectator, in accepting the critical description of the work, undergoes a renewed experience in light of that description. Criticism, that is, aims at illumination. The democracy of such enlightenment is secured in the conversation we have about art. Provided a suitably sensitive spectator is open to the suggestion of criticism, she will be able to accept or reject aesthetic description just according to whether the critical content with which she is provided shows up in her experience. Thus the spectator is engaged in a critical attitude toward the work in her attempt to fit her experience to the critical descriptions made available to her.

By contrast, if any and all responses to works of art are equally valid, we would not know what to make of a particular work of art, since any thought we now have might be succeeded by another, and that by another, and so on. Since, *ex hypothesi*, there can be no reason to move from one thought to another, any mere succession of thoughts can have no argumentative value. Therefore *no* present thought could establish itself; not even as a peculiar or personal *judgement* – since judgement implies the assessment of something beyond its mere appearance to the subject. Moreover, the endurance of a thought would have nothing further to recommend it, since such a *thought* would have the status simply of a tickle or pain – something that can come or go, can subsist for a while or might perish in a trice. Nothing in the thought is substantial enough (again, *ex hypothesi*) to provide adherence between it and the objective world beyond. On a similar matter let us turn to an unlikely source. In fact I find St Paul refreshingly rigorous in a manner that presages Kant and, later, Wittgenstein. (There are clear echoes in Wittgenstein's famous attack on the idea of a *private language* and Paul's resistance to *unknown tongues*.) St Paul, in his attempts to get clear about speaking in tongues, writes to the Corinthians,

> [Y]et in the church I had rather speak five words with my understanding, that by my voice I might teach others also, than ten thousand words in an unknown tongue.
> (I Corinthians 14: 19)

And later:

> If any man speak in an unknown tongue, let it be by two, or at most by three, and that by course; and let one interpret. But if there be no interpreter, let him keep silence in the church.
> (I Corinthians 14: 27–8)[13]

I leave it to the reader to consider the parallels between these thoughts of St Paul – directed at the hollowness of tongues – in his letter to the decadent Corinthians, and the theoretical junk and jargon pursued in art and architecture schools in the attempt to rid the community of any sense of critical standards. The celebration of the so called 'end of master narratives' is really no more than fashionable gibberish designed to accompany the posturing of *artists* who attempt to live on their personalities as modern celebrities. Whilst I am not a Marxist, nor am I a practising Catholic, I find myself – like Marxists, Christians, Jews and Muslims – wanting the return of some overriding sense of what we are as a people that might give meaning to the arts by which we seek to be identified and thereby personified.

Let us, at last, turn to a work of architecture which I do not believe should be considered as anything much improved upon some average undergraduate project. The piece I have in mind is Daniel Libeskind's ORION building, the Graduate Centre for the London Metropolitan University in North London's Holloway Road. Libeskind is a prominent architect of our times. His Berlin Holocaust Museum; the proposed Victoria and Albert Museum extension; and the proposed Ground Zero monument have made him arguably the most renowned architectural celebrity of the moment. But let us look at the Graduate Centre. What might we say of it; and how might we approach our *looking* at it?

It is unusually shaped for a building and has stainless steel cladding, which is not that unusual. Its unusual shape is designed to disrupt the flow of building along the Holloway Road and is meant to *cock a snook* at its neighbour, a piece of stark and undistinguished modernism that is also a university building. As a graduate centre, we might assume that this juxtaposition is aimed at thinking of post-graduate study as freed from the edifice of learning that has to be undertaken and mastered at undergraduate level. The creativity of postgraduate work in any of the university's disciplines, we might be encouraged to think, lies outside of the established framework of material that is mastered when studying for one's bachelor's degree.

Both in materials and in form, we must see the ORION building as in conflict with the rational building techniques of modernity, embedded in the adjacent building mentioned above. Gone are the clear implications of plan and elevation for the organisation of interior space. We can no longer 'read' the building from its exterior facade. Instead we are treated to an exciting formal arrangement of planes and interpenetrating solids, gleaming or mute according to the weather. Here is what the man himself has to say:

> The Orion project has an enlivening impact on the wider urban context and particularly on the image and accessibility of the University. The three intersecting elements that form the building strategically emphasise certain relationships: one creates a connection between the public, the new building and the university behind, one form gestures from the university toward the tube connection to the city and one more regular form stitches the new building into the context of Holloway Road. A small plaza at the entrance provides an accent and an engaging gateway.[14]

> The interior spaces are simple, bold volumes which provide multi-purpose flexibility for programmatic events.[15]

I find none of this convincing. Having stood in the Holloway Road on a number of occasions attempting to arrive at some judgement on the work, I think that the gesture is unreadable, for one thing. The connection is nothing but a bridge that crashes into both new and old building in a way that is not yet architecturally resolved. (Think of the way that either modernists or Baroque architects have treated the corner of a building where two facades meet. If this is done well, we have the feeling that a *problem* has been *resolved*.) Moreover, the expression of the volumes according to no comprehensible scheme serves to alienate the spectator, rather than interest or engage her.

Libeskind is quite right to point up that the building is meant to provide an 'image . . . of the university'. As such it is to be seen less as a building and more as a emblem. Little wonder that his work is more sculptural than architectural. However, architecture is not sculpture and we do not appreciate its works as works of sculpture. As Kant reminds us,

> In architecture the main concern is what *use* is to be made of the artistic object, and this use is a condition to which the aesthetic ideas are confined. In sculpture the main aim is the mere *expression* of aesthetic ideas . . . For what is essential in a *work of architecture* is the product's adequacy for a certain use. On the other hand, a mere *piece of sculpture*, made solely to be looked at, is meant to be liked on its own account.[16]

I doubt very much that the building works as sculpture in any case, but that is not our present concern. As a building I think it lacks aesthetic value. Once we are accustomed to the strangeness of its shape (as a building) there is little to recommend it. The floor plate crashes into the corner window and the interior shows the institutional doors with the glazed strip that is a standard office fixture. The interior, that is, has no relation to the exterior in its sense of refuting the tenets of modernism. In short, apart from plonking a pretty unpleasant shape in the Holloway Road, the building itself is unimaginative and pursues the rather lumpen institutional interior trends that is the mark of most modern university buildings. My feeling is that the building is half-baked. It attempts to be cutting edge without having any clear idea about what that might mean. I conclude with a nuanced interpretation of a much quoted passage from Saint Paul's letter to the Corinthians:[17]

> Though I speak with the tongues of men and of angels, and have not charity, I am become as sounding brass, or a tinkling cymbal.
>
> (I Corinthians 13: 1)

Sometimes *charity* is translated as *love* and this is often preferred in the Nuptial Mass. However, taken as an expression of the binding of a community together, we might think of charity as the mark of what public art and architecture bring to a community – as an expression of its values. That is, we find our home in such bonds as can be expressed in public art and architecture. The cult of celebrity into which we are rapidly descending can be resisted only if we recognise that some of the loudest claims voiced in the name of increasing democracy are but sounding brass or tinkling cymbals. We need to put aesthetics back into the heart of our thinking about art, architecture, charity and democracy.

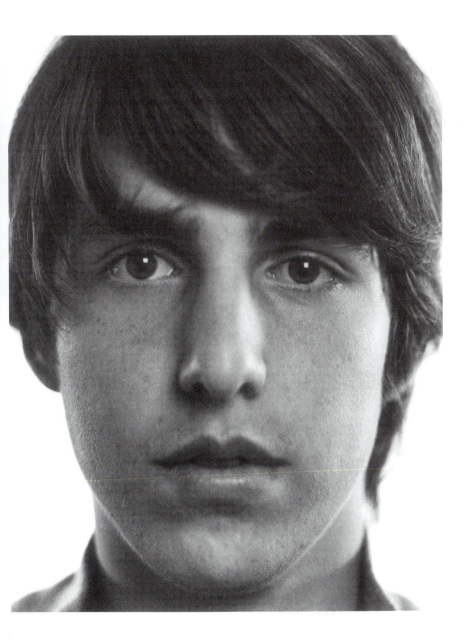

A-List Architects

17

Torsten Schmiedeknecht

The confident title of this one-day conference, organised by *Building Design* (*BD*) and *Corus*, suggested that one already knew, first, how to define an *A-List* architect and, second, why one would want to become one.[1] But even without this prerequisite knowledge I decided to attend. I went to enhance my understanding of the intriguing and arcane world of architects' public relations and self-promotion. The conference was linked to the *2004 Young Architect of the Year Awards* taking place the same evening (a competition very much in line with the trade press' obsession with treating architects as celebrities – albeit minor ones – however little they have built). This, then, was the warm-up. For £245 + VAT, 12 invited speakers, ranging from Ricky Burdett, former Director of the Cities Programme at the London School of Economics, to Keith Blanshard, a director of *Yorkon*, a company producing prefabricated building units, would present their thoughts on how to become A-List.

What exactly an *A-List* architect might be was surely an important question to address. The conference – and in particular the architects among the speakers – implied that becoming one was unquestionably a desirable aim. With one exception (the engineer Hanif Kara stated right at the beginning of his talk that he did not believe in them) the agreed tenor was that whoever did not aspire to get on the list clearly had to sort themselves out. But – individual egos apart – where might the real benefits lie?

There were two sessions: the morning's theme was *Winning Work* (press and publicity, working with developers, tailoring your pitch); the afternoon's, *Collaboration* (with consultants, contractors and manufacturers). In his introduction, *BD* editor Robert Booth said that the audience could expect some practical advice from the speakers on how, for example, to increase their public profile and how to 'get under the skin of developers' to convince them of one's worth as a designer who could bring something special to a project. This 'something special' would lead to 'added value' – one of the buzz-terms of the day.

Ricky Burdett's opinion was that architects tend to view buildings as objects disconnected from their urban context; his advice was for them to see themselves as part of a bigger picture and actively to seek collaboration with other professions when bidding for projects. So far, so prosaic. David Rosen from Pilcher Hershman ('one of the most influential people on the property scene', as the programme said) was full of admiration for architects and on several occasions during his talk described their profession as the most wonderful of them all. His advice was simple and unpretentious: don't delegate, treat people with respect, publish till you drop, increase your exposure, be original. But even if Rosen's analogy of architect as film director and developer as film producer were correct, argued Lee Mallett (who swapped his editor's chair at *BD* to become a developer a few years ago), no films are made without money. In that sense, architects were just another risk a developer had to take.

It was time for architects to assert themselves but Caroline Cole (whose firm, *Colander*, advise architects on how to do just that) noted that, in her experience, and rather unsurprisingly, the chemistry between client and architect was much more important than the latter's quality as a designer.

Paul Monaghan's entertaining chat recounted his firm's success story by showing connections between different projects and their histories. It felt for a moment as if everything was somehow linked to everything else, life was beautiful, made such perfect sense, and was all in the name of (good) architecture. To end his talk, Monaghan had put together a list of 10 lessons to be learnt – from his firm, Allford Hall Monaghan Morris (AHMM), one presumes. Particularly noticeable on the list was number seven, *gongs and mags*, where the architectural press were likened to music magazines promoting young pop or rock bands. True, Robert Booth, introducing Monaghan, had mentioned that AHMM had been known in their early days as *The Fab Four*, but surely architecture and pop songs are very different things?

The architect was a hero (Rosen) but a liability (Mallett), should be an alchemist (Cole), might become a pop-star (Monaghan). But beyond the familiar tips of working hard, getting published, collaborating with other professions and networking, networking, networking, what did the day deliver? For me, the very existence of the conference raised some interesting questions. How do we as a culture select, reward and sustain architects and kinds of architecture? Why wouldn't any *A-List* consist of works of architecture that have stood the test of time in a broad context rather than the work of architects who have allowed their vanity momentarily to get the better of them? And finally, in these circumstances, how long would it be until we see Dani mud-wrestling with Zaha on UK television's *I'm a celebrity . . . get me out of here!*?

It was a frivolous thought, but when ex-Richard Rogers Partnership man Robert White (now apparently an expert in negotiating the best possible fees for architects) happily declared that his love for Kung Fu movies provided him with the necessary inspiration and panache for his daily business, I began to wonder.

Note: A version of this text was previously published as 'How to Become An A-List Architect' in *Architectural Research Quarterly*, Volume 8, Issue 1, p. 90.

The Fall and Rise of Craig Ellwood

18

Paul Davies

I've loved Craig Ellwood's architecture for a long time. Of course I haven't seen any of it in the flesh. Craig Ellwood may be the first master of modern architecture where this is generally the case because it's so difficult to find anything in Los Angeles. In LA, architecture just vanishes, gets torn down, reconstituted or just overgrown in impenetrable vegetation and security, at least it does when I try to see it.

Craig Ellwood became famous as a prominent contributor to John Entenza's Case Study House Programme of the 1950s. Sponsored by the magazine *Art and Architecture*, these ephemeral constructions, light in touch and equally ephemeral in time, are now best found in libraries. The most famous, Pierre Koenig's Case Study 25, still blinks at you from the hills above Sunset Boulevard just west of The Chateau Marmont. It is now a museum piece preserved in perpetuity for advertising shoots. Paradoxically we see it all over our cities now, on billboards under the guise of promotion for British Airways, or Barclaycard, or Robbie Williams records.

Ellwood was himself a great self-publicist, he employed the best photographers and made the most photogenic buildings, he'd always try to see to it that we got a glimpse of coolsville (his word). However the means were limited, and Ellwood had a predilection for bundling his photographs off to Domus in Italy rather than more prosaic publications. So despite those efforts, 20 years ago, my enthusiasm was founded on one copy of Domus found in the RIBA library and a B&W paperback '*Case Study Houses*' by Ester McCoy, on cheap paper.

Another 20 years, and we are now getting a much better look at coolsville, because the publishing industry has caught up with Ellwood. Two volumes appeared in 2002, one, a fine monograph by Neil Jackson published by Lawrence King. The interesting thing about this book is not the perennially fashionable look of California modern that has itself found something of a revival amongst today's cool architects. It is more the biographical material that titillates. Here we have Jackson's attempt to tell a faithful tale of an utter louse. OK, a spirited louse. Now Jackson would prefer to be discrete about his subject's behaviour, it is after all, an Architectural Monograph, but there is no such coyness in Alfonso Peres Mendes volume '*In the Spirit of the Time*' whose promotional blurb yelps 'Ellwood wasn't his name, he wasn't a licensed architect, and he drove a red Ferrari'.

Notwithstanding that while still not officially an architect, Ellwood designed these buildings that became the epitome of LA style, Ellwood was married four times (including Miss Delaware), had a penchant for very fast cars and hung with some very dubious pals (one of whom, Robert Runyan, is just the spitting image of Tom Selleck in Magnum PI). Ellwood was a good time boy who upset a lot of people as much as he must have enchanted others. In a letter distributed to interested parties by e-mail on publication of Jackson's book, one son declares his father was a sex addict.

This is quite believable, wife three confesses to Ellwood 'knocking her socks off' on page 177, but the son's main memory of childhood remains the time he was ushered in to a hotel bar to be told by Ellwood he was running off with a girl the age of his sister.

Meanwhile colleagues in the office never seemed to get the credit they deserved and accountants stormed off at the sight of another Ferrari. His academic life, such as it was, is characterised by a paper paradoxically titled *Nonsensualism*.

Claiming the demands of constant schmoozing were a drain on his creativity, Ellwood finally gives it all up, first to race cars at Le Mans and then to be a silver haired painter in Tuscany, reading Tolkien and St Expury and getting spiritual as only Californians know how. Thankfully, and true to script, the paintings are satisfyingly awful. Suffice to say none of the ex wives, sons and daughters get a cent when he dies.

Perhaps it was Mark Girouard's book on Jim Stirling that started it, but readers are slowly but surely finding themselves as tantalised by the personal lives of our heroes as by their work. Jim's pies and affairs (he pops up in here too, and so does Girouard) simmer just below scandal, Ellwood might be considered to be the first modern architect to have been killed off by sexual appetite.

But he will certainly not be the last. When working on designs for the content of the Millennium Dome I was myself charmed in to working with one of the finest creatives, and furious lothario's, it has ever been my pleasure to meet. When a national scandal blew, he was delighted to have made it in to the Observer with a cartoon showing a signpost to 'The Erogenous Zone', of the doomed attraction.

And I am no scholar of Vasari, but I understand they did that sort of thing in the Renaissance, but it's unusual to find your mind comparing an architectural stars life to those of, say, the members of Fleetwood Mac at their most hazy. I'm sure this made the methodical Jackson just a little queasy. For Ellwood's social antics bring great quotes, in notes and stories overheard at parties. But I don't think Ellwood read the books Jackson would have liked. Anybody who advertises for a secretary with:

GIRL FRIDAYSVILLE
Int'nat'ly-known arch'firm needs bright attrac.unkooked recp-sec'y who digs Mies van de Rohe, Miles Davis and Jax clothes . . .

does not have time. Jackson, no doubt disappointed, hunts for evidence of substance with the tenacity of a forensic scientist. He doesn't find much but thank goodness for his thoroughness because otherwise I might have got upset to have my images of coolsville tainted. As it stands, I can no more imagine Ellwood reading Thomas Aquinas than I can myself, and I'm relieved there is finally an architectural monograph that makes you feel good reaching for another vodka gibson.

Such are the dangers of fame, the flip side is infamous, and infamy is more entertaining and sells more books. Ellwood had his serious side, the personal Mies connection a puzzle. Ellwood blagged a meeting with the master and Craig put on his best suit. They got on well, and Ellwood even became Mies's envoy for the opening of The National Gallery Berlin. Now my favourite picture of Ellwood has him super casual wearing a flowery embroidered shirt and denim jacket, smiling broadly in front of a picture of Mies, suited, in black, perched on one of his uncomfortable chairs. They look centuries apart and, you imagine, thought centuries apart. It's hard to imagine the laid back Ellwood shooting the breeze with the by then Brandoesque Mies. At least, if I can read something in to Jackson's tale, they'd enjoy the same dirty jokes, fine cigars and strong drinks.

Jackson, I think, would prefer the intellectual link to Mies to be stronger, but the most re-assurance I got was of Ellwood's undoubted skills as a detailer of clear construction (no matter how many abused underlings thought they deserved credit for the designs).

And on closer inspection, despite the sobriquet of California's answer to Mies van de Rohe and those distracting parties, there are some difficulties in Ellwood's buildings that belie the imagery. As soon as you scaled down Mies pavilion genre to the scale of a family house in Hollywood, you found yourself with some terrible planning problems and some prickly sociology. Not letting freely floating walls touch the envelope of the building could be a recipe for domestic disaster. The solution more often than not was to extend the floating planes beyond the envelope (as in Case Study 16) giving a bit of privacy and a frisson with the garden landscape. Rooms in the traditional sense, despite their obvious utility, were a problem.

But Ellwood didn't ever hang around to witness family strife or a Hollywood caste system at work, which demanded domestic remodelling on demand. Quick as a flash he'd populate the house with other people's wives and furniture for photoshoots and pop the shots in the post to Domus.

Forty years ago, the power of modernity was still strong enough to send the architectural intelligentsia apoplectic when Case Study House 17 was draped in Doric columns and set designers mansards (and probably divided up in to rooms). Ester McCoy and John Entenza were still considered evangelists.

If today monograph writers, either for the sake of genuine scholarship, or sensationalism, find themselves outlining ever more salacious detail, some critics have also caught up to deliver a dose of the bleeding obvious. John Chase had the courtesy to point out to us in his excellent, *'Glitter Stucco and Dumpster Diving'* (Verso 2000) the disarming and completely reasonable truth. How could you expect Hollywood clients to do anything else than add Doric columns and set designer mansards to their modernist classics? That's what Johnny Mathis had. With that I'm afraid, bang went modern architecture, until it becomes fashionable with the next Johnny Mathis that is.

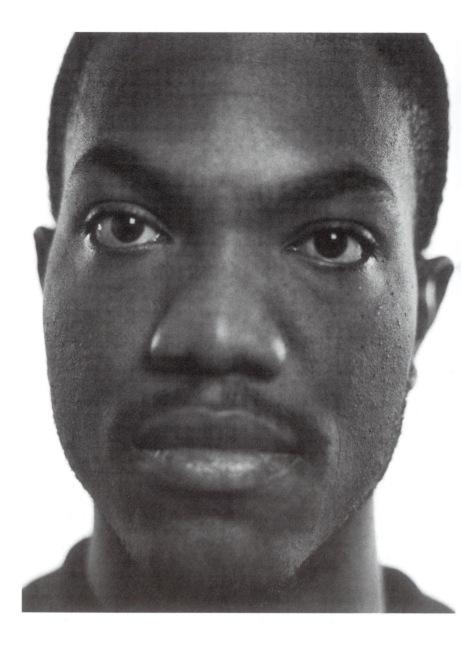

Situating Dalibor Vesely

19

Richard Patterson

Zeno, the ancient Greek philosopher, once arrived at an interesting conundrum with reference to the principles of Euclidean geometry. As a line is made up of an infinite number of points, he noted, we can readily apprehend that in moving between any two points, it will be necessary first to arrive at the point midway between them. Secondly, to get to that midpoint, it will be necessary first to arrive at the point midway between it and the origin, and similarly, by way of this infinite regression, he argued it would be impossible ever to arrive at one's destination. Yet, paradoxically, as a result of our 'being in the world' – being, that is, in a particular situation – we know that we are able to get somewhere; that whatever are the coercions of geometric rationally – that is, of abstraction, of theory, of the limitations of self-consistent, instrumental represension – we are in actual, experiential fact free. Yet, for the age in which we live, now, it is precisely the limit of the conceptual language of instrumental rationality that stands as the real. The reification of our alienation from emotion (we might say), from sensuous knowledge and the symbolic, existing as we do in the 'condition of postmodernity', subject that is to the reduction of meaning to a play of signifiers, to a series of algorithms formalising relationships in which the only allowable value is that of quantification, are all for Dalibor Vesely the product of this particular mode of representation. But as Vesely observes, *pace Zeno*, this representation is now *divided* from its other, and that the paradoxical nature of the condition in which we live is as a result structurally inaccessible to us.

Born and raised in Prague, Vesely's cultural influences are those of the pre-war *avant-garde*, the architects Havlicek, Honzik, and Fragner with whom he studied and with whom he came to work. The orientation of his point of view is due to exposure to the historians of the Baroque Hans Sedlmayr and Hermann Bauer, the Hegelian Alexandre Kojeve, and the humanists Ernesto Grassi and Jan Patocka, the latter of whom introduced him to the phenomenology of Merleau-Ponty, Husserl, and Heidegger.

This experience was broadened in initial contact with Western Europe through a UNESCO grant to study in Munich in 1962. In 1964, Vesely came to England for a month where he began to acquaint himself with the architectural scene, systematically visiting prominent individuals. He met the Smithsons and met several people through the Design Centre and the RIBA but mostly through the Architectural Association. It was through an otherwise inauspicious suggestion at the Llewellyn Davis Partnership that he made contact with Joseph Rykwert, who, at that time, was librarian at the Royal College of Art. In 1966, Vesely returned briefly and looked him up again. Rykwert had just been appointed Head of the Department of Art at Essex University by the radical VC, Albert Sloman. It was Sloman who gave Essex its early radical outlook, in many ways epitomising the intellectual climate of the late 1960s. There was a belief current at the time in the possibility of a new type of intellectual, one possibly formed by an unorthodox academic experience, and possibly only having just managed to survive the authoritarian distortions of institutional education with an intact sensibility. At Essex this translated as the possibility of acceptance on a course of study without any formal qualifications. The general notion at the time was to establish academic provision on, so to speak, a different tack. This suited Rykwert temperamentally very well. It was a good time to be associated with architecture, as architecture seemed to adumbrate a more generalised praxis, as epitomised, for example, in the fundamentals of Situationism. As it was, Rykwert, working to a very different agenda to the SI, wanted to get architecture on the curriculum and the most straightforward way to do so was to set it up as an MA, which he did as the MA in the History and Theory of Architecture. At the time, it was the only one of its kind in the country. By 1968 events in Prague led Vesely to turn his sojourns to the West into a permanent relocation. He initially arrived in Paris shortly after the student uprising, only to discover that nothing was happening in the academic world. Moving on to London, he met up with James Gowan, who introduced him to James Stirling, for whom he began to work for three days a week. In 1969, John Lloyd gave him a job teaching for one day a week at the AA. He also had one day a week teaching on the MA at Essex, where he joined Dawn Ades and T.J. Clark among others. By this time, the Essex course had begun to attract an exceptional group of students as well, including Daniel Libeskind, David Leatherbarrow, Brian Avery, Mohsen Mostafavi, David Porter, Helen Mallinson, Alberto Pérez-Gómez, and Robin Evans to mention some of them. In 1976 Rykwert went on sabbatical and the course stopped.

In 1975–6, Vesely was in Princeton with Anthony Vidler, and teaching studio with Michael Graves. On his return, he continued to work full-time at the AA, which he continued to do until 1978, when, at the suggestion of Robin Middleton, he began teaching at Cambridge as well. Mohsen Mostafavi had been a student at the AA and by 1978 had begun running Vesely's unit with him. This was the period when Eric Parry arrived from the Royal College of Art to do the AA Dipl. It was also the beginning of the Kentish Town projects, which Vesely had originated around the concept of a territory of sharing [which he now refers to as symbolic or communicative space], in opposition to the more anonymous and operationally neutral principle of *public realm*. The projects had a fairly pragmatic beginning. Kentish Town had a substantial amount of derelict railway land, offering the potential of linear urban sites, in other words, an English development type. The direction the studio took, however, brought into focus the method that became Vesely's concept of praxis, the ethical response to situations raised by the situation itself as it was given and by the process of design. Credit for the graphics associated with these landmark schemes, Vesely gives to Homa Fardjadi and to Eric Parry.

This was also the time of the 'struggle' to set up an MPhil at Cambridge along the lines of the Essex model. It was largely a battle with the traditional degree structure, and when finally achieved was the first of its kind at the university. This was indicative of Vesely's growing commitment to Cambridge, and St. John Wilson, who was Professor and Head of the Department at the time, came to insist that he give up the London job. This was the end of the Kentish Town projects, which were effectively summarised in the AA Files publication *Architecture of Continuity*. In 1983, Vesely spent 6 months at Heidelberg University working with

Hans Georg Gadamer. In 1985 he also made contact with Paul Ricoeur, initially at Cambridge and then in Paris. Gadamer and Ricoeur, along with Patocka, were the most profound influences in his development. Gadamer and Ricoeur remain his most important interlocutors. In 1985, Rykwert left for Philadelphia, so that Vesely ran the MPhil for the next 20 years with Peter Carl and later also with Wendy Pullan. The Cambridge design projects were the ground of formation for the themes presented in Vesely's publication in 2004 of *Architecture in the Age of Divided Representation, the question of creativity in the shadow of production.* These include a range of methodological tropes, including the use of the fragment, the metaphorical study, composite drawings, etc., feeding what he there refers to as poetics of architecture.

The trajectory of Vesely's calling begins with work in the studio, reflection upon which then leads to writing. He is emphatic, that he does not write theory. The writing arises as a reflection on work in the studio. In completing the circle, Vesely's calling is the constitution of an architectural praxis, a situational approach to architecture. His writing, prior to *Architecture in the Age of Divided Representation* occurred as a series of articles, most of which came to function as fragments, reflections on immediate situations, rhizomes that colonised into that final text. The overall theme, for example, came into focus with a piece for *AA Files* entitled the *Conflict of Representation*. Chapter 8, 'Toward a Poetics of Architecture', began with a piece in *Daidalos*, while 'The Rehabilitation of Fragment' was produced for Alvin Boyarsky's festschrift, edited by Robin Middleton as *AA Files, Idea of the City*. For this reason, *Divided Representation* is, as has been described by Robin Middleton, 'unlike any other study in architecture'. What gives it coherence is that it is essentially an intellectual autobiography, representative of the completeness of a working life's ambition and discipline. It arises as such as a form of individual critical praxis – arises in studio work and reflection – that falls outside the format of standard intellectual production. It is not like history, nor is it like a theory. It is not like history in that the historical material is so situationally embedded and illuminative of historical practices. By asking the question how was it possible to make sense of historical events at the time, he has, for example, radically reinterpreted the facts of the development of perspective in the Renaissance. By situating perspective within the objectives of representation, he has been able to demonstrate how, rather than simply an epistemological break, a harbinger of Cartesian space, perspective was conceived as a spiritual development, following on the objectives of medieval philosophy of light. Similarly, in *Divided Representation* there are statements which sound like theory, but they are statements which are coached in a rhetoric of openness, rather than one of prescription or exclusion. The pronouncements are more provisional than final, in that they remain subject to adaptation to different situations. Hence, the key to Vesely's work is that the past is not a post-rationalised justification of the present and the future is not limited by formal knowledge. What is proposed in the text and lived as a form of praxis is an ethical exploration of the possibilities arising out of typical human situations.

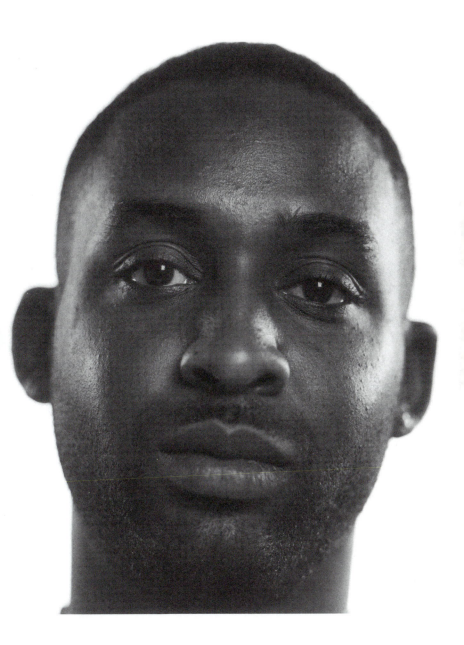

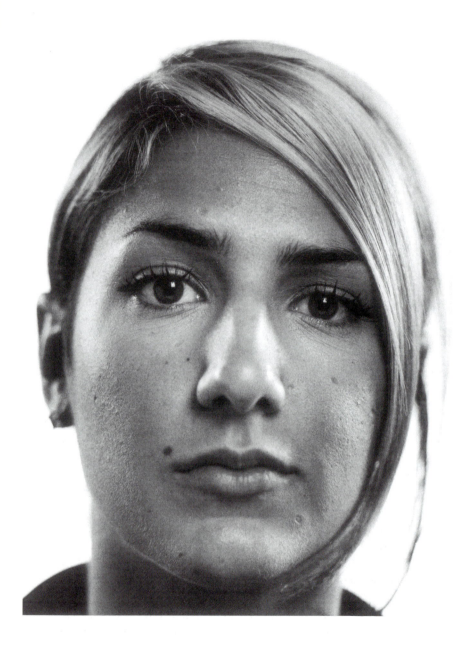

The Psyche of the Unit Master

20

Carlos Villanueva Brandt

The what of the what? The psyche OK, the unit OK, but what about the master? Unit masters come in all shapes and sizes. Both physically and psychologically they can be S, M, L and XL. Their physical differences are of no importance, but the variations in their psyche are important.

Their psyche makes the unit work. This is all well and good but, at times, their psyche and their ego can become blurred and this confusion inevitably creates those who believe themselves to be true *Masters*. Some are philosophical scientists, some are cultural icons, some are religious leaders, some are masters of the universe, some are barking up the wrong tree and, fortunately, the majority are just good teachers.

For some, being a unit master can be a good stepping-stone on to the slippery ladder of architectural fame. Generally this is a process of self-promotion rather than an advancement of the unit, it all relates to the individual's personality and his or her psyche rather than to the entity of the unit. To my mind, the question we should really be asking is what is the psyche of the unit? Unit masters operate, network, promote, theorise, publish and become famous; this process is predictable and no different to any other career strategy.

The unit, on the other hand, is a different animal. If its psyche is right it can, unlike the unit master, bypass the usual steppingstones to success in order to achieve its objectives. In the A to Z of units, Unit X is good, Unit Y is prosaic and Unit Z exceptional; whereas Unit Master X is good, Unit Master Y is a *Star* and Unit Master Z is unknown. It is not quite as simple as that but the moral is clear and, luckily, there are always units that rise above their unit masters.

Having been a unit master for many years, I still feel elated when any unit appears to have a life of its own. Facilitating this vitality and independence is the key role of the unit master but of course there are many 'Masters' who would not agree.

My unit, Diploma Unit 10 (Dip 10), at the Architectural Association, has a long tradition dating back to the 1970s, it encourages and has always encouraged the students to act for themselves, to participate in and inhabit the city and to see how they can influence it directly without having to adhere to the demands of hype or the etiquette of the profession.

Bernard Tschumi, Nigel Coates, Robert Mull and me: masters or 'Masters'?

In this particular unit's case, as the students have proved, it would appear that talking to the likes of Ken Livingston, Kate Hoey or Stella Rimmington is much easier if you are not famous. The students themselves, not the unit master, get directly involved. This involvement generates all sorts of interventions and is a form of direct action.

Direct action, and by this I do not mean burning buses or the like, can easily side-step the treacherous process of self-promotion, personality cult and celebrity status that afflicts a large number of *Masters*.

> Does direct action or direct architecture work? I don't know, but do Daniel Libeskind's glasses contribute to the future of the city?

On numerous occasions, Dip 10 has gone out there and taken the city's problems into its own hands. The unit master still sets the agenda, but it is the students who participate and inhabit, they are the agents who seem to dig deeper and venture further to uncover the true city. It is the unit who intervenes.

> Would any unit master ask the students to break a leg, play Pooh Sticks or sell a shadow?

In Glasgow, Amir Sanei, who had recently broken his leg whilst attempting to gain the taxi driver's *knowledge*, took on the problems faced by the disabled only to be labelled as a 'Madman Who Bans Escalators' by the local press. In contrast, from the disabled point of view he was seen as entirely sane and as a true architect.

He decided to act. After looking at the then current planning applications which appeared to pepper the entire surface of Glasgow, he identified that this phase of the city's making was the appropriate point to act. As an objector or an applicant, he realised that he could contribute to the design of the city in ways that eased access for the disabled.

He befriended 12 disabled individuals who he formally photographed on one roll of film with his favoured Rolleiflex camera, then he provided each one of them with a disposable camera and asked them to record the specific locations where they felt there was a need for a design change. The 12 then photographed the points where, for them, the city became inaccessible and returned the cameras to the architect. There were 12 frames, or portraits on the Rolleiflex and 27 frames on each of the disposable cameras which, if each frame was successful, would lead to a total of 324 design changes. The films were processed and the frames printed.

Although many of the issues raised in relation to the disabled and the city were discussed with the powers that be, the council, members of parliament, lobby groups and interested parties, this consultation process proved to be ineffective. In contrast, when the architect turned the 324 photographs into individual planning applications Glasgow suddenly found itself with 324 design changes that needed to be addressed. This action was now impossible to ignore.

Where was the unit master? Not there.

Similarly, in West Belfast, Thor Kleppan decided that direct action, maybe, could do something that John Mayor, Bill Clinton and Gerry Adams seemed to be unable to do. The Peace Process and Cross Border Institutions were all the rage, but in reality they were having little effect on the experience of the West Belfast sectarian divide.

By spending time in both the Falls and the Shankill Roads, a possibility for a cross over was identified. Participation was the key.

Assuming his role of architect, he surveyed the territory of West Belfast, traced the geography and psychogeography (thought about the Situationists), made drawings, considered the troubles which he diagnosed as symptoms (thought about Freud), made more drawings, made friends and continued to inhabit until, finally, he decided to focus on the course of the River Forth that flowed and transgressed through protestant and catholic areas and harnessed common memories of an undivided past.

But what could he as an architect do with these memories?

Not an easy question, but he designed his way out of it and devised a plan. The answer was to act.

He mapped all the points in West Belfast were the river was still visible, worked out how long it would take to walk from point to point and the total time needed to cover the chosen stretch of river and, strangely, inspired by the adventures of Pooh Bear, decided to use the water's flow to play Pooh Sticks.

He set a date, finalised a timetable, made some wooden sticks. He added a timing clock, and put them into a box. On the chosen day, he set off with the box to play Pooh Sticks in West Belfast. The box itself caused some problems: what was this box, what were these sticks and why the clock? After some explanations it all began. At each point of open water, people joined in to play Pooh Sticks. The game was played; he recorded it and then moved on to the next point according to the set timetable. At first it was mainly children who joined in, but eventually the grown-ups also started to play. They played Pooh Sticks and traced the course of the river. When at one point the sticks ran out, someone went and made more and throughout the day they continued to travel across West Belfast. People played, watched, commented and talked about the river. They traced the course of the river, crossed boundaries, walked through protestant areas and walked through catholic areas until they reached the end of the scheduled timetable. People had just joined in and, just for once not caring about it, they had crossed and re-crossed the normally impossible social divides.

Again not a question of individual's contribution, unless you count Pooh Bear's, just the right action in the right place and at the right time.

Where was the unit master? Not there.

And in Liverpool, Thomas Hildebrand discovered that the Anglican Cathedral was adversely influencing its surrounding public spaces. This was not an issue of religious beliefs, but an issue of ownership and property development.

After spending some time inhabiting Cathedral's Garden, a former quarry and then a cemetery, situated next to the cathedral he was informed that this public space had been earmarked to become part of the cathedral's planned expansion. Another public space could surreptitiously become private. The influential Dean of the Cathedral, Reverend Derrick Walters, had previously been directly involved in developments around the cathedral which were fenced off, controlled by cameras and protected by security guards. These developments were exclusive and were creating a buffer zone between the cathedral and the public.

Cathedral's Garden worked well as a public space, so the question was what could be done about the proposed development?

With an open mind, he began to survey the area and attempted to identify all the factors that made up the public spaces around the cathedral. He ascertained that the cathedral's shadow, the actual shadow cast by the building, inevitably crossed over the surrounding spaces which were disparate and strictly divided. The dynamic quality of this constantly changing shadow could provide the means to counterbalance the permanent and restrictive plans of the cathedral. What could he do as an architect?

He proceeded to plot the shadow and to delineate the resultant space. He established that the shadow created a recognisable and quantifiable territory. He concluded that he would have to find a way of working with the territory of the shadow. The drawings and the models of the shadow were somehow insufficient; he would have to act. He decided that he might be able to sell the shadow. By selling the shadow and claiming its ownership he could transform this transient space into a more permanent social space.

He set out, on a chosen date, to trace the perimeter of the shadow and this action allowed him to meet a representative group of people that lived within the area of the shadow. He suggested to them that they could become owners of the shadow and therefore have a more communal influence on the area surrounding the cathedral.

He finalised the drawings of the shadow's territory and proceeded to issue *Liverpool Cathedral Shadow Property Certificates* to those who wanted to become owners of the shadow. It worked. The residents took part, became owners and created a shadow community that could have a say in the future of the surrounding public spaces. This community, formed from within the shadow territory, now had the power to counteract the exclusive and divisive developments generated by the Anglican Cathedral.

Where was the unit master? Not there.

To date these interventions continue, each one generated by the city and enacted by an individual. They vary enormously but, in a sense, they all are a direct response to the social and physical contexts that are clearly well beyond the control of the unit master, let alone his psyche.

Still there are those who believe themselves to be *Masters*, those who believe – like a guru – that they have the knowledge, those who purport to know the right process or technique and those who believe dogmatically in their own creed. Some are good, some are bad and some are brilliant, but the world is not too concerned about their psyche.

What appears to us be much more important is the psyche of an idea.

21 The Psyche of a Depressed and Disappointed Unit Master

Jonathan Harris

[Henry James's] determination to excel on stage was perversely at odds with his deepest instincts. In his rash impulse to leap from private study to public stage, he behaved for a while like a don trying desperately to break into television.

> . . . 'Well, in comparison, architects have never been backward in coming forward, have they (or we, should I say)? Take that loud-mouthed huckster Daniel Libeskind, for example. On TV – or garrulously issuing writs – whenever the chance presents itself. 9/11 was the making of him, of course, though the Holocaust didn't hurt either . . .

. . . Woken, too abruptly, then, from my sleep. Well, not really sleep: comatose empty-minded musings and speed-reading the *London Review of Books* before my 10 o'clock lecture, actually. Trying, dimly, to imagine how to re-invigorate a discussion of Al Speer's romantic fascination with terrible Aryan scale and even more terrible order. Trying, equally dimly – and hopelessly – to fashion a means to really communicate with all 85 of my second year undergraduates, especially with the Chinese from Shanghai who keep themselves to themselves too remorselessly. What could have happened to my ambitions to end up doing this? Did my cutesy post-doctoral attempts to deconstruct 'form-follows-function' conventions *have* to end up with my own de(con)struction? (Never mind conning myself.) Should purely academic theory have replaced practice so decisively in my own life, I wonder?

Never mind designing a 'signature' building; these days I have trouble designing my signature ('architects', like most of the 'artists', in inverted commas *and* comas, who teach in universities, seem to have trouble expressing themselves, and end up not being able to 'teach' nor 'practice' at what is still, laughably, called a *profession*.) From architecture, then, to that euphemistic black-hole called 'architectural studies': studies that are shaped like a leaky boat with most of the dirt luckily below the waterline of popular intelligibility – real horrors such as 'building management science', 'energy conservation modelling', 'construction economics theory', *portable buildings*, for god's sake! Right down in the bowels of the pedagogic machine, then, slopping around with the shit-shovellers in 'Civic Design Studies', or what ever they call themselves these days.

Fame, it appears to me, has *nothing to do* with teaching – or at least teaching in a university. 'Academic celebrity' is a shop-soiled, fifth-rate, oxymoronic non-commodity. The star *communicators* (that Enlightenment/Habermassian buzzword!) in architecture are really not grovelling about undertaking Research Assessment Exercises and having the quality of their educational provision assured. That's a reference to the contemporary British university system, for you American or Australian *educators* who wonder what the hell I'm talking about. (No doubt you have your own local miseries to deal with.) No, Libeskind, and that sexy structures semiotician from the 1970s – what's his name . . . Charles Jencks – do *their* 'educating' and 'communicating' only on national television, or at one-off 'master-classes' at MIT or Stanford . . .

. . . Eyeing them on their way in, now. Trying, hopelessly, all to sit in the back three rows, but the lecture theatre can't tolerate that – it throws them up, forward, so I can see their spots and sweaty armpits too clearly. The Shanghai Seven lope in, deep in esoteric communal exchange, cigarettes in the bin, gum in the mouth. What to say to them this time then? How to perform this performance for the nth time? . . .

Academics are terminally type-cast, I'm afraid. And there is something intrinsically comic (and, more to the point, tragic-comic) about them now as a category of professional person. In the days of dons – Gods – and quads, and '*quad erat demonstratum*'[1] – that is, when knowledge was the recognised province of a minority and only those from the suitable backgrounds went up to English and Scottish universities – the 'system', meaning a closed world of privilege and passage into the Establishment, made some sense. Now, in the age of what the government calls 'lifelong learning', with the guaranteed human right of all 21 year olds to a 2:1 degree (that's nearly perfect for you Americans), the life of the 'dons' (!) is very different. We're as ten-a-penny as the students are: 'cultural democracy' is what some wit in the 1960s thought to call it. Compound that with the doubtful contemporary public profile of architects – style-merchants, chancers and would-be 'artists' – and 'town planners' – inevitable fascist overtones there! – and you have a truly lethal cocktail.

If 'Howard Kirk' was the demonized Marxist sociologist in Malcolm Bradbury's campus novel *The History Man* (1975) – portrayed by 'latte liberal' Bradbury as an egomaniacal Stalinist always trying to bed his women students – then who might be a candidate for the modern-day 'architectural studies' equivalent? Jencks, I suppose, was a kind of 'Morris Zapp' (the fictional character in David Lodge's novel *Small World* (1984)[2] based loosely, but legibly, on the real literary theorist Stanley Fish, and made to seem an entirely opportunistic individualist perpetually sitting in business class flying between master-classes of literary-hermeneutic brilliance on both sides of the Atlantic).

But there *is* no real or fictional equivalent in architecture. Or rather, public figures like Libeskind, or le Corbusier for that matter, have become personas in their own right: media-fictive inventions, practically ectoplasmic spectacular projections of Design Will and energy buzzing through your TV tube, or down the radio aerial into your kitchen, irritating you when you're trying to make the dinner. Issuing sound-bites of startling would-be profundity: their language, like their architecture, turned into sculpture, really – madly active, undulating, autistic, tourettes syndrome stuff, like the Imperial War Museum North, in Manchester (England, i.e. not New Hampshire, though you Americans will be getting the Pentagon equivalent, brought to you by Halliburton, soon, don't worry) . . .

> . . . Shuffle my notes, clear my throat, test my two slide projector clickers like the buttons of an ejector seat or, better still, the 40 mm canons on a Spitfire over

Normandy. Eat lead, you miserable bunch of dummies! Turn off the mobile phones, cease the chat to your neighbour, prepare to be communicated to . . .

'Robert Lane' is the fictional town-planner in Raymond Williams' novel *The Fight For Manod*, the third story in his 'Welsh trilogy' of books that deals with the social history of a family from the time of the General Strike in 1926 up to the late 1970s.[3] In the previous volume, *Second Generation*, Lane had appeared in the guise of the supervisor of the chief character's PhD on the history of the depopulation of Wales. Even this fictional academic, then, managed to see how sad and naff the role was and got himself reinvented as a member of staff for the Department of the Environment! And if manipulating people and resources to engineer some kind of miserable post-industrial future for a fictional depressed Welsh town called Manod (remember the Jam's 1980 song: 'A Town Called Malice'? – that was about town-planning too) involves alienating intervention and control from outside, *from the English*, then the same could be said, couldn't it?, about university education now.

Whose interests are really, finally, at stake?

'Mathew Price', the son of the railway signal man in the first volume of the trilogy, *Border Country* (modelled on Williams's own father), musing on the future for Manod, gets the central question right:

> . . . there could still be approval, significant approval: not just the design of a city but the will of its citizens . . . I don't mean nationality. I mean that the storms that have blown through that country – storms with their origins elsewhere – should now be carefully and slowly brought under control. In one place at a time,

one move at a time, we should act wholly and consistently in the interests of that country, and those interests, primarily, are the actual people now there, caught between rural depopulation and industrial decline . . .[4]

But the crucial difference is that students, unlike towns and cities, come and go, don't they? If you're the lecturer, that is. You have to do the Speer thing again next year. You have to think of something witty and yet suitably deprecating to say about Norman Foster's Gherkin in the city of London, or Libeskind's next new what-ever-it-is. Somehow, teaching architecture studies has to appear to be a wily and knowing commentary on the predictable mistakes of other simpletons given hundreds of millions of dollars or pounds or euros to spend on some whacky tube or black coily-shaped thing they came up with that will re-energise Birmingham or symbolise a brave post-modern future for Coventry. Or Fresno, or where ever . . .

> . . . over then. They troop out, tripping over chairs and waste-paper bins. None the wiser, on the whole. Stick that in your pipes and smoke it! Look forward to your 'feedback'! NOT . . .

Teaching, like architecture, remains basically authoritarian: what I say goes. It's about as democratic as allowing the sheep to decide who ambles into the abattoir first. There is no real *independent learning* any more than there is *independent architecture*: do-it-yourself Taj Mahals, or Scottish Parliament buildings (£400 million and counting . . . You really think it's 'finished'?!). The interests and wealth dominating the *structure* come from outside, and the products are designed to fit and reproduce the *structure*. It's a flat-pack, a multi-purpose box, a build-it-in-a-day and 'repent at leisure' affair – education, I mean, and, ugh, architecture. And as for fame and celebrity in academia's architecture: remember the 'factory'?

Not, this time, the car plant in Oxford, up the hill from the dreaming spires (and the not-so-dreamy Said Business School Oxford, UK), at the shabby end of 'Between Towns Road'.[5] A 'factory' was what Andy Warhol called his 1960s Soho studio in Manhattan – the place where the silkscreen prints dealing with fame and celebrity were rolled out and off the art production line, along with those sister images of death and disaster. Marilyn, Jackie Kennedy, and Liz Taylor; electric chairs, tuna fish disasters, Bellevue Emergency Room, and jets crashing. Fame is the gaudy after-image glow that Warhol added in to those lugubrious icons and situations – smudged lips and eyebrows, bleached whites, yellows, pinks, and reds. Multiples of multiples, more of the same. But 'fame' in academia – as opposed to academics on TV – is an afterglow of that afterglow, an infinitely receding and diminishing point of light, minor cultism in the classroom, surface without depth: *quad erat demonstratum.*

Seeking Peter Zumthor

22

Kit Allsopp

We came from Basel to Chur in the East of Switzerland on a wet February afternoon in 1997 hotfoot from three days of early Herzog and de Meuron and a flying visit to Gehry, Hadid and Grimshaw at Vitra. We had also listened to Tschumi and Koolhaas rambling on about big and global at a conference in Basel where we got rotten drunk. You can overdose on all that stuff and I for one was anticipating a different diet in thinner air.

Zumthors fame, fuelled in part by his reputation as a prickly and reclusive sage, the hermit of the mountains, had crept out of the country on the back of a handful of small and exquisitely crafted projects and we were eager for the hands-on experience. We had maps, journals, woolly hats and scarves, and on foot, by train and by coach we scoured the countryside in search of him and his progeny.

When we found them the buildings seemed quieter and more self-effacing than their pictures, each one tailored perfectly to its site and programme, from the elegant simplicity of the Old Persons Home in Chur to the magical poetry of the chapel at Sogn Benedetg. The students were nonplussed – had we come all this way for so modest an experience – what were we to make of it? And the weather – where were the glittering snow-clad mountains?

They were close by, and so was the big one, the almost sacred encounter with the Thermal Baths at Vals. The sun came out and short of £15 apiece we trooped through reception to a long corridor, and clutching our rented swimmers arrived in the sensual decadence of the changing rooms, soft leather and floaty drapes, a world of pleasure and touch. This we had not been expecting, nor were we ready for the descent to the baths, the dark and the damp, the contrasts in scale and temperature, the sheer luxurious minimalism of the total experience. There should be one of these in every town but none could match the awesome mountain backdrop seen through a giant picture window as we swam seamlessly from inside to outside, from the gloom into the light.

Contact made with the great hermits office we were granted an evening audience and set off to Haldenstein, the village where he lives and has his studio. The studio is just like his famous pencil drawing, a simple shed clad in silvery vertical wooden battens. There is a trademark copper porch, a narrow hallway, and a straight flight of wooden stairs to the first floor studio.

Herr Zumthor, every inch the famed recluse, tall, grey bearded, and of a serious countenance, bade everyone remove their shoes and coats, mount the stairs, and sit in a semicircle before him. He talked about his career to date and his concern that with larger projects there might be a loss of control and quality, and one was struck by his complete commitment to his work and his wry and self-deprecating humour.

'How did you get so smooth a finish on the chapel benches?' We used many many sheets of a very fine sandpaper.

On our last day we trudged for miles from the nearest station to find the Gugalun House perched like an exquisite chest of drawers on the side of a mountain. Everywhere was frozen, there was no-one at home, the house and its setting were serenely beautiful. We had found Peter Zumthor.

The students, of course, had gone snowboarding.

The encounter with Peter Zumthor happened as part of a field trip organised by Ivana Wingham for BArch students at the Manchester School of Architecture in February 1997.

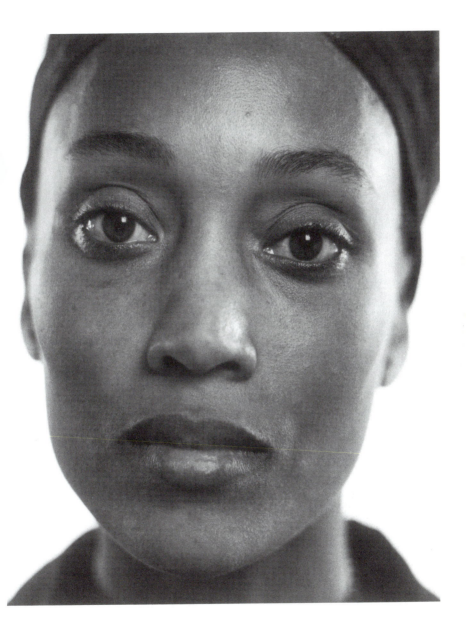

The Chapter According to St John

23

James Soane

They used to say to students that if you wanted a job with me, then you brought your portfolio down to the St John on a Friday night and bought me a beer . . .

Site

Thus spoke a venerable architect now on his second practice, reminiscing to me about the good old days, pint in hand. Picture the scene if you will. It is the Friday before the weekend before Christmas, in the bar of the renowned London St John restaurant, well-known haunt of architects. It is raining outside, now that we have brown Christmas' not white as a result of global warming; the well-worn concrete floor is slippery grey, with a film of beer, broken glass and fag ends. A group of lawyers have been in since lunch time and don't seem to have left yet. The space is rammed with black polo necks, furry parka hoods and graphically challenging tee shirts.

Perhaps a bit of background is called for; what is this place the St John? Beloved by food critics and architects alike, the St John is a restaurant with a bar on the side. Set up by Fergus Henderson, son of an architect, in October of 1994, it occupies a former smokehouse. The room itself is worthy of note as it has a ceiling height of 20 ft topped by a row of saw-tooth roof lights. The location is also significant for two reasons; first, it is adjacent to Smithfield meat market and second, it was one of the first restaurants to open in Clerkenwell, now recognised as one of the centres of urban regeneration-chic in London. The meat market, which is still in operation, provided a hook for the menu, described as 'nose-to-tail eating' by the establishment, and features such delicacies as bone marrow, chittlings and squirrel along with whole carrots, cabbage and mash. . . . this no-frills-honest-to-God style of food has found favour with those who enjoy severely edited choices by someone they can trust. It is hard to say which comes first; the fashionable avant-guard restaurant and bar followed by urban regeneration, and accusations of yuppification; or was it always going to happen and the bar just snuck in there first. Either way architects have something to do with both phenomena. In the pre loft-revolution St John Street was a collection of rickety warehouses and a couple of hip pubs. The artist Alan Jones has lived around the corner forever in one of Piers Gough's early works, the Vic Naylor bar a couple of doors down has always drawn in a motley crew, while Allies and Morrison had a go at designing the posh Steven Bull restaurant up the road. The offices of architects YRM were opposite for many years and Janet Street Porter built 'that' house. Until then, however, there was hardly a pin stripped suit in sight. There are now loads of new bars and restaurants in the vicinity including the ever-popular Wells Mackereth designed Smiths, which is heaving nearly every night of the week – but not with architects. It is a neighbourhood that sums up the zeitgeist; both edgy but safe, popular but not over-run, on the edge but accessible, urban and not suburban. It is a thesis project in the making; it could be in the next Rem Koolhaus book as a case study for normal life. A formula for the future: C19th meat market (still working) + mixed use warehouses + sad 1960s offices + artists + money = C21st neighbourhood. The photos would be slightly blurry, post Dazed and Confused, showing the latest Derwent Valley scheme in a brochure designed by Studio Myerscough. There would be a map showing the hundreds of places you can go to eat and drink, the lifestyle gyms, the grimy workmen's cafes, the bondage nightclubs and the boutique hotel. Welcome to the 'glocal' age (where global meets local). They have the equivalents from Hamburg to Vienna, San Fransisco to Montevideo, Sydney to Barcelona. Cities are still able to regenerate themselves into new identities; the architect is the surgeon who repairs the body of the city, inserts a transplant and sews it all up again.

Story

Back in the smoke filled bar, just before Christmas, Project Orange had secured a key table next to the counter, carefully depositing bags and coats around the back of the tables opposite the wall, so as not to aggravate the waiters collecting pre ordered drinks; believe me, it's a hazard. Scarcely through the door when Ken Mackay grabs my arm, perching in the corner next to the metal stair up to the restaurant and on top of the open floor drain. As we pounce on our table we are greeted by the posse from Diamond Architects, who have been on the go since lunchtime. Looking left I see the determined face of Kevin Rhowbotham, striding towards the bar, if that is possible in a crowd situation, but being stopped en route no doubt by one of his ex students. . . . Next through the door is the office of DSDHA having returned from their Christmas jolly which involved hiring a mini bus and driving out to the East End, eating chips and beans at a greasy cafe, surveying a bit of docklands and now venturing back into town for some action. Good call. They are immediately joined by the Über fashionable Soft Room, whom I must have missed coming through the door, as I was now catching up with Fran, our last-year's-year-out student who had knowingly stopped by to catch up with the architectural world . . . . By now Jamie Shorten is on the Vodkas and taking a pew and catching up I fancy with the AA's very own Tony Swannell. Over in the far corner, next to the working bakery, is Dominic Cullinan on the very chair where I once spied Joseph Fiennes; the same day that Zoe Wannamaker brushed passed me on the way to the bathroom. The only people who weren't there were the AHMM crew, regulars of a Friday night any week of the year, only not this night as it was their Christmas Dinner; taking place at that other East London architectural restaurant, Eyre Brothers, down the road. There you have it, the story unfolds.

Scene

As my friend Jeremy Melvin pointed out recently, in the *Architect's Journal*, there is indeed a tradition of architects gathering for Friday night drinks at the St John. It is a scene. This is neither a prescribed ritual nor a complete co-incidence. There is one obvious factor above all others that attracts this crowd. No music. It is that simple; name one pub or bar that does not have some sort of pumped ambience; from 1980s compilations to the latest electro-pop?

Either way it can often be anti-social and not conducive to chat; if you are over 21 that is. It also helps that there is plenty of standing space, as well as tables where you are not obliged to eat at. That said it is the characters that are the real draw. In the past the still editor of the *Architect's Journal*, Paul Finch, could often be heard testing out next weeks headlines on a small but select audience, while his rival Lee Malett, Editor of Building Design, was working out his next deal. In a profession which has numerous small practices, counting from 1 to 10, whole offices appear to relax and exchange ideas, gossip, see who is in and what is out and bitch about contractors who don't read drawings and complain about book reviews in the *Architect's Journal*. Architecture's very own PR guru Carolyn Larkin pops in to catch up on the *news*, exchange *news* with the girls and to steal a lead on the others. I have met visiting critics from China there, the Bartlett hired the whole place for Phil Tabors leaving party, and I know of at least one architectural wedding held there. There have been dinners held by Cedric Price, celebrations for Britain's architectural A-List; even Terence Conran is regularly spotted taking a break from his empire. Importantly, however, there is no velvet rope; it is open to all.

Specificity

There is an inherent irony about the place in that while many architects engage in the business of designing buildings, homes, restaurants and bars, the very one they choose to congregate at is a non-signature space. It is the *object type* of bars, discovered and not created; it feels real. Sure there are some neat touches. The ordering device of the lights, the choice of only three materials, stainless steel, white paint and concrete, as well as the inherent character of the *found* space, all add up to a coherent whole. The place has a certain austerity about it, a back-to-basics quality, and above all possesses a sense of authenticity. It is a genuine place that does not prescribe the kind of people who enter through the door; even though a certain kind of person may come again and again. There is one interpretation that may suggest that the space is rendered neutral, and that to a disparate group of architects the room itself provides a haven of calm, an emptiness of design, allowing conversation to flow without any concern over having either to 'fit in' to the customer profile or to feel dominated by the character of the room. There is no competition of ego in a place that has no design attached. This is the antithesis of what architects do most of the time. When designing there is a specific desire to create a building, a place, an interior which is characterised by it's own particular configuration. We talk about light, space and materials; but there is more than that. There are memories, associations, smells, tactility and references to deal with. These are less easy to prescribe and it is too simple to associate them with matters of taste and fashion. But this is only one theory. Another might be that for whatever reason a group of architects happened upon the bar, liked it and returned. They told their mates, and by word of mouth it garnered a reputation as the place to meet up, even if you had not arranged to see anyone. It therefore reaches a kind of cult status, a place that has been created by urban mythology, the recognition of which goes beyond the boundary of the local to one that is international. It has become a destination. Last but not least, it opened when there was still a recession in architecture. People needed a place to network, find out who had the jobs and to mull over the state of the nation.

Salon

It has always struck me that for many architects the profession itself is quite alienating. You are exposed to people with lots of money, building quite particular and sometimes expensive projects. The architect is then expected to empathise, understanding the often complicated requirements of the client, and to go out of their way to provide a *service*. The tension between the pursuit of a wider agenda than the project is tempered with the possible outcomes and constraints. This process of negotiation is not something that is taught, it is a skill that is acquired, quite invisibly, away from the computer screen or boardroom table. It relies on shared experiences and exposure to situations. You need to talk about it, reflect and question both motives and outcomes. You often need to do this over a pint. There is something quite normal about going to the pub and downing a few beers, or many even. From the outside this situation could be interpreted as being elite, even though it isn't. Maybe it would be nice to think that there was a certain notoriety about the St John; the times that were had there, the people who pass through the door, the scene that develops of a Friday night. Well, it's the same in all bars. There are regulars there are locals and there are visitors, good nights and bad ones, fights and affairs. Every minute a hundred conversations happen, information is exchanged, arguments had, good times recalled and opinions formed. It goes on until it all ends at 11.00, when the bar shuts. The waiters and waitress' are still brisk to the point of being rude and there are never enough chairs.

A bell is rung and 'last orders' is shouted from the bar. The lights are turned full on and the broken glass is swept up. The chapter over.

'I suppose that even the world itself could not contain all the books that should be written'. The final verse of the Gospel according to St John.

Notes

1. What is it about the Smithsons?

1. Smithson, P. 'Reflections on Hunstanton'. *Architectural Research Quarterly*, **2** (4): 32–43 (1997). The paper was based on a talk Peter Smithson gave at the Architectural Association and on conversations with Peter Carolin, who wrote it out and edited it.
2. Preface to the revised edition of Waugh, E. *Brideshead Revisited* (Penguin Books, Harmondsworth, 1980) p. 7. The novel was first published in 1945; this preface was written in 1959.
3. Banham, R. 'Machine Aesthetes'. In M. Banham et al. (eds), *A Critic Writes: Essays by Reyner Banham* (University of California Press, Berkeley, 1996) p. 26. The essay was originally published in the *New Statesman*, 16 August 1958. It begins 'You don't have to be very clever to find a link between the New Brutalists and the Angry Young literaries, but you don't do yourself much good in the process'.
4. Johnson, P. 'School at Hunstanton, Norfolk'. *The Architectural Review*, **116** (693): 148–162 (1954).
5. Banham, R. 'The New Brutalism'. In *A Critic Writes, op. cit.* The essay was originally published in the *Architectural Review*, **118**: 354–361 (1955). The French expression (the quality of not giving a damn) comes in a linguistic flurry where a number of contemporary buildings are excluded from the Brutalist

canon for being more *suaviter in re* than *fortiter in modo* (more gentle in manner than resolute in deed).

6. 'Secondary School at Hunstanton'. *Architects' Journal*, 120 (3107): 336 (1954).

7. Smithson, A. and Smithson, P. *Without Rhetoric – An Architectural Aesthetic* (Latimer New Dimensions, London, 1973) p. 14.

8. Smithson, A. 'House in Soho, London'. *Architectural Design*, **32** (12): 342 (1953).

9. Smithson, A. and Smithson, P., *Ordinariness and Light* (Faber and Faber, London, 1970) p. 9.

10. Sergison, J. '6 Lessons Learnt from Alison and Peter Smithson'. *made* (1): 10–19 (2004).

11. Cook, P. 'Regarding the Smithsons'. *The Architectural Review*, **172** (1025): 36–43 (1982).

12. Watkin, D. *The Rise of Architectural History* (The Architectural Press, London, 1980) p. 154.

13. Smithson, A. and Smithson, P., 'Architectural Principles in the Age of Humanism' (letter). *RIBA Journal*, 59 (4): 140 (1952).

14. Smithson, P. 'Reflections on Hunstanton'. *op. cit.*

15. Smithson, A and Smithson, P., *The Charged Void: Architecture* (Monacelli Press, New York, 2001) p. 323. What they wish to imply here (and did state elsewhere, e.g. in *Italian Thoughts*, 1993) is that, just as the Renaissance ('an architectural language whose intentions were wholly new') was founded by the three generations of Brunelleschi, Alberti and Francesco di Giorgio, so Modernism's fresh start was founded by the three generations exemplified by Corbusier, the Eames, and the Smithsons themselves. The charge of presumptuousness stands.

16. Smithson, A. and Smithson, P. *Signs of Occupancy*. Tape/slide lecture, Pidgeon Audio Visual (PAV 793), 1979.

17. Walsh, V. *Nigel Henderson: Parallel of Life and Art* (Thames and Hudson, 2001) p. 54.

18. *ibid.*, p. 16.

19. Pearson, F. *Paolozzi* (Trustees of the National Galleries of Scotland, Edinburgh, 1999) p. 18.

20. The quotation is from an unpublished text by Alison Smithson. I am indebted to Angela Williams and Peter Hawley for lending me their copy.

21. Smithson, A. and Smithson, P. *Changing the Art of Inhabitation* (Artemis, London, 1994).
22. Walsh, V. *op. cit.*, p. 54.
23. Smithson, A. and Smithson, P. *Ordinariness and Light. op. cit.*, p. 45.
24. Banham, R. *The New Brutalism* (The Architectural Press, London, 1966) p. 70ff.
25. See, for example, *Urban Structuring* (1967), *Ordinariness and Light* (1970), *Without Rhetoric* (1973) and *The Emergence of Team 10 out of CIAM* (AA Publications, London, 1982).
26. Smithson, A. and Smithson, P. *Urban Structuring* (Studio Vista, London, 1967) p. 5. On the humanising aims of Team 10, Aldo van Eyck would later remark that 'Initially Team 10 responded to the new dimension. John Voelker [the other English member of team 10], with whom I talked a lot, certainly did. When I discovered that his name had been struck from the tiny list you'll find on page two of the Primer [the *Team 10 Primer*] which was edited and published in England, I was sad and worried. For me, in a way, Team 10 died when that happened; it made a slip into a groove not far removed from that of CIAM.' (Aldo van Eyck, *RIBA Journal*, April 1981.) Alison Smithson wrote Voelker out of Team 10 history.
27. Smithson, A. and Smithson, P. *Ordinariness and Light. op. cit.*, p. 104.
28. Smithson, A. and Smithson, P. *Urban Structuring. op. cit.*, p. 18.
29. *ibid.*, p. 22.
30. Frampton, K. 'Team 10, Plus 20: The Vicissitudes of Ideology'. In *Labour, Work and Architecture: Collected Essays on Architecture and Design* (Phaidon Press, London, 2002) p. 140. The essay was first published in *L'Architecture d'Aujourd'hui*, **177**: 62–65 (1975).
31. Smithson, A. and Smithson, P., *Ordinariness and Light op. cit.*, p. 48.
32. Martin, L. and March, L. 'Speculations'. In Martin, L. and March, L. (eds), *Urban Space and Structures* (Cambridge University Press, Cambridge, 1972) p. 35.
33. Curtis, W. *Modern Architecture Since 1900* (Phaidon Press, London, 1992) p. 320.
34. Smithson, A. and Smithson, P. *Ordinariness and Light. op. cit.*, p. 11.
35. An effect all the more surprising when one considers the lack of interest shown in their British contemporaries. One thinks of Michael Brawne, Trevor Dannat, Howell Killick Partridge and Amis, Powell and Moya, Douglas Stephen, Colin St John Wilson,

James Stirling and James Gowan: all were born within 3 years of Peter Smithson.

36. Bowness, A. *The Conditions of Success: How the Modern Artist Rises to Fame* (Thames and Hudson, London, 1989).
37. Cook, P. *op. cit.*
38. Smithson, A. and Smithson, P., *Ordinariness and Light. op. cit.*, p. 28.
39. Larkin, P. 'Basie'. In *Required Writing* (Faber and Faber, London, 1983) p. 306.
40. Goffman, E. *The Presentation of Self in Everyday Life* (Pelican Books, London, 1972) p. 225.

2. The Archigram Group

1. Cover cartoon, Concerning Archigram, Ed Dennis Crompton, 1998, Archigram Archives.
2. The answer I think should have been, 'rent another pod'.
3. 'A Necessary Irritant', Barry Curtis in Concerning Archigram, *op. cit.*
4. 'Street Fighting Man' has been attributed as a response to both the demonstrations in Chicago at the Republican convention of 1968 and Jagger's realisation of his own difficulty as a wannabe participant of the Grosvenor Square demonstrations in London.

3. Boyarsky and the Architectural Association

1. I will later argue that it was Boyarsky's distrust of curricula that was unique. He inherited the unit system from John Lloyd his predecessor, who had copied it from normal practice in the US.
2. Boyarsky was trained as an architect at McGill and then went to Cornel to undertake graduate work with Rowe. According to Rowe, Boyarsky only completed one of the studies Rowe suggested to him. They travelled extensively in Italy together. See Rowe's Eulogy in *As I was Saying, vol. 3: Urbanistics* (The MIT Press, Cambridge, MA, 1999). Colin Rowe's biography has yet to be written.
3. Nowhere comprehensively written up but an account by Sir Leslie Martin was published in the second number of the ill-fated journal *Architectural Research* published by the RIBA.
4. Young Fabian Pamphlet number 5, published in March 1963.

5. Crossmaw was Minister for Housing in Harold Wilson's government.
6. A. Caragonne (ed.), *As I was Saying, Vol. 1: Texas, pre-Texas*, by Colin Rowe (The MIT Press, Cambridge, MA, 1996), pp. ix–xii. Much of my interpretation derives from a reading of the 3-volume collection of Colin Rowe's writings, *As I was Saying*.
7. Reyner Banham, 'In-architecture Illustrated, a review of *British Buildings 1960–64* by Douglas Stephen, Kenneth Frampton, Michael Carapetian'. *New Society* 7(183): 33 (1966). Fairly accusing Rowe as being part of an in-group, and it must be added that Frampton and Carapetian both worked at that time for Stephen who himself admitted to this author that he had 'discovered' Terragni before Rowe. On in-groups, Banham with the editor of New Society, Paul Barker, Cedric Price and Peter Cook formed a fairly powerful in-group themselves.
8. Interview with Leon von Schaik, by Diane Baird, 1996 at http://ultibase.rmit.edu.au/Articles/june97/schai1.htm
9. See *Architectural Design* April 1972 for a report, pp. 218–243. Boyarsky's slightly hyped image made the cover of the magazine and thereafter till 1980 *Architectural Design* was to all intents and purposes the house magazine of the AA.
10. Peter Cook, 'Conversations' *Arena* 84(923): 18 (no date).
11. A recent symposium at the Canadian Center for Architectural research considered the periodicals of this decade and the previous one.
12. Boyarsky, Editorial. *AA Files* 1(1): 2 (Un-numbered) (1981–2).
13. See Caragonne, A. *The Texas Rangers* (The MIT Press, Cambridge, MA, 1995).

4. Fame and the Changing Role of Drawing

1. Of course historians and philosophers of science would be quick to point out that this too is not as stable a definition as it might at first appear, but we are making a relative point here.
2. See Spiro Kostof (ed.), *The Architect: Chapters in the History of the Profession* (Oxford University Press, New York, 1977) and J.J. Coulton, *Ancient Greek Architects at Work: Problems of Structure and Design* (Cornell University Press, Ithaca, 1977).

3. See L.R. Shelby, 'The Master Mason in English Building'. *Speculum* 39, 1964.
4. Andreas Palladio is widely considered to have first developed and used the set of orthographic drawings that any modern architect would recognise – indeed, his built production is often seen as somehow over-determined by drawing, as an embodiment of elevational thinking through drawing in particular.
5. E.L. Eisenstein, *The Printing Press as an Agent of Change: Communications and Cultural Transformation in Early Modern Europe* (Cambridge University Press, Cambridge, UK, 1979), p. 24. Quoted in Edward Robbins, *Why Architects Draw* (The MIT Press, Cambridge, MA, 1994).
6. Robbins, *op. cit.*, p. [. . .].
7. Henri Lefebvre, *The Production of Space* (Blackwell, Oxford, 1991), pp. 360–361.
8. Abstract space, Lefebvre writes, 'emerged historically as the plane on which a socio-political compromise was reached between the aristocracy and the bourgeoisie (i.e. between the ownership of land and the ownership of money)'. Henri Lefebvre, *ibid.* [. . .]
9. Robbins, *op. cit.*, p. 30.
10. *Ibid.*, p. 46.
11. Robin Evans, 'Translations from Drawing to Building'. In R. Evans (ed.), *Translations from Drawing to Building and Other Essays.* (Architectural Association Publications, London, 1997), pp. 153–193.
12. Robbins, *op. cit.*, p. 42.
13. Manfredo Tafuri, *Architecture and Utopia: Design and Capitalist Development* (The MIT Press, Cambridge, MA, 1996).
14. Robbins, *op.cit.*, p. 39.
15. Robbins follows cultural theorist Raymond Williams' dialectic definition of 'culture' and 'society'.
16. Robbins, *op. cit.*, p. 46.
17. *Ibid.*, p. 48.
18. A phrase used by Simon Alford of AHMM at a lecture in the Technical Studies series at the University of Westminster, 2. December 2004.
19. Manfredo Tafuri, *The Sphere and the Labyrinth* (The MIT Press, Cambridge, MA, 1995), p. 267.

20. Cadai is an architectural software developed by Halli Bjornsson and Murray Fraser. See M. Fraser and H. Bjornsson, 'Real-Time Digital Modelling in Design Education and Practice', *Urban Design International*, Writer 2004, pp. 1–10.

5. Switzerland – Botta: Fame and Scale

1. Loderer, B. 'Roman with Modern Forms'. In: Pizzi, E. (ed.), *The Complete Works of Mario Botta* (Birkhaüser für Architektur, Basel, Switzerland, 1998), pp. 6, 7.
2. *Ibid.*, pp. 6, 7.
3. Fleig, K. and Aalto, E. (eds) *Alvar Aalto: The Complete Works*, 3 vols (Birkhaüser für Architektur, Basel, Switzerland, 1963–78). Boesiger, W., Stonorov, O. and Bill, M. *Le Corbusier: The Complete Works*, 8 vols (Birkhaüser für Architektur, Basel, Switzerland, 1995).
4. Lambot, I. *Norman Foster: Buildings and Projects*, Vol. 1 (1964–73); Vol. 2 (1971–78); Vol. 3 (1978–85); Vol. 4 (1982–89) (Birkhaüser für Architektur, Basel, Switzerland).
5. Cathédrale d'Évry, France, 1988–95. The San Francisco Museum of Modern Art, California, USA; 1988–95 (with Hellmuth Obata and Kassabaum).
6. Prominent members of the group included Tita Carloni, Aurelio Galfetti, Ivano Gianola; Flora Ruchat and Luiggi Snozzi.
7. Brown-Manrique, G. *The Ticino Guide* (Princeton Architectural Press/ADT, Princeton, NJ, 1989), Introduction, p. 16.
8. Wrede, S. In: Bee H.S. (ed.), *Mario Botta and the Modernist Tradition* (The Museum of Modern Art; New York City, USA, 1986).
9. Frampton, K. 'Mario Botta and the School of the Ticino'. *Oppositions* (A Journal for Ideas and Criticism in Architecture; The Institute for Architecture and Urban Studies and the MIT Press, Cambridge, MA, USA, 1979) pp. 1–25.
10. *Ibid.*, p. 25.
11. Of particular note is the introduction by Christian Norberg-Schulz to the edition of GA Architect dedicated to Botta's work, published in 1984 in Tokyo.
12. Frampton, K. 'Critical regionalism: modern architecture and cultural identity'. In: *Modern Architecture: A Critical History*, Revised edn. (Thames and Hudson, London, 1985).

13. 'Mario Botta'; curated by Stuart Wrede in the Department of Architecture and Design at The Museum of Modern Art, New York City, USA, 20th November 1986 to 10th February 1987.
14. See, e.g. Petit, J. *Traces d'architecture photographies* (D'architecture de pino musi, Fidia Edizioni d'Arte, Milan, 1994).
15. As when in 1971, the newly formed and relatively unknown partnership of Piano+Rogers won the architectural competition to design the Centre Pompidou in Paris.
16. Frampton, *op. cit.*, p. 3; see Note 11.
17. In 1996, Botta was put in charge of devising the programme for the newly created Academy of Architecture in Mendrisio-Ticino, part of the new Swiss–Italian University.
18. See the article by Catherine Slessor: 'Swiss Civility'. *The Architectural Review* (April): 63–65 (2003).

6. Italy – Rossi: Fame and Familiarity

1. Olmo notes that the success of *The Architecture of the City* 'has been entirely independent from his architectural production' taking issue with 'an aesthetics of mirroring' between texts and buildings ('Across the Texts' in *Assemblage* N5 February, 1988, pp. 90–120).
2. Karen Stein (following Moneo) defines four stages in the development of Rossi's reputation: the 'fascist' or 'communist' of the 1960s; the 'radical' supporting the student movement of the early 1970s; the 'conservative' radical (admired for his 'common sense') in the 1980s, and the 'cult hero' who acquires the status of 'official hero' on being awarded the Pritzker Prize in 1990, in Stein, K. 'Il Celeste della Madonna'. Adjmi, M. (ed.), *Aldo Rossi: The Complete Buildings and Projects 1981–91* (T+H, London, 1992), pp. 269–271). Other critics have made finer distinctions about early developments.
3. They may concretise his theories; become a commodity (like his tea service); present an autobiographical record of his designs and preoccupations, or simply provide an outlet for poetic reverie.
4. The IAUS journal. All three publications are framed by 'editorial' prefaces, introductions or postscripts: *Aldo Rossi in America: 1976 to 1979* (IAUS Catalogue, New York, 1979); Rossi, A.

A *Scientific Autobiography* (MIT Press, Cambridge, MA, 1981); Rossi, A. *The Architecture of the City* MIT Press, Cambridge, MA, 1982). Given this focus, discussion is limited to texts translated into English. The Italian background has been well covered elsewhere.

5. Daniel Libeskind's essay ' "Deus ex Machina"/"Machina ex Deo" Aldo Rossi's Theatre of the World' in *Oppositions* n21, 1980, is significant in the context of Rossi's own response to Libeskind's drawings in the latter's *Chamberworks* (Architectural Association, London, 1983).

6. As he notes himself (interview *Domus* n722, December 1990) until then his clients had been primarily Italian municipalities.

7. The attempt to theorise this in *A Scientific Autobiography* is generally taken to represent a break with his 'rationalist' past identified with *The Architecture of the City* (1966) published 15 years earlier.

8. Psychological assumptions about ownership and value condition the evaluation of a life's-work, but also the desire to deliver a moment of personal insight in the form of an anecdote or reminiscence.

9. Over 100 buildings were completed, administered from branch offices of his studio in Milan, in New York, Tokyo, Berlin and The Hague.

10. Proposed as an 'alternative vision' distanced from 'ideology' but comfortable with a certain morality or spirituality; this perception is shared by Vincent Scully in his postscript to *A Scientific Autobiography*.

11. *Casabella* September 1997. Substituting portrait for text, in homage to a 'master'. His arms are folded into the creases of a loose white shirt; the shadows reminiscent of an earlier portrait taken in Athens in 1971, where he stands with anthropomorphic intent next to columns on the Acropolis, in a display of *chiaroscuro*. Both photographs recur in publications on his work.

12. The drawings, printed on cream paper, are centred on the page, mostly as single images with wide borders, and prefaced by a black page featuring his projects (*Oppositions* n26, Spring 1984).

13. *Times* 18/09/97. Jonathan Glancey noted (with a degree of sarcasm) that Rossi's international reputation 'precluded him building in Britain' (*Guardian* 06/09/97), while his influence on ex-students Herzog and de Meuron, as architects of the Tate Modern, surfaced in *Building* (12/09/97). The 'spare style' of this building was associated with Rossi, though its 'transformation' epitomises Rossi's view of the role of the *primary element* in the city.

14. Reiterating the Pritzker jury citation of 1990.

15. He contrasted the 'harsh reality' of the architecture with the 'hypnotic power' of drawings in which it was endlessly reproduced. Rossi himself talks evocatively of everyday life in Milanese working class tenements, though John Foot has contextualised this social mythology as stereotypical in *Milan Since The Miracle* (Berg, 2004), p. 24.

16. This is evoked at one remove from a working-class social life concretely remembered, yet understood in deference to the abstract 'types' of corridor, balcony and courtyard. Rossi in *A Scientific Autobiography* talks of the image of fog infiltrating Alberti's Basilica in Mantua as the 'unforeseen element that modifies and alters' like 'stones worn smooth' by use; stolidity of form substantiating the effect of its occupation. Aesthetic perception is one thing, social reality another.

17. Attributes he associated with Rossi's floating *Theatre of the World*, another temporary building, which is seen to manifest Rossi's abstract practice of displacement (qualified by the very real experience of seasickness inside).

18. Moneo cautions that 'following Rossi's . . . principles in no way compels the formal choices he has made', which is not to disregard the veracity of Rossi's thinking, or the insight it offers into his architecture. The double imperative of his final footnote, decrying the 'purity' of Rossi's imitators, supports Moneo's own work of this period, but also casts doubt on a transparent relationship between Rossi's writing and building.

19. Or, as David Dunster prefers it, 'anti-humanist', overbearingly 'rational' and dependent on 'history' (*Architects Journal* 11/09/97).

20. They raid 'The 'Case' of Aldo Rossi' in his *History of Italian Architecture, 1944–1985* (Cambridge/London, MIT, 1989). Written in 1982 this presented Rossi as 'the only 'school leader' capable

of constantly fuelling around his ... works and self a controversy ... that ended up affecting the very concept of
architecture'.

21. Rossi notes: 'The meaning of the title of this catalogue, chosen
by Peter Eisenman and signifying my relationship with America,
perhaps is not very apparent in the designs' – concluding
warily 'though I thought I chose these thirty designs with a
precise reference to America, in reality I did not, because that
would be looking for a pre-established theme that does not exist'.

22. Its fragmentation signifying the effects of the capitalist
economy (though the author further philosophises its iconography). The IAUS catalogue duplicates a sketch 'study for a
grand composition' on its cover, a playful combination of
anecdotal still-life, axial and linear composition, but lacking
any reference to America.

23. As if they were primarily of art-historical interest. Eisenman
later defers this, talking instead of 'the unconscious process
which informs the making of his imagery' which allows 'an
understanding of the working method itself' rather than
'a series of art historical 'origins'.

24. Or in his terms a 'memory'. Several of the drawings evoke New
York in the form of a skyline constituted by an assembly of
towers (which include the twin towers of The World Trade
Centre, and the Chrysler Building).

25. John Berger comments of Giorgio Morandi's late paintings:
'Because there is no density and no colour the objects there
don't distract us. And we realise that what interests the artist is
the process of the visible first becoming visible, before the
thing seen has been given a name or acquired a value', 'They
are not objects. They are places ...' 'Giorgio Morandi', in *The
Shape of the Pocket* (London, Bloomsbury, 2002), pp. 144–145. For
all the attention given to Rossi's objects, Rossi himself notes
'Today I know that it is sufficient to look at things; art is the
singular life established through this relationship of seeing.'
('My Designs and Analagous Architecture' in *Aldo Rossi in
America: 1976 to 1979, op. cit.*, p. 15).

26. Though whether in response to an American condition is
inconclusive. Rossi is ambivalent about this: 'In New York it is
precisely the application of Beaux-Arts architecture on a giant

scale that produces these abnormal effects...I tried to express this concept of emotion in several of my New York drawings...I do not wish to interpret these drawings here because I wish to avoid becoming facile and mechanical...the images follow different directions, or are superimposed, because of the ways the land settles' (Rossi, *A Scientific Autobiography, op. cit.*, p. 61). An unsettling experience, and the emotion identified with it, is quickly deferred in a straightforward description of physical settlement.

27. Noting that the use of 'analogy' in architectural drawing is part of a 200-year tradition (though the use of the term is vague), only later to qualify this.

28. 'The house of the Dead as the City of Survival' in *Aldo Rossi in America: 1976 to 1979, op. cit.*, p. 9.

29. Rossi's interest in Daniel Libeskind's drawings develops this notion: 'Perhaps it was our common comprehension, or perhaps in our common understanding in work, that we both saw and came to know quite precisely the colour and form of a 'key' or 'cypher': and we are not afraid to look at it, to repeat it, immersed as it is in a complex of hieroglyphics. Yet in continually returning to it, we know we will lose it and we must ask if ours is a flight or a search.' ('Simply a Path' in *Chamberworks, op. cit.*)

30. For their internal coherency and their evidence of formative process. Both are characteristic of his own thinking. He appears to mean 'formative' in a theoretical rather than instrumental sense, which suggests a representational theory displacing design procedures.

31. His earlier observations on the drawings' suspension, or collapse, of time, are totally contradictory: 'they make history present'; 'they exist outside time at the same time as they condition time', and 'it is not the capacity to stimulate historical association which is at issue' (*Aldo Rossi in America: 1976 to 1979, op. cit.*, p. 11). Rossi's view of memory appears to be largely as 'observation', whereas Eisenman rarely turns down an interpretative opportunity.

32. The psychological dimension to Rossi's repetition has been addressed by Mary Louise Lobsinger in 'That Obscure Object of

Desire: Autobiography and Repetition in the Work of Aldo Rossi', *Grey Room* 8, Summer 2002.

33. 'Serious' credentials are flagged up by Guarini's conical projections (Baroque episodes) on the dust-jacket (embossed on the hardcover), and the funereal black pages at start and finish (illustrations alternating on black or white backgrounds in the main text).

34. Four separate consecutive sentences: 'I felt that the disorder of things, if limited and somehow honest, might best correspond to our state of mind'; 'But I detested the arbitrary disorder that is an indifference to order, a kind of moral obtuseness, complacent well-being, forgetfulness'; 'To what, then, could I have aspired in my craft?', and 'Certainly to small things, having seen that the possibility of great ones was historically precluded'. This qualified reflection, and question and answer, flag up the discursive nature of the text.

35. Despite the rhetorical title, a degree of fragmentation or dislocation would be a more accurate, and less emotive, description of the forms in this image. Rossi himself celebrates at one point, an unforeseen crack in the Parthenon giving 'immense strength in unanticipated beauty'. He actively enjoys 'errors on the construction site', where an ideal of order is subjected to practical changes. This signifies 'the failures of human weakness' he notes philosophically.

36. He has Venturi in mind – the Italian vernacular is taken for granted. Acting in conjunction with 'a sharp gable' the forms of the four-square window idealise 'something . . . more traditional, basic and enduring' than modern design, he argues, something 'international' yet also 'familiar' as an object of affection.

37. He later repeats this: 'Americans cannot help but think of Louis Kahn once more' perhaps with his own monograph *Louis. J. Kahn* (Brazillier, New York, 1962) in mind.

38. Scully on the one hand wishes to distance himself from Fascism; on the other he sees its influence 'endowing' Rossi's forms with a special aura. He resolves this contradiction noting Italian Fascism's evocation of tradition, both classical and vernacular. Rossi, he claims regains tradition 'more vitally because he is operating through memory rather than ideology'. Here, having noted its ideological use, history acquires a sanction of its own.

39. But this judgement he sees adopting 'the functionalist criteria of modernist criticism'.
40. 'Something deep is touched' he suggests in the 'coupling' of Aymonino and Rossi's buildings. The sexual connotation seems to have more to do with his need to project an exaggerated psychological aura onto the work, than Rossi's building.
41. The project established a mature vocabulary of form, but the theoretical attention paid to the project initiated a critical 'rite of passage' which strongly influenced attitudes to Rossi's subsequent work.
42. It is associated with a second phase of his career, following his earlier association with *Casabella*, identified with *Gruppo Architetturra* and a didactic period of teaching and writing. Generally thought to be a consolidation of his teaching practice (associated teaching 'notes' for students being published as *Architecture for Museums*), it reads in many respects as if a set of lectures: systematically structured in four chapters (each broken down into titled sub-sections). A 'personal' introduction to the main sections of text competes with a rhetorical recapitulation of what has gone before, and the occasional digression, or anecdote, surfacing within an otherwise logical structure plays as if to an audience. For the Italian background see D'Amato 'Fifteen Years after the Publication of *The Architecture of the City*', Olmo 'Across the Texts', and Bandini 'Aldo Rossi'.
43. His preface, and lengthy introduction *The Houses of Memory: The Texts of Analogue*, influenced how the new publication presented what was already, a historical text (yet one endowed with a canonical contemporary status).
44. A conventional 'note' from the translators Ghirardo and Ockman concerning their editorial role is missing. Given the unique importance attached to the role of 'repetition' in Rossi's work, this editing down might be problematic.
45. The claim is framed in grandiose terms out of key with the immediate text of the book, and implies perhaps that it is the trilogy of IAUS publications that constitute a 'treatise'.
46. Where drawings and texts are seen as 'analogous instruments'.
47. A metaphorically natural flow, in a 'current that washes back and forth from drawing to drawing, and from writing to

writing', is seen to connect parallel activities. Eisenman resorts to the phrase 'a kind of analogy of an analogy'.

48. Eisenman's degree of editorial control points to his own likely contribution to the editing of the main text.

49. Rossi himself is realistic enough to temper his moments of despair, with contrasting epiphanies.

50. He over-emphasises, repetitiously, what he calls Rossi's conception of the 'autonomous researcher. The concept of 'autonomy' does surface from time to time in Rossi's text, but it is usually used with reference to analysis of the structural characteristics of city form. This has a practical inference, but one exaggerated by Eisenman who often uses the term as a synonym for 'transformation'. This identification with autonomous form, has been explicitly denied by Rossi as a relative matter.

51. 'His drawings of the city – become part of it 'not just a representation of it'. A concern with the legitimacy of architectural drawing conceived, in itself, as 'architecture', surfaces during the 1980s in the work of several architects. For Eisenman the drawings come to concretely 'embody' Rossi's thinking as architecture, rather than acting as a record of his 'designs', or representing aspects of his thinking. Rossi's expedient reworking of his drawings for publication in *A Scientific Autobiography* suggests otherwise.

52. 'The shadow of the humanist poet hovers continuously behind the figure of the autonomous researcher. The potential transformation of the individual into the collective subject is left in suspension. Ambiguously, the object of the analogous city begins to define the subject once again, not so much as a humanist-hero, nor as the psychological collective, but as a complex, divided, and shattered solitary survivor, appearing before, but not withstanding the collective will of history.'

53. Indebted to phenomenological thinking, and revealing a poetic intent just 'where epistemological effort becomes more complex' D'Amato, C. 'Fifteen Years after the Publication of *The Architecture of the City* by Aldo Rossi', in *The Harvard Architecture Review* 3: p. 101 (1984).

54. In fact a constructed 'memory'. The later image of Cologne cathedral standing in the ruins of the city centre, for example,

prompts a perception of 'analogical thinking' (Rossi *The Architecture of the City, op. cit.*, pp. 22.124).

55. Rossi, *The Architecture of the City, op. cit.*, p. 22.
56. And the yellowed honeymoon photographs that Rossi collected (Rossi, *A Scientific Autobiography, op. cit.*, p. 62). At the outset of Diane Ghirardo's obituary, the iconography of Rossi's 'polaroids' (recording visitors to his apartment, against the backdrop of his kitchen mantelpiece and the Torre Velasca outside), serves to highlight Rossi's understanding of the relationship between immutability and transience (*Journal of Architectural Education* 51(3): 146; 1998).
57. Rossi's thinking elides two conceptions explored in Theodor Adorno's influential essay *Valéry Proust Museum*, where he discusses the polarity, at the end of the C19th, between the two writers' views of the museum and its contents (Adorno, T. *Prisms* (The MIT Press, Cambridge, MA, 1997)).
58. While he distances himself from his hasty judgement of post-war Cologne, on the other hand 'The analogy of the value of monuments in destroyed cities serves . . . to clarify' the singularity of the monument, understood through its relationship with other 'urban artefacts', which points to Rossi's subsequent formulation of 'an analogical architecture' (Rossi, *The Architecture of the City, op. cit.*, p. 124).
59. Arnell, P. and Bickford, T. *Aldo Rossi: Buildings and Projects* (Rizzoli, New York, 1985). This is to marginalise Italian monographs like the earlier comprehensive Braghieri, G. *Aldo Rossi* (Zanichelli Editore, Bologna, 1989).
60. The Electa 'Opera Completa' came later in 1987, 1992 and 1996.
61. Loos, A. *Spoken into the Void: Collected Essays 1897–1900* (MIT Press, Cambridge, MA, 1982), p. viii.
62. Rafael Moneo 'Postscript', in Arnell and Bickford, *op. cit.*, p. 312.

7. The Netherlands – Koolhaas and the Profession at Play

1. Burton Hamfelt, Lecture Academie van Bouwkunst Rotterdam, 19 February 2003.

2. The same myth has it that modernism has strong roots in the Netherlands and that the current international interest in collectives like OMA, UN, MVRDV, NL, West 8 and others is the self-evident products of an uninterrupted modern movement. 'Superdutch' this movement is labelled in plain English. The term is as rash as it is shameless and is remarkable for many reasons. It is an English title of a Dutch book, which is in the Netherlands less usual than it may seem. The term serves a promotional goal and is in itself an export product. Also, the term is without much ado chauvinistic. 'Super' suggests that the architects under this flag have outgrown their Dutchness and count the global setting as their natural habitat. 'Superdutch' exploits the modernist Dutch architectural legacy for an exclusive group of designers. Superdutch is the energetic term for architects aware of their origin, full of self-confidence that their native country has become too small for them.

3. NRC Handelsblad is a Dutch daily newspaper.

4. For instance, Hulsman, B. Een sublieme fantast die niet normaal doet, architect Rem Koolhaas bouwt met het mes op tafel. *NRC Handelsblad*, 16 February 2004.

5. *Pars pro toto* is Latin for synecdoche, or '(taking) a part for the whole'. When used in a context of language it means that something is named after a part of it (or after a limited characteristic, in itself not necessarily representative for the whole). For example, 'glasses' is a *'pars pro toto'* name for a complicated structure to put on a human's nose, and implying also other materials than simply two pieces of glass.

6. Weeber has remained unknown abroad, but has been an influential force in Dutch architectural thinking throughout his career.

7. van Dijk, H. Rem Koolhaas, de reïncarnatie van de moderne architectuur (Hans van Dijk: Interview Rem Koolhaas). *Wonen TA/BK* 11 (1978).

8. Koolhaas, R. How Modern is Dutch Architecture? In: Crimson with Speaks, M. and Hadders, G. (eds), *Mart Stam's Trousers, Stories from behind the Scenes of Dutch Moral Modernism* (010 Publishers, Rotterdam, 1999).

9. 'Rem Koolhaas of OMA is less obviously a Rationalist, but uses Rationalist compositional processes to precipitate the unpredictable and the irrational'. In: The Netherlands. *The Architectural Review* 1055: 39 (1985).

10. Crimson: Re-Urb, *Nieuwe Plannen Voor Oude Steden* (010 Publishers, Rotterdam, 1997), p. 46.

11. Koolhaas, R. *Delirious New York* (010 Publishers, Rotterdam, 1994), p. 238.

12. Crimson: Re-Urb, *op. cit.*, p. 48.

13. Colenbrander, B. and Bosman, J. *Referentie: OMA: De Sublieme Start van een Architectengeneratie* (NAI Uitgevers, Rotterdam, 1995).

14. *Ibid.*, p. 6.

15. *Ibid.*, p. 7.

16. Hans van der Heijden: *On certainty and negotiation*, a+t #13 1999.

17. '*Gnadenlos gute Laune*', phrase coined in German by Marcel Meili, recorded in Stuhlmacher, M. 'Vakkundige smaakmaker', *De Architect* September (2001).

18. Koolhaas, R. Studie om in hoofdlijnen na te gaan of het bestaande huis van Bewaring 'De Koepel' te Arnhem bruikbaar kan worden gemaakt voor een tijdsduur van circa 50 jaar, rekening houdend met huidige inzichten betreffende de huisvesting van gedetineerden. Unpublished Design Report (London, 1980).

19. Koolhaas, R. and Mau, B. *Small, Medium, Large, Extra-Large, Office for Metropolitan Architecture* (010 Publishers, Rotterdam, 1995), p. 354.

20. Leupen, B. *IJ-Plein Catalogus* (Afdeling der Bouwkunde TH Delft/ Stadsdeelraad Amsterdam-N, 1986). Leupen, B. *IJ-Plein, Amsterdam, Een speurtocht naar Nieuwe Compositorische Middelen* (Uitgeverij 010 Publishers, Rotterdam, 1989).

21. Koolhaas and Mau, *op. cit.*, pp. 130, 195.

22. *Born naked*, interview by Dirk van den Heuvel, Vincent Kompier and Sanna Schuiling in Oase 47, 1997. See also, van der Heijden, H. 'The Diagram of the House'. *Architectural Research Quarterly* 5(2): 110 (2001).

23. SMLXL for instance was amongst others supported by the Netherlands Foundation for Fine Arts, Design and Architecture, the Netherlands Foundation for Architecture, the Dutch Ministry of Education, Culture and Science, the National Buildings Agency, Prins Bernard Foundation and the Rotterdam Arts Council.

8. Germany – (Un)edited Architecture: *Wettbewerbe Aktuell*

1. Ramona Buxbaum, Architect, in conversation with the author, Frankfurt, August 2003.
2. Dorothee Stürmer, Architect, in conversation with the author, Frankfurt, July 2004.
3. Prof Johann Eisele in conversation with the author, Darmstadt, August 2003.
4. Prof. Max Bächer, Darmstadt (Architect and juror of competitions); Dipl.-Ing. Peter Karle and Dipl.-Ing. Ramona Buxbaum, Darmstadt (Architects); Prof. Nicolas Fritz, Darmstadt (Architect and juror of competitions); Prof. Johann Eisele, Darmstadt (Architect and juror of competitions); Dipl.-Ing. Thomas Hoffmann-Kuhnt, Freiburg (founding owner–editor of *Wettbewerbe Aktuell*); Dipl.-Ing. Dorothee Stürmer, Frankfurt (Architect); Dipl.-Ing. Frau Gesine Ludwig, Wiesbaden (Architect and Presently Head of the Competitions Department of the *Architekten -und Stadtplaner Kammer Hessen*); Dipl.-Ing. Cornelia Zuschke, Fulda (Architect. Presently Chief Urban Planner (Stadtbau Dezernentin of the City of Fulda, responsible for Urban Developments and Architecture Competitions).
5. Equivalent to the Architects Registration Board in the United Kingdom. However, in Germany registration is a federal rather than a central state matter.
6. Prof Max Bächer in conversation with the author, Darmstadt, August 2003.
7. Peter Karle, Architect, in conversation with the author, Darmstadt, August 2003.
8. Until the very recent past open architectural design competitions were the standard means of procurement for publicly funded buildings and UDPs (*Bebauungsplaene*) in Germany. It is still the case that by law architecture funded by a public body has to be procured by competitive selection process if the fees exceed the threshold value. This, however, includes competitive interviews and invited/restricted competitions which are now becoming equally common means to select an architect. There is a distinction to be made between local or regional competitions in which the status quo presents the rule not to

be broken (a town hall), and large national competitions were signature architecture or projects challenging the status quo are more acceptable if not required (Reichstag).

Until 1993 competitions were usually organised as open (by area) and anonymous contests. The submission usually had to consist of b/w drawings in a scale not larger than 1/100 (mostly 1/200) and massing models in a scale not larger than 1/200 (mostly 1/500). Since 1993 and the implementation of the European Services Directive (92/50/EEC) for the procurement of public services both the format of competitions and the rules and opportunities for participation have changed. Open competitions are extremely rare now, having been replaced by invited competitions and competitive interviews and the format of submissions has shifted towards a stronger emphasis on three-dimensional representation, the latter being a direct result of the advent of advanced computer technology in architectural practice.

In this context it is also worth remembering that in Germany both the title *Architect* and the activities of the profession, i.e. who is allowed to do what, are protected. Participants in competitions have to be registered architects, hence providing the profession with a monopoly in the field of planning and building.

The rules as to from which size project one needs to be a registered architect vary but generally anything beyond a single dwelling requires the designer to be qualified and registered. This also explains why Germany probably has the highest density of architects in the world.

The threshold value for a project to have to be procured by competitive selection process is currently €200,000 for consultant's fees.

9. It was shortly after their successful run of competitions that both partners were awarded Professorships.
10. Prof Nicolas Fritz, in conversation with the author, Darmstadt, September 2003.
11. Ramona Buxbaum, Architect, in conversation with the author, Darmstadt, August 2003.
12. Peter Karle, Architect, in conversation with the author, Darmstadt, August 2003.

13. A verdict is achieved by vote, eliminating projects in a number of rounds until, depending on the size of the project, about eight schemes are left in competition. The number of prizes awarded in a competition varies depending on the size of the individual contest, but on average 1st to 5th prize plus a number of commendations are awarded. The client is obliged by law to employ the architect of one of the top five schemes in case the project proceeds.
14. At the other end of the spectrum it can also be safely said that well known international practices like Herzog and De Meuron, OMA or Coop Himmelblau have not really got to where they are by building successful competition schemes in Germany. In most superstar cases the contrary applies with the architects persistently employing any possible media at hand to promote their ideas independently, subsequently gaining direct commissions and then invitations to limited competitions where the chances of winning are higher and they find themselves in the company of other stars against whom to lose is presumably more acceptable.
15. Prof Johann Eisele in conversation with the author, Darmstadt, August 2003.
16. One exception is the section *Wettbewerbe weiterverfolgt* in which architects are invited to give their own account of how a project developed from competition win to completion.
17. Prof Johann Eisele in converstion with the author, Darmstadt, August 2003.
18. Prof Max Bächer in conversation with the author, Darmstadt, August 2003.
19. The journal *Architektur + Wettbewerbe* (Karl Kraemer Verlag, Stuttgart), collects competitions on the same building type and publishes them as volumes, hence the information is never as up to date as in *Wettbewerbe Aktuell*. It also tends to publish just one or two winning schemes per competition.
20. The 14 categories are Urban Planning; Housing; Schools; Education, Science & Research; Culture; Sacral; Healthcare; Leisure, Sports & recuperation; Tourism; Traffic; Administration; Government & Local Authorities; Business, Industry & Services; Design & Detail.

21. Thomas Hoffmann-Kuhnt, Owner, Publisher and Editor of *Wettbewerbe Aktuell*, in conversation with the author, August 2003.
22. The *pre-editorial* control of the journal's contents takes place in the competition juries.
23. Despite featuring model photographs – albeit of mostly poor quality, taken on the occasion of the competitions public exhibition – and some photographs of buildings in the section showing built projects, the main content of the journal are drawings.

9. Spain – The Fame Game

1. Amongst those featured in *The Praise of Light* were Rafael Moneo, Oscar Tusquets, Alberto Campo Baeza, José Antonio Corrales, Álvaro Siza, Dolores Alonso, César Portela, Oriol Bohigas, Juan Navarro Baldeweg, Cruz y Ortiz and Luís Peña Ganchegui y Alejandro Zaera.
2. Other outstanding names include Josep Lluis Sert, José Antonio Coderch, Javier Sáenz de Oiza, Miguel Fisac, Alejandro de la Sota, Emilio Pérez Piñero, Juan Daniel Fullaondo, Félix Candela, Javier Carvajal, Antonio Fernández Alba, Enric Miralles, Carme Pinós, Rafael Moneo, Oscar Tusquets and Studio Per, Oriol Bohigas and MBM, Juan Navarro Baldeweg, Alberto Campo Baeza, Albert Viaplana, Josep Lluís Mateo, César Portela, Salvador Pérez Arroyo and Alejandro Zaera. The list of architects is getting longer and denser every year and new offices appear on the map like Iñaki Ábalos and Juan Herreros, Federico Soriano, Eduardo Arroyo, or the young couple Efrén García y Cristina Díaz (*Cero 9*).
3. Coderch de Sentmenat, J.A. 'It's Not Geniuses We Need Now'. In: Ockman, J. (ed.), *Architecture Culture* 1943–1968 (Rizzoli, New York, 1993) (first published in *Domus*, November 1961).
4. Within this context, a novel initiative in approaching the public was further made by The Architectural Association in the Region of Murcia when it organised the prizes for architecture in the year 2004, with a catalogue in which the columnist of the *El País* newspaper, Vicent Verdú, wrote the introduction. Big posters showed the portraits of the winner architects and were hung up in different places in the city and published in the local newspapers. Attached to each portrait, were the architect's

answers to a short questionnaire that showed his/her 'human' side, narrations from his personal life. The answers to questions like the wife's name (there was only one female architect prized), the favourite food, the necessary object in order to be able to work, or what dream he would like to fulfil, were followed closely by the press.

5. Later, Elías Torres and Martínez Lapeña followed in no 61, two monographs on Rafael Moneo no 64 (I) and no 98, the issue no 72 (II) was dedicated to Miralles alone and was followed by a third one with the issue no 100/101 with Benedetta Tagliabue and a monograph on Juan Navarro Baldeweg was published in no 73 (II).

6. Anatxu Zabalbeascoa 'Arquitectos Estrellas' in El País Semanal, 29th February, 2004.

7. In a conversation with Lola Fernández. Published in the web-page magazine El Mundo.

8. From Federico Climent Guimerá: Sáenz de Oíza. Mallorca 1960–2000, proyectos y obras. Palma de Mallorca, 2001, p. 149.

9. Anatxu Zabalbeascoa, *op. cit.*

10. USA – Ground Zero: 1,776 ft into Thin Air

1. Daniel Libeskind in his *German Architectural Prize Speech*, Berlin, 1999, in: Libeskind, D., *The Space of Encounter* (Universe Publishing, New York, 2000), p. 73.

2. Muschamp, H. In: Lutyens, D., *Man of the Moment* (Time Out Guide to The London Design Festival, London, 2003), p. 7.

3. Libeskind, D. and Crichton, S. *Breaking Ground: Adventures in Life and Architecture* (Riverhead Books, 2004).

4. See, Lutyens, *op. cit.*

5. E-mail sent by Studio Libeskind, see also: http://archlog.editthispage.com/2003/02/07

6. Studio Libeskind, *Ibid.*

7. Zizek, S. *The Plague of Fantasies* (Verso, London, 1997), p. 153.

8. See, Lutyens, *op. cit.*

9. Richardson, V. 'That Libeskind Touch'. *Spiked*, Mar 7th, 2003.

10. See, Tafuri, M. *Architecture and Utopia, Design and Capitalist Development* (MIT Press, Cambridge, MA, 1976).

11. Libeskind, D., introductory text to the Ground Zero proposal, see: www.daniel-libeskind.com
12. Koolhaas, R. 'White briefs against filth, The Waning Power of New York'. In: AMOMA, Koolhaas, R. (ed.), *Content* (Taschen, Cologne, 2004), p. 239.
13. http://www.renewnyc.com/News/DisplayStory_130.asp
14. Libeskind, D. In: Glancey, J. 'You've got to have faith'. *Guardian* G2, 04/08/04, p. 12.

11. Editors – *Architectural Design* in the 1970s and 1980s

1. Prak, Niels L, *Architects: the Noted and Ignored* (Wiley, New York, 1984).
2. Interview with Haig Beck, October 2004.
3. Interview with Andreas Papadakis, November 2004.
4. Interview with Haig Beck, October 2004.
5. Interview with Haig Beck, October 2004.
6. Interview with Andreas Papadakis, November 2004.
7. *AD* vol.70, no. 5, pp. 98–101, 2000 (Wiley).
8. Interview with Haig Beck, October 2004.
9. Interview with Andreas Papadakis, November 2004.
10. Interview with Martin Spring, November 2004.
11. Interview with Andreas Papadakis, November 2004.
12. Interview with Haig Beck, October 2004.
13. Interview with Haig Beck, October 2004.
14. *AD* Vol. 47, no. 5, 1977 (Acroshaw).
15. *AD* Vol. 47, no. 1, 1977 (Acroshaw).
16. Interview with Haig Beck, October 2004.
17. Interview with Haig Beck, October 2004.
18. Interview with Haig Beck, October 2004.
19. Interview with Andreas Papadakis, November 2004.
20. Interview with Andreas Papadakis, November 2004.
21. Interview with Andreas Papadakis, November 2004.
22. Interview with Andreas Papadakis, November 2004.
23. Interview with Andreas Papadakis, November 2004.
24. Interview with Andreas Papadakis, November 2004.
25. Interview with Andreas Papadakis, November 2004.

26. Interview with Andreas Papadakis, November 2004.
27. Interview with Helen Castle, November 2004.
28. Interview with Andreas Papadakis, November 2004.
29. Interview with Andreas Papadakis, November 2004.

13. All The Kings Men

1. Shaw, G.B., from *'The Doctor's Dilemma* (1911) Act 1.
2. Smith, A. 'Of wages and profits in the different employments of labour and stock', Chapter 10. In: Cannan, E. (ed.), *An Inquiry into the Nature and Causes of the Wealth of Nations* (Methuen and Co., Ltd., London, 1776; 5th edn., 1904).
3. Smith, A. 'Of the expencesof the sovereign or commonwealth', *Ibid.*, Chapter 1.
4. architect /'a:kitekt/ *n.* (1) A designer who prepares plans for buildings, ships etc., and supervises their construction. (2) (foll by *of*) a person who brings about a specified thing (*the architect of his own fortune*). French *architecte* from Italian *architetto*, or their source Latin *architectus* from Greek *arkhitekton* (as ARCH, *tekton* 'builder').
5. 1993 poll of public perceptions of the architectural profession in Britain.
6. In reality, he states, their main reward is *honour*, as their actual recompense is never quite enough to take into account the true value of their work.
7. Sagens, C. 'Professionalism and Public Interest'. In: Pressman, A. (ed.), *Professional Practice 101* (John Wiley & Sons, New York, 1997).
8. 'The Professionalization of everyone?' *The American Journal of Sociology* IXX (September 1964), Wilensky, H.L.
9. Taken from the obituary eulogium given by Vice-president George Godwin, for Earl de Grey who he stated, 'brought together in support of the Institute the most distinguished persons of all classes, whether belonging to the aristocracy of rank or talent'.
10. Godwin, *Ibid.*
11. Gotch, J.A. 'The Royal institute of British Architects'. In: Gotch, J.A. (ed.), *The growth and work of the Royal Institute of British architects* (RIBA, Simpson & Co, London, 1934).
12. Gotch, *Ibid.*

13. Jenkins, F. 'Architect and Patron' (Oxford University Press, London, 1961).
14. Jenkins, *Ibid.*
15. The initial meeting of what was then called the Society of British Architects, resulted in its first disagreement. After the first meeting a committee was set up to produce a report as to an appropriate set of rules for membership. According to Barrington Kaye, this related to the original intention to admit architects and architect–surveyors. A break away group met to agree an alternative report and proposed a far more exclusive set of rules. The intention was to preclude its membership from involvement in building contracting, the supply of materials and the measurement or valuation of work on behalf of builders or tradesmen. The second full meeting of the Society found itself in receipt of two reports and two proposed sets of rules. The more stringent set of rules were agreed after a vote and the architect–surveyors were excluded. Those architect–surveyors, who were not prepared to give up what was a lucrative additional source of income from 'measuring', formed the Society of Architects and Surveyors. However, in an interesting manoeuvre to start the new Society of British Architects with a solid membership, the committee informed an approved selection of the architects who had voted against the more exclusive proposal, that they had been elected to the Society of British Architects, on the previous night, in their absence!
16. There were three classes of membership. Fellow, for those practising civil architecture as a Principal for more than seven years; Associate, for those over 21 years who had practised or studied architecture for less than seven years and Honorary, for 'noblemen who shall contribute ... not less than 25 guineas and gentlemen unconnected with any branch of building as a trade or business', always providing they could meet the fee. Others who were eligible for membership, were persons with 'eminent scientific acquirements'. These were admitted for free.
17. *Transactions*, Vol. 1, Part 1 quoted in Barrington Kaye. The Development of the Architectural Profession in England (1960) George Allen and Unwin.
18. The suggestion that it is only in recent years that younger members of the profession have failed to take into account the

financial consequences of their designs, appears therefore misplaced.

19. Gotch, *op. cit.*
20. And as the position of President of the RIBA offers no salary and only expenses, the cost of running for office, and then holding office for two years, means that only those of sufficiently independent means, or supportive partners or fellow directors or with the energy not be able to not give up the day job, need apply.
21. Jenkins, *op. cit.*
22. Letters from Dean Bourke to James Gandon, an entrant in the Dublin Royal Exchange competition of 1768, quoted in Jenkins, F. *Architect and Patron* (Oxford University Press, Oxford, 1961).
23. *Journal of the Royal Institute of British Architects*, 8th December 1906.
24. Lanchester, H.V. in 'Competitions' a chapter in Gotch, J.A. *op. cit.* H.V. Lanchester was one of the members who summoned the Council to the Special meeting and who resigned from Council in protest.
25. Report of the discussion at the Special General Meeting held 28th April 1907. Published in the Journal of the *Royal Institute of British Architects*, 15 June 1907, p. 551.
26. Crinson, M. and Lubbock, J. *Architecture: Art or profession?* (Manchester University Press, Manchester, 1994).
27. Fletcher, H.M. in 'Education', from Gotch, *op. cit.*
28. *Ibid.*
29. RIBA Proceeding, 1889 new Series, V, 339 reprinted in Barrington Kaye, *The development of the architectural profession in England* (George Allen & Unwin, London, 1960).
30. Shaw and Jackon (eds), *Architecture: a Profession or an Art* (1892).
31. Jackson cites 7 and Blomfield cites 8.
32. The examinations were the Preliminary, Intermediate and Final Examinations.

14. All The Kings Men and a Few Women

1. The original RIBA response to the Warne Report had been to support it. The thinking being that this would remove any

other control on the profession other than that of the RIBA and would allow them to make the title Chartered Architect, the sole definition of architectural quality. After an outcry from its membership, it supported Warne's alternative proposal that if registration was to be retained, the RIBA was the most obvious body to hold the register.

2. Hansard, April 1st 1996, House of Lords in Committee, on the proposed Housing Grants, Construction and Regeneration Bill.
3. It was in fact to be entered for the RIBA Regional Award programme, not the Stirling Prize.
4. Scorpio, BD August 23rd 1996.
5. Report in 'In Brief' section of AJ September 5th 1996.
6. Martin Pawley, 'Martin Pawley on some bad advice from the Bureau', AJ 5th September 1996.
7. Building Design, September 6th 1996.
8. Letter from Mira Bar-Hillel, London SW19, printed in Building Design October 4th 1996.
9. Letter from Stephen Buzas, London W8, printed in Building Design October 4th 1996.
10. Daniel Libeskind is not on the Register of Architects as held by ARB at the time of writing, 10/10/2004.

15. The Portraits

1. Royal Institute of British Architects.
2. Quality Assurance Agency.
3. Peter Cook speaking on 28.10.04 at the Bartlett at the launch of an AD publication on architectural education edited by Michael Chadwick.
4. See the special edition of *New Scientist*, 2.10.04, 'The Secrets of the Face'.
5. It was fitting that South Bank graduate David Adjaye's portrait was gracing the cover of Icon magazine two weeks later (Issue November 2004).

16. Art, Architecture, Artists and Architects

1. Leonard Cohen, 'Everybody Knows' from the album *I'm Your Man*.
2. Leonard Cohen, 'The Future' from the album, *The Future*.

3. Immanuel Kant, *Critique of Judgement*, Werner S. Pluhar (trans.), Hackett Publishing Company: Indianapolis/Cambridge, 1987.
4. *Ibid.*, section 46, pp. 174–176.
5. Thus the culture of the modern art student is something akin to the Cargo Cults that sprang up in the wake of the Second World War. In parts of Borneo tranches of rainforest were hacked down to make landing strips for allied forces to set up base in their war efforts against the Japanese. The tribesmen were bribed with trinkets, cloths, mirrors and other things that glitter. Naturally enough, the tribesmen thought of the aircraft landing, with the white men emerging from them, as chariots carrying gods. Long after the war, members of the indigenous community were cutting down swathes of forest and setting up camp praying for the arrival of yet more gods with gifts from the sky. Just think of these poor folk sitting around the edges of crudely cut airstrips and waiting and waiting. The East End of London is now full of recently graduated art students with their firsts and two-ones busily having ideas and waiting for the new galleries to take them up and waiting.
6. I am much amused by this term, which I owe to a former colleague at the University of Westminster, Alan Lamont, whose desperation with the current lack of thought in architecture brought us together as fellow travellers for a short time.
7. Leonard Cohen, 'Here It Is', from the album, *Ten New Songs*.
8. Dr Penny Florence was part of a delegation from the Slade School of Fine Art in a research seminar at West Dean College in July 2004 concerned to look at interdisciplinary convergences between Artists, Art Historians and Philosophers.
9. See Winters, E. 'Art, Architecture and their Public'. *The Journal of Architecture*, 7(4), 2002.
10. Leonard Cohen, 'Democracy' from the album, *The Future*.
11. Consider the notion of single issue *referenda*. Asked if they would like their tax burdens reduced it is almost certain that a majority will return a positive response. However, ask the same sample group if they would like to see public services improved and there will be an equally strong response in favour. Whilst these two 'wants' are not *logically* incompatible, they are almost certainly *practically* incompatible. (Notwithstanding this fairly

obvious truth, political parties issue policy statements in favour of increased investment in public services to be paid for by efficiency gains, whilst at the same time promising to reduce personal levels of taxation.) My point is that democracy is only really effective when those in a position to formulate policy can effectively persuade an electorate that their *raft of policies*, taken of a piece, is worth voting for.

12. Leonard Cohen, 'The Future', from the album *The Future*.
13. I am much indebted to Edward Stourton's book, *In the Footsteps of St Paul*, London: Hodder and Stoughton, 2004. Stourton quotes the passages given here in the context of Paul's intellectual commitment to the development of Christianity. Stourton wryly observes that much of what passes in contemporary 'charismatic Christianity' is the meaningless other-worldly noise that St Paul was attempting to defeat. There is a Wittgensteinian flavour to Stourton's distrust, if not distaste, of charismatic Christianity.
14. Daniel Libeskind, website address: daniel-libeskind.com/
15. *ibid.*
16. Immanuel Kant, *op. cit.*, pp. 191–192.
17. The nuance is Edward Stourton's. See Stourton, *op. cit.*, p. 62.

17. A-List Architects

1. How To Become An A-List Architect, Conference Centre, Great Russell Street, London, 25 March 2004.

21. The Psyche of a Depressed and Disappointed Unit Master

1. *What you see is what you get . . .* more or less.
2. Terry Eagleton, 'Living as Little as Possible', *LRB* 23 September 2004: 23 (review of David Lodge *Author, Author: A Novel* [about Henry James]) I attempt here experimentally to create my own hybrid form somewhere between fiction and academic essay prose – though never simply, or securely, one or the other – partly to have some play with notions of identity and status in university teaching. The best accounts of academia as 'lived

experience', and its 'small world' of fame and celebrity for those teaching English, or Sociology, or Architecture and Town Planning, are clearly works of fiction: the so-called 'campus novel'. See the stories mentioned here by Malcolm Bradbury, David Lodge, and Raymond Williams (those his *Second Generation* is also really a hybrid form – in literary terms 'Between Towns Road' itself, indebted particularly to D.H. Lawrence in its treatment of changing identities and social relations within urban industrial capitalist society).

3. Williams, R. *The fight for Manod* (London: Hogarth Press, 1988 [1979]).
4. *Ibid.*, pp. 193–4.
5. 'Between Towns Road' appears early on in Raymond Williams' novel *Second Generation* (London: Hogarth Press, 1988 [1964]: 9), set in Oxford, which explores the social and spatial relationships between the communities there that constitute academia ('gown') and the workers at the car-production plant ('town').

Biographies

Editors

Paul Davies was born in 1961 in Colchester. Educated at Bristol University and The Polytechnic of Central London through the eighties. He lectures in architecture at London South Bank University and The Architectural Association, London, usually on the subject of Las Vegas. He is married to photographer Julie Cook.

Torsten Schmiedeknecht is an architect and currently a lecturer and course director at the School of Architecture, University of Liverpool. He studied architecture at the TH Darmstadt, The Polytechnic of Central London and The University of Liverpool and has practised in Germany, France and the UK. Together with Julia Chance he edited *Fame and Architecture* (John Wiley, 2001).

Contributors

Kit Allsopp is Professor of Architecture at London South Bank University and Chairman of SCHOSA (Standing Conference for the Heads of Schools of Architecture).

Halldóra Arnadottir PhD (The Bartlett, UCL) is a freelance art historian. Her work on architecture and design has been published in magazines, daily newspapers, exhibitions and TV programmes.

Stephen Bayley is one of Britain's most famous commentators on culture, something he achieved after failing to become an architect. He studied at Manchester University and Liverpool School of Architecture and was an academic before the lure of money and fame led him to the harsh, bright world of media. A columnist for The Daily Telegraph and The Independent on Sunday, he is also the author of many books. In 1989 he was made a Chevalier de l'Ordre des Arts et Lettres by the French Minister of Culture. He has a letter from the Queen saying he may use the title, but elegantly refuses to do so.

Carlos Villanueva Brandt was born in Caracas, Venezuela in 1957, studied at the Architectural Association, London between 1977 and 1982 and founder member of NATO in 1983. He has taught Unit 10 at the Architectural Association ever since.

Julie Cook was born in 1960 in St Albans and studied photography at Westminster University and The London College of Printing. Her award winning book *Baby Oil and Ice, Striptease in East London* was published in 2002. Other recent publications include: *Zeropolis* (Reaktion, 2003) and *Stripping Las Vegas, A Contextual Review of Casino Resort Architecture* (El Verso, 2003).

David Dunster was educated at the Bartlett, University College London between 1963 and 1969 during the reign of Llewellyn Davies and the student revolt. Having worked for James Gowan and for Colin St. John Wilson he taught at

Kingston Polytechnic moving to the Bartlett in 1983 then to a chair at South Bank University. He has been Roscoe Professor of Architecture at the University of Liverpool since 1995.

Judi Farren Bradley is a Principal Lecturer and Course Director at Kingston School of Architecture and Landscape. She teaches, writes and researches in the area of Professional Practice and Sustainability. She is married with 2 teenage children, neither of whom intend to follow their parents into architecture.

Jon Goodbun was educated at the Polytechnic of Central London, University of East London, and The Bartlett School of Architecture. He is a director of WaG Architecture and is a senior lecturer and design Tutor at the University of Westminster, where he co-founded the Polytechnic research group. His research interests include interface design and the history of expressionist architecture.

Jonathan Harris teaches art history in the School of Architecture at the University of Liverpool. He has a first degree in art history from University of Sussex and a PhD from Middlesex Polytechnic and has taught at Leeds Polytechnic, Keele University, and since 1999 at Liverpool University. He is the author and editor of several books.

Karin Jaschke was educated at Technische Universitat Berlin, The Bartlett and Princeton University where she is currently completing her PhD. She has taught and lectured at Bauhaus-Universitat Weimar, Princeton University, Reading University, Westminster University, The TU Berlin and Waseda University, Tokyo. Her interests include primitivism in modern architecture, modern architecture in the Netherlands and ecological concepts in architecture.

Laura Iloniemi is a specialist in architectural PR. Born in Finland, she set up in London to run her agency in 1996. She has worked with clients such as Arup Associates, Rafael Viñoly Architects and Ushida Findlay Architects who are featured in her recent book on publicity and architecture called *Is it all about image?: How PR works in architecture* (Wiley, 2004). Iloniemi studied architectural philosophy at The University of Cambridge and Arts Promotion at The Ecole du Louvre in Paris.

Ryan McCrudden and **Mathew Witts** wish to use the results of their investigations to benefit their own future careers as recent graduates from the University of Liverpool.

Markus Miessen studied at Glasgow School of Art, UdK Berlin and the Architectural Association in London after working for Daniel Libeskind in Berlin. He is the author (with Kenny Cupers) of *Spaces of Uncertainty* (Müller & Busmann, 2002).

Richard Patterson is an architect and Academic Programme Leader in Architecture at the University of Brighton. He has published on early 17th architectural theory and the origins of modernism.

Andrew Peckham teaches Architecture at the University of Westminster.

Charles Rattray is an architect. He teaches at the Robert Gordon University in Aberdeen and is Associate Editor of *Architectural Research Quarterly*.

Dr Javier Sánchez Merina is an architect and a teacher of design at the Alicante School of Architecture.

James Soane is an architectural practitioner and teacher working in London. He studied at Cambridge and the Bartlett going on to become a director at Conran & Partners. In 2001 he became a founding partner of Project Orange, an architecture and design studio of ten people. He is also the author of *New Homes* (Conran Octopus, 2003) and *Catalogue*.

Hans van der Heijden graduated from the technical university in Delft in 1988. After working in design practices such as Mecanoo, he established BIQ with Rick Wessels in 1994. His writing on architecture has been published in *De Architect*, *Archis* and *Architectural Research Quarterly*. He has lectured and taught at universities in the Netherlands, England, Switzerland and Belgium.

David Vila Domini studied architecture in Spain and the UK. He teaches at the Robert Gordon University in Aberdeen.

Rob Wilson is a curator and freelance writer who trained as an architect. He currently works at the RIBA in London and recently co-curated with the Hayward Gallery the exhibition 'Fantasy Architecture 1500–2036' which has toured to five UK cities.

Edward Winters trained as a painter at the Slade School of Fine Art before reading Philosophy at Birkbeck College London. He wrote his PhD in Philosophy at University College London. He has written on the philosophy of visual art for academic journals and has written critical pieces for art and architectural journals. He is Senior Lecturer and Research Fellow in Visual Arts at West Dean College, The Edward James Foundation.

List of Images

Index